The Nature
of Communism

Books by Robert V. Daniels

A Documentary History of Communism

The Conscience of the Revolution: Communist Opposition in Soviet Russia

The Nature of Communism

ROBERT V. DANIELS

The Nature
of Communism

RANDOM HOUSE

New York

First Printing

© *Copyright, 1962, by Robert V. Daniels*

All rights reserved under International and Pan-American Copyright Conventions. Published in New York by Random House, Inc., and simultaneously in Toronto, Canada, by Random House of Canada, Limited.

Library of Congress Catalog Card Number: 61–6254

Manufactured in the United States of America by Kingsport Press, Inc.

Acknowledgments

I am indebted to my wife, Alice M. Daniels, and to the following friends and colleagues, who have read all or parts of the manuscript and have been most helpful with their suggestions and criticisms: Arvid Brodersen, Paul Evans, Merle Fainsod, Lewis Feuer, Harold Fisher, Nathan Glazer, George Little, Paul Power, and Albert Sadler.

R.V.D.

To Helen, Irene, Bob, and Tom—
may theirs be a saner world

Table
of Contents

Introduction

It is human nature, where weighty affairs
of state are concerned, to make the world and the
issues which agitate it seem clear and simple.
Where much is at stake, and political affairs are
highly charged with emotion, people are particularly inclined to conceive of their problems as the
result of uncomplicated, if bitter, conflicts of competing states, groups, or principles. The more serious the challenge, the less are people able to study
it dispassionately and to appreciate what may be
the complex reality of its true nature.

Never in modern history has this been so true
as it is now in the conflict between the Western
democratic states and Communism. This grave
situation, threatening a struggle of mutual annihilation between the nuclear-armed halves of a divided world, is unprecedented in the history of
mankind. Formidable obstacles lie in the way of a
resolution of the tension and hostility that
threaten world-wide destruction—obstacles posed
by conflicting principles and values embedded in
the very nature of the contending democratic and
Communist systems. Differences of this sort demand the most painstaking effort to understand
the other side in all the detail and variety of its real
nature. Only thus can we prepare either to resist

the opponent or reach an accommodation with him.

Unfortunately, the tendency to simplify under stress heightens the sense of unavoidable conflict between the competing systems, and makes perceptive mutual understanding all the more difficult. The purpose toward which I hope this work will contribute is to break the vicious circle of fear, hostility, and oversimplified misunderstanding. Communism is simple only to the superficial glance. If I succeed only in demonstrating the complexity of Communism, in showing that it cannot be described or explained by any one principle, force, or formula, I will consider my effort successful.

The subject of this book is the modern political movement that calls itself Communism. The theoretical notion of "communism" as an ideal form of society is not our concern, and we will find that in large measure it is irrelevant to the study of the movement which has adopted that name. The Communist movement is a discrete entity, with recognizable organizational bonds. We are not studying a class of movements that have some feature in common (as would be the case if we were dealing with "socialism," for example), but one particular movement in all its particular aspects. Communism is a movement specifically of the present century, with definite historical origins in prerevolutionary Russia. We will treat the movement as a world-wide phenomenon, though we must not lose sight of the central importance of Russia in the movement. The movement was formed in Russia, made powerful by events in Russia, and shows the stamp of Russian influence everywhere. Our primary concern naturally will be to understand the nature and development of Communism in Russia.

The objective of this study is a definition of the Communist movement. What is its real nature? How has it developed? What distinguishes it from other political movements and systems? What does it mean to say that an individual, an organization, or a government is Communist? What, apart from nomenclature, do all Communists have in common? What are the sources of such common denominators of the movement? We will try to establish, in short, what the Communist movement *is,* in distinction to what its spokesmen or its enemies may say it is.

The difficulties to be encountered in the pursuit of this aim need hardly be stressed. Passions run high with regard to the subject. The hostility which oversimplification and misunderstanding reinforce is itself an obstacle to more accurate understanding. It is hard to be objective when often a particular interpretation or explanation of the opponent is attractive just because it reinforces a particular political commitment or emotion. The fatal step, which the Communists themselves took long ago, is to cease governing politics by understanding, and instead to allow explanations to be dictated by political expediency.

Objectivity is not the only serious difficulty in the study of the Communist movement. The subject itself is agonizingly complex, despite the simplification afforded by the totalitarian structure of Communist society. The essence of the movement has changed with time. Differences between theory and practice, changes in theory, changes in interpretation without alteration in the literal doctrine, make it difficult to comprehend or even to define the Communist movement. We must try to dispel the haze of doctrinal obfuscation, though to do so is to challenge the emotions of people who are attached to the original Communist doctrine as a basis for either liking or disliking the movement.

There are still other difficulties which are inherent in the very nature of the investigatory enterprise. The history of human events becomes ever more complicated and less reducible to social laws, the closer we approach the present. "The further back we go in the examination of events," writes Tolstoy, "the less arbitrary they seem to us." With a problem of recent development and contemporary import like Communism, it is exceedingly difficult to take all factors into account and to give all variables their proper weight. Further, the complexity of the recent past is aggravated by the paucity of efforts among serious students to work out schemes of causal relationships to describe and account for the pattern of recent events. The abundance of documentary and monographic material on recent history, including most aspects of Communism, confronts us with an embarrassment of riches, while the work of synthesis, which could provide a foundation for studies such as this one, has not kept pace. At the same time, some crucial developments in Communism, especially the central politics of the Soviet government since Stalin became dictator in 1929, have transpired within the shroud of official secrecy, and are less documented than the Dark Ages. To guesswork, loose generalization, and the impromptu decreeing of historical laws we must unfortunately, but necessarily, have recourse. Otherwise we cannot even attempt the definition of Communism. We must try to do our best, be content with an approximation, and not claim more.

The approach which we shall follow toward a definition of Communism is intended to correct the one-sidedness which is so common in this field. Most studies of Communism seek to explain the movement as a member of a certain class of events or systems. This is quite valid as far as it goes; the trouble is that only one context or perspective is employed. It is common to treat Communism as a conspiratorial movement, *or* as a secular religion, *or* as the reincarnation of tsarism, *or* as the studious application of the principles of Karl Marx (whether the observer endorses or abhors them). Each of these approaches may be meaningful up to a point, but if it is pursued to the exclusion of the others a woeful distortion will result. Efforts to weigh the various points of view usually turn into controversies as to which *one* is the most significant. The fruitless debates as to whether Communism is governed by Marxist ideology *or* a conspiratorial power drive *or* Russian imperialism are familiar to all students of Soviet affairs.

In this study we shall not attempt to choose among the various possible interpretations of Communism, but shall try to utilize each of them for whatever insight it may yield. Under each heading we shall describe that aspect of the Communist movement toward which the particular interpretation points, and shall try to assess the validity of that interpretation as a partial approach to the problem. In this fashion we shall examine Communism first as the orthodox application of Marxist principles; next, as the creature of the Russian Revolution; then as a party conspiracy; as a struggle for world power; as a product of Russian history; as a rebellion against the West; as a form of the industrial revolution; as totalitarian society;

and as a secular faith. As we proceed we shall attempt to interrelate and accumulate the insights
derived from the various approaches. In the end,
hopefully, we shall have a realistic working definition of the Communist movement.

The Nature
of Communism

1 Communism and Marxist Theory

Communism is grounded in illusion. Both its adherents and its enemies are entranced by a mythology. Both commit the mistake of taking Communist doctrine at its face value. The terms in which Communism describes itself—the philosophy of Marxism—cannot be avoided, for they are immediately encountered in the most casual contact with Communism, but they must not be taken for granted. Marxism, however much it may be hailed or cursed in the present world struggle, does not really provide the true motive, the real guide, or even an accurate description of the Communists.

Over the years Marxism has been almost completely recast by the Communist leaders in Russia. Contrary to its own claims and the assumptions of most outsiders, the Communist movement has undergone step by step a radical transformation in its innermost nature. In no real sense does it represent the working class socialism predicted by Marx. Their dedication to Marxist theoretical ideals has not prevented the Communists from adapting to the practical realities of a world that Marx never envisioned. At the same time, they cling to the forms of Marxist belief and terminology, for they are determined to appear to the world and to themselves as the orthodox heirs of a dynamic movement.

The necessary first step in the study of Communism is to penetrate the ideological fog which surrounds the movement. We must work through the official explanation of themselves which the Communists have contrived over the years, in order to reveal what the movement actually is in down-to-earth terms. At the same time we will be able to explore how Communist doctrine and practice have diverged. Finally, through examining the way Communism has used and developed its doctrine, we may begin to achieve some insight into the movement's real nature.

1 MARXISM

Marxism—or Marxism brought up to date by Lenin, and "creatively applied" by Stalin and Mao, and then polished down by Khrushchev—is regarded by every Communist as the scientific foundation of his belief and the sufficient justification for every violent step a Communist regime takes. This is the dogma—but dogma governed by totalitarian politics, not by intellectual conviction—and the dogma has been shaped to suit the movement. A little inquiry will reveal how very unscientific, and how far stretched from the original theory, is the faith of the present-day Communist. Marx is supposed to have declared, when confronted with some of the notions of his followers, "All I know is that I am not a Marxist." Were he to return to earth today in one of the professedly

Marxist countries, he would probably be purged for an anti-Marxist deviation.

Marxism is primarily a theory of history, a set of propositions about human society and the way it is supposed to behave over the course of time. The theory was, in its time, a remarkable step in the direction of a science of society, even if we cannot call it adequate. The core concept of Marxism is the doctrine of "historical materialism," loosely synonymous with "economic determinism" or the "economic interpretation of history." On this foundation Marx constructed an elaborate system of sociological analysis and political prophecy, with conclusions pointing imperatively to revolutionary action.

The basis of human social life, according to Marxism, is production. This is more than a truism, for Marxism asserts that the conditions of economic activity, the "forces of production" and the "relations of production," are "in the last analysis" responsible for the form which all other aspects of social life take. "In the social production of their life," Marx wrote in his *Critique of Political Economy,* "men enter into definite relations of production which correspond to a definite stage of development of their material productive forces. The sum total of these relations of production constitutes the economic structure of society, the real foundation, on which rises a legal and political superstructure and to which correspond definite forms of social consciousness. The mode of production of material life conditions the social, political, and intellectual life process in general. It is not the consciousness of men that determines their be-

ing, but, on the contrary, their social being that
determines their consciousness."

For Marx, the key to the understanding of
events was the idea of classes and the class struggle. "The history of all hitherto existing society is
the history of class struggles," proclaims the opening line of the Communist Manifesto. Economic development gives rise to classes, according to Marx,
when people assume different relationships (as
owners, workers, etc.) to the process of production.
Various classes, in the historical sequence, struggle
for domination. Political organizations and ideas
are in large measure auxiliary to the historical
struggle, created or molded to further the domination of a given class. As economic conditions
change, new classes arise. New doctrines express
their interests. The class struggle intensifies: "At
a certain stage of their development, the material
productive forces of society come in conflict with
the existing relations of production. . . . From
forms of development of the productive forces
these relations turn into their fetters. Then begins
an epoch of social revolution. With the change of
the economic foundations the entire immense superstructure is more or less rapidly transformed."
Finally, in the act of revolution, the old ruling class
is displaced by a new one which in turn asserts its
domination.

Marx discerned, after the primitive communal
society, five historical types of society, each distinguished by the domination of a certain class:
ancient slave-holding, Asiatic, feudal, bourgeois or
capitalist, and socialist. In the socialist society, for
the first time, the masses—i.e., the industrial proletariat—would come to power. On the basis of
mass-produced abundance the classless society
would be ushered in, when "society [can] inscribe

upon its banners: from each according to his ability, to each according to his needs." Marx thus proclaimed his faith in progress, with the conviction that the age-old misery of mankind was coming to an end.

This millennial upheaval Marx envisioned as the inevitable consequence of the development of the capitalist mode of production. Bringing wage laborers together in factories, capitalism made it possible for them to become conscious of their interests as a class, and to combine in defense of those interests: "The advance of industry . . . replaces the isolation of the laborers, due to competition, by their revolutionary combination, due to association." The workers, progressively impoverished by the growth of monopoly, but stimulated by revolutionary intellectuals whose grasp of the Marxian "science" showed them the true course of history, would inevitably become a revolutionary force capable of sweeping away the old order. Relationships of property (private ownership of the means of production) would conflict more and more with the actual collective character of industrial production. The capitalist system would reach a limit, indicated by deepening economic crises, when it would impede the further development of production and arouse ever more vigorous revolutionary opposition. Capitalism, like every system before it, contained "the seeds of its own destruction"—"the development of modern industry . . . cuts from under its feet the very foundation on which the bourgeoisie produces and appropriates products. What the bourgeoisie therefore produces, above all, are its own grave-diggers. Its fall and the victory of the proletariat are equally inevitable."

On the nature of the revolution and on the

character of the ensuing socialist order Marx and
Engels expressed themselves in terms much vaguer
than their sharply etched critique of capitalism.
While convinced of their correctness about the
general trend of history, they hesitated in their
prophecy when it came to details. In one way or
another the proletariat would take over the power
of the state—the "executive committee of the ruling class"—and turn the exploiters' own weapons
against them. For the model of revolutionary procedure Marx relied largely on an actual historical
event, the ill-fated Paris Commune of 1871. This
short-lived rising of the Parisian workers in the
dark days of defeat after the Franco-Prussian War
was to Marx the first manifestation of the real
proletarian revolution. He idealized the actions of
the Commune as the "smashing" of the old state
machinery, with direct democracy and measures to
keep the new officialdom from rising in status
above their fellow workers.

While Marx and Engels expected violence in the
proletarian revolution, they did not insist upon it.
Marx conceded that the revolution could come
peacefully in countries such as Britain and
America, where parliamentary traditions out-
weighed the forces of bureaucratic repression. A
year before his death in 1895 Engels reached the
conclusion that thanks to advancing democratic
opportunities in the modern parliamentary state,
armed insurrection was a thing of the past: "The
irony of world history turns everything upside
down. We, the 'revolutionaries,' and 'rebels'—we
are thriving far better on legal methods than on
illegal methods and revolt."

However instituted, the revolutionary regime
would "expropriate the expropriators" by nation-

alizing the monopolistic enterprises of the capitalists, and would as rapidly as possible put an end to
"wage slavery" and the whole capitalist ethic of
money-making. From here on the prophets of
Marxism did not venture specific directives, except
to caution that the process of transition to the
classless society could not take place overnight. In
the end, however, they looked to the "withering
away of the state," as the demise of class antagonisms eliminated the need to use political force.
The revolution would proceed on an international
plane, capitalism having made the world an economic unit, and the diplomatic and defensive functions of the state would similarly be obviated. Finally, with the elimination of classes and the
unfettering of the potential of modern industry,
society would enter an era of blissful abundance.

This utopian program of Marxism was distinguished from its predecessors in the same vein by
its underpinnings of elaborate economic analysis.
Marx's socialism did not count on a master phi-
lanthropist or a monastic sect to introduce it. Socialism was to proceed naturally and inevitably
from the existing economic system, which was
busily creating the industrial prerequisites for the
new order. Industry was the foundation for the
classless bounty to be achieved under "communism," and the indispensable role of capitalism's
industrial revolution in creating this basis was
fully acknowledged. Here was the guarantee that
nothing could go wrong: the industrial development which was the prerequisite for socialist
equality was itself the force which would cause the
obsolescence and break-up of capitalism. Outbreak
of the socialist revolution before the prerequisites
were ready was an eventuality never contemplated

by Western Marxists. But in Russia this was the actual path of events, with profound tribulations as its consequence.

In the work of Marx and his collaborator Engels there are obvious inadequacies, confusions, and oversimplifications. It is hardly necessary to point out how wrong most of their predictions have been. However, a detailed critique is not our purpose here; we are concerned with the influence of Marx's doctrine on his followers. The force of Marxism is clear enough when we note that no other nineteenth-century writer still compels critics to exhume and refute his theories day after day.

We must give some attention, however, to certain broad conclusions in the Marxian scheme of things which do not necessarily follow even from Marxian premises. These are the ideas that the proletariat will become the next ruling class, and that the historical travail of class struggles will come to an end after the next revolution. Feudalism, in which the nobility exploited the peasants, was not succeeded by the rule of the downtrodden tillers of the soil but by an order in which a new ruling group, the capitalists, took power. By analogy, it would be more logical to expect the capitalists to be displaced, not by the working class and the classless society, but by still another ruling group basing its social position on the latest conditions of production. Such a trend in the present century has actually been suggested, with the "managers" or bureaucrats, public and/or private, taking over. This is James Burnham's thesis of the "managerial revolution." The expectation that the proletariat will become the next ruling class has no logical foundation in Marx's own analysis of history; it is sheer prophecy, wishful thinking. Events in fact have made it clear that the working class as such has nowhere become the ruling class and is nowhere likely to do so, although individual workers may be recruited in large numbers into the new bureaucratic strata. This opportunity and the purely verbal label of the "workers' state" are the only things "proletarian" in the actual Communist regimes.

A further element in Marxist myth-making is the philosophy of the "dialectic" which Marx adopted from his German philosophical mentor Hegel. According to the dialectical philosophy, all things are in a state of change, which occurs in a prescribed fashion: a given state of affairs (the "thesis") generates contrary forces (the "antithesis") which, when they accumulate sufficiently, cause a sudden reordering of things into a new state (the "synthesis"). Marx applied the scheme to his class struggle, and envisaged the prospects for the future accordingly—change would come naturally through the growth of the proletariat (the "antithesis" of the bourgeois "thesis") and the socialist revolution. Marxism thus represents revolution as the natural manner of social change, when in reality it has been exceptional. Gradual evolution, even if not placid, has been the form of real progress most of the time in most places. But Marx's stress on revolution was typical of the radicalism of the first half of the nineteenth century, which could anticipate little amelioration of the human condition without a fundamental reconstruction of the social order. "Revolution is necessary," asserted Marx and Engels in one of their early works, "not only because the *ruling* class cannot be overthrown in any other way, but also because only in a revolution can *the class which over-throws* it rid itself of the accumulated rubbish of the past and become capable of reconstructing society."

The dialectical fallacy of inevitable revolution reflects the general Marxist habit of regarding abstract notions as the real thing, and of forcing the complexities of life into the neat pigeonholes of theory. This is the way social classes are treated, for example: bourgeoisie and proletariat are virtually personified, and we can almost visualize them meeting in wager of battle. The "proletariat" is discussed as something quite apart from the individual proletarians, who may actually deviate from the approved norm in every way. Thus, oddly enough, the "materialist" Marxists incorporate a good deal of philosophical idealism in their style of thinking, which puts a premium on verbal formulas and ideal types.

Marxism was and is, despite its "materialist" terminology, an intensely ethical and idealistic movement. The opposition of "materialism" and "idealism" must be understood in three separate respects—metaphysical, historical, and ethical. Marxism is, of course, vehemently materialist in its metaphysics; it not only denounces supernatural religion but is sharply antipathetic to any philosophic notion which seems to question the prime reality of "matter" as common sense has it. Even more fundamental to Marxism is historical materialism, the proposition that events are the product primarily of material conditions and economic interests, while ideas serve less to guide actions than to justify them. But in the ethical sphere quite the contrary is the case: Marxism was, at least originally, an anguished protest against the materialist spirit of capitalism, against the profit motive, against the mechanization and dehumanization of all classes of people in the service of industrial production.

In connecting every human thought and action with the class struggle, Marxism endeavors to deny that there is such a thing as an absolute moral standard, and to assert that values are all relative to a particular class or social order. This notion has been especially significant in the development of intellectual controls in Communist countries—ideas of which the state does not approve are "bourgeois" and hence taboo. Nevertheless, Marxist thought has never been entirely content with this pure relativism. Exceptions are made for the proletariat, whose ideas can approach absolute validity because (unlike other classes) it is assertedly in step with the march of history and needs no illusions. More significantly, the whole moral atmosphere of Marxist thinking is heavy with the implication of higher, universal ethical standards, against which class society is judged and found wanting. Marxism makes much of the economic argument that capitalism is doomed by its organizational inefficiency and its crises, but the real reason for attacking it is moral: capitalism is based on the "exploitation of man by man," it is unjust and inhuman.

It is in its moral aspect that Marxism has made and still makes its great appeal. Whoever fails to see this will miss the point altogether. Marxism has gathered much more force as a moral rebellion than an economic one. In Russia, the Far East, much of Western Europe and America, the driving force in the Marxist movement has not been the working class, but morally disaffected members of the educated and presumably "ruling" strata of society. While Marxism does take some account of

the revolutionary role of "bourgeois intellectuals,"
the actual role of such elements in the Communist
parties (which Lenin stressed intensely) goes far
beyond what the theory of Marxism can explain.
The historical materialism of Marxism is confuted
by the character of the very movement which professes it.

Despite these limitations, Marxism has played
a prominent role in the history of thought, not only
as the inspiration of revolutionary movements,
but as a significant step in the growth of social
science. Here Marxism was important not for its
specific conclusions but for the questions which it
posed and the attention which it directed to previously neglected aspects of life. No one can now
neglect the role of economic circumstances in history, any more than attribute exclusive importance
to them. The interrelationship between the various
aspects of life—economic, social, political, intellectual—has to be faced. To Marxism we must credit,
as Edmund Wilson puts it, "the technique of analyzing political phenomena in social-economic
terms." In the view of the skeptically minded English historian Herbert Butterfield, "The chief contribution of the Marxists has been that they, more
than anybody else, have taught us to make our history a structural piece of analysis—something
which is capable of becoming more profound than
a piece of ordinary political narrative."

The animating spirit of Marxism is deeply embedded in the intellectual traditions of Western
European civilization. Virtually every major idea
produced in Europe since the seventeenth century
is reflected in Marxism. Science and a rationalist
approach to human problems were fundamental
elements in the development of the Marxist outlook—society is to be studied rationally in a search

for the "laws" governing its behavior and evolution. Marxism also shares the optimistic European
faith of the two centuries past—that man is not
condemned by his nature or Adam's sin to suffer
hopelessly as long as he remains on this earth,
and that the natural course of history is upward,
"progress." Marxism holds that prosperity for the
masses is desirable and attainable, and thus endorses implicitly the utilitarian test of institutions
and social systems. If man is in misery or chains,
it is the institutions and the social system which
are to blame, not man himself; rational criticism
and a political overturn will set things right.

Marxism's intellectual distinctiveness lies only
in the particular combination which it makes of
the elements it took over. It presents a program
of revolutionary improvement, and at the same
time endeavors to prove the inevitability of its goal
by a supposedly scientific analysis of history. The
critical revolutionary spirit of the eighteenth century and the evolutionary science of the nineteenth
are merged. The result is a pseudoscientific belief
neatly tailored out of the intellectual materials of
its age, with the emotional force of a religious
faith. Nevertheless, there are serious weaknesses in
the Marxist intellectual amalgam, and these had
much to do with the paradoxes in the later development of Marxian belief.

Strictly interpreted, Marxism leaves little room
for individual will or initiative in determining the
course of events. If there is to be a revolution, conditions will make so many people strive for it that
the decision of any one individual pro or con is
immaterial. Marx, to be sure, calls on man to act
and change the world, but by no means does he
rely on individual wills alone. Man makes history,
but history makes man. Engels wrote in 1885, to

caution the enthusiastic Russian revolutionaries, "People who boasted that they had made a revolution have always seen the next day that they had no idea what they were doing, that the revolution *made* did not in the least resemble the one they would have liked to make." Men are likely to be the unwitting agents of a necessity beyond their ken, as they strive for a certain goal, rationalize it with a certain ideology, but produce effects which may be of a very different nature, depending on the circumstances of their society. The Russian Revolution is no exception to this rule.

Marxism has never been sufficiently consistent, however, to view the efforts of its own adherents in this light. Presuming perfect knowledge of the laws of history, Marxism complements its doctrine of historical inevitability with a program of necessary and unerring revolutionary action. The marriage of these two elements suffers from as much logical incompatibility in the case of Marxism as elsewhere (*cf.* the Calvinist combination of predestination and individual striving).

Psychologically the fusion of determinism and voluntarism—reliance on history and reliance on will—makes a great deal of sense. Students of the Marxist movement often make the mistake of assuming that Marxists are revolutionary because they believe in the Marxian doctrine; it is much closer to the truth to say that Marxists believe in the doctrine because they are revolutionary. People rebel because social conditions make them want to. As Nikolai Bukharin put it, when he was still one of the top Soviet leaders, "Marxism does not deny the will, but explains it. When Marxists organize the Communist Party and lead it into battle, this action is also an expression of historical necessity." Communists embrace Marxism as an

"ideology," not because it is demonstrably true (it
does not adequately account even for its own believers), but because it is effective as a rationalization of the desire of the rebelling group for social
overturn. Economic or moral rebellion against the
existing order draws sustenance and reinforcement
from the belief that the cause is just and is guaranteed ultimate victory.

We can shed light on this state of affairs by applying Marx's own concept of "ideology." An ideology, according to Marxism, is a system of beliefs
—including legal, philosophical, religious, and
other ideas—generated in a given society and serving to justify the status quo and the interests of
the ruling class. "The ideas of the ruling class,"
wrote Marx and Engels in 1846, "are, in every age,
the ruling ideas. . . . The dominant ideas are
nothing more than the ideal expression of the
dominant material relationships . . . which make
one class the ruling one." Here is an application of
the dictum that it is men's "social being that determines their consciousness." Such beliefs need
not be deliberately contrived; ideology grows
through the selection and conditioning of thought
by social pressures and influences. Ideology is not
ordinarily a conscious fraud, but is taken seriously
by its beneficiaries. It is a myth, "false consciousness," believed and enforced by the ruling class,
but not necessarily corresponding to reality. The
Marxist movement itself proves to be no exception
to this type of thinking. The vision of the proletarian revolution and Soviet rationalizations about
the workers' state are just as fanciful as any bourgeois hypocrisy about liberty for the unemployed
or medieval appeals to the will of God.

It follows that the actions of Marxists are not
determined by Marxist theory, but only orna-

mented with it. Marxists, with few exceptions, have
never acted in practice as though they really believed in the inevitable triumph of the revolution.
Some have striven mightily to make the revolution
occur. Others, of a contrary spirit, have rested content with their verbiage, satisfied that the revolution really *isn't* going to occur. Thus we have the
two latter-day offshoots of the Marxist movement:
Russian Bolshevism, with its premium on violent
willful action, and Western Social Democracy, committed to a future of gradual reform. Isolated sec-
tarians aside, there are no genuine Marxist movements left in the world today. In the West, the
Marxist Social Democrats had become by 1914 either explicitly or implicitly "revisionist." Marxism
was revised and desiccated by them, with the elimination of revolution in favor of reform through the
democratic process and trade unionism. Toward
this undogmatic gradualism the Russian Bolsheviks and their foreign sympathizers reacted with
the most violent antipathy, but the stand of these
committed revolutionaries was no less a break with
the original doctrine: militant faith and totalitarian government were to sweep all economic obstacles before them.

2 LENINISM AND THE
RUSSIAN REVOLUTION

A serious and not infrequent error in the study
of Communism is to assume, as the Communists
do, that Lenin is all Marx and all Marx is in Lenin.
Lenin, of course, always affirmed his orthodoxy in
vigorous terms, but this should only signal the more
caution in judging him. Actually, the transplanting of Marxism from the West into Russia

wrought fundamental changes in the meaning of the doctrine, no less than in the anatomy of the country where the Marxist revolutionaries triumphed.

Marxism did not begin to figure as a political force in Russia until the very last years of the nineteenth century, half a century after its principles were first laid down. It came as the latest in a series of revolutionary fashions to be adopted by the radical "intelligentsia," the rootless and alienated educated classes of a country half in transition to modernity and half submerged in the feudal mire of the ages. Subjected to the disputations of Russian ideologues, Marxism was quickly given more diverse interpretations than it had been before in all its history in Europe. By 1903 the Russian Marxist movement, newly organized as the Social-Democratic Workers' Party (mostly of intellectuals), was badly split.

The issue in the party schism was Lenin, a rising star among the Russian revolutionaries and as headstrong a leader as history has ever witnessed. Lenin provoked the cleavage of the Russian Marxists into Bolsheviks and Mensheviks (the factions so styled from their temporary status as "majority" and "minority" respectively) by propounding and insisting upon a distinctly new conception of what the party ought to be and do. In contrast to the Western idea of a mass opinion-mobilizing organization espoused by his opponents among the Marxists, Lenin urged an organizational model largely inspired by Russian antecedents and much more closely adapted to the exigencies of underground politics in a country where the tsarist police were a constant threat. The party was to be a tightly organized and disciplined body of "professional revolutionaries," dedicated to the promotion of a revolutionary mass movement and the overthrow of the autocracy.

Lenin's organizational scheme and his tactical precepts had enormous significance for the future development of Communism. Equally decisive were the implications of Lenin's doctrine of the party for Marxist theory. Without acknowledging the fact, and probably without even realizing it, Lenin introduced (or at least set in motion) momentous changes in the substance of Marxian belief.

The form of party organization was acutely important for Lenin because of the role which he felt the party would have to play. He began with the premise, not unwarranted under Russian circumstances, that the masses, if left to themselves, would *not* become revolutionary. "The history of all countries," he sweepingly asserted, "shows that the working class, exclusively by its own effort, is able to develop only trade union consciousness." The working class movement would be made revolutionary only through the leadership of inspired intellectuals, guided by Marxism, who would impart to the workers the proper socialist mentality. In a patent contradiction of Marx, Lenin asserted, "Class political consciousness can be brought to the workers *only from without,* that is, only from outside of the economic struggle, from outside of the sphere of relations between workers and employers." To supply this consciousness and thereby *create* a revolutionary mass movement was the task of the party.

From this position of Lenin's the implications range far. The revolution is not really the result of natural forces, of the conditions of capitalist production, as Marx would have it. The revolution, for Lenin, is the result of willful intervention by the

party to *divert* the natural course of history. However, there is no automatic assurance that the
party will arise, steel itself, and properly act to
bring about the revolution. This depends on the
historically accidental factors of the right doctrine
(Marxism) and unflinching leadership (Lenin
himself).

In Lenin's scheme doctrine assumes the utmost
importance. For here, and not in the social com-
position of the movement, is the only guarantee
that the party will preserve its revolutionary vigor.
Lenin demanded a doctrinal commitment without
reservations: "The *only* choice is: either the bourgeois or the socialist ideology. There is no middle
course. . . ." Because doctrine was the key to political success, it followed that any ideological dissension was tantamount to treason. After the revolution even worker-critics were denounced as
"petty-bourgeois" because they committed the doctrinal error of questioning the "socialist" character
which the Soviet regime ascribed to itself. Purity
of doctrine was essential. Only the vigilant repression of heterodoxy could insure the revolutionary
virtue of the party and prevent its contamination
by "reactionary" notions.

Here is Communist thought control in embryo.
It stems not from Marxism but from the use to
which Lenin put Marxism. Lenin started and led
a movement which contradicted the basic propositions of Marxism: he was determined on revolution
through sheer organizational force. This he proclaimed boldly—"Give us an organization of revolutionaries, and we shall overturn Russia." Marxism was neither his motive nor his guide, but only
his justification and his faith, giving the necessary
sanction for his revolutionary drive. Coming to
power with this faith, Lenin then had to cover

up its divergence from the original doctrine: the
Inquisition was a logical step.

Before the revolution, Russian Marxists of all
shades were acutely aware of the gap between
Russian conditions and their revolutionary expectations, and the problem was debated at great
length. The Menshevik faction, which had taken
shape in opposition to Lenin's organizational ideas,
added doctrinal differences to the cleavage by insisting on a strict reading of Marxist theory as applied to Russia: the path from feudalism through
capitalism to socialism, while it might be traversed
at an accelerated rate, could not be avoided. Russia
stood at the beginning only of the "bourgeois"
revolution, and no more ambitious program could
be entertained than a democratic government per-
mitting the most rapid development of private industry. (Curiously, doctrinaire Marxism in Russia
was almost an apology for capitalism.) The socialists could function only as a sort of "loyal opposition" until economic development and the growth
of the working class made the socialist revolution
feasible.

Such a prospect was utterly unacceptable to
Lenin, who was by temperament a revolutionary
above all else. His recourse was a maneuver which
has become characteristic of Communism: the manipulation of doctrine in order to justify a predeter-
mined political objective. Lenin wanted the party
of the proletariat—i.e., his Bolsheviks—to take
power; if Marxism seemed to pronounce this impossible under the existing Russian circumstances,
the doctrine would have to be reinterpreted. Lenin
decided that while the coming revolution could be

"bourgeois," it would have to be carried out by the most radical party, his own; he would establish a "democratic dictatorship of the proletariat and peasantry," to hold the ground until full measures of socialism became feasible.

In these manipulations by Lenin, words become mere slogans, incantations; all true meaning is lost in a tangle of contradictions. What clarity can come from speaking of a "democratic dictatorship"? How can the revolution be meaningfully "bourgeois" if the bourgeoisie does not conduct it? While the Bolsheviks had their rationalizations for such questions, fixity of definition in their theoretical concepts was being lost. For the Communists, like Humpty Dumpty, words have come to mean whatever the people in power say they mean.

A third approach to the problem of revolution in Russia, distinct from the Leninist and Menshevik views, was especially significant, for it actually guided the Bolsheviks in their seizure of power and justified for them their attempt at establishing a socialist society. This was the theory of the "permanent revolution" developed by Trotsky (who was at the time a left-wing Menshevik). The theory was so termed because of its two basic propositions: (1) the revolution in Russia would begin as a "bourgeois" revolution but it would remain in progress continuously or permanently as the workers' party came to power and began trying to introduce socialism; (2) a permanent state of revolution would ensue internationally as the uprising of the proletarian minority of Russia inspired the outbreak of the socialist revolution supposedly brewing in all the advanced countries of Europe. The two aspects of the vision were interdependent— Russia was, for the most part, so backward that the revolutionary workers' government was doomed to go under in a short time unless aid came from the Western proletarians.

When the Tsar fell in February 1917,* and confirmed the expectation of the Mensheviks by giving way to a bourgeois Provisional Government, Lenin was exhilarated by the prospect of seizing power in the name of the workers. Returning to Russia from his Swiss exile, he swung his party around to just the sort of course outlined by Trotsky (who at the same time joined the Bolsheviks) : the party would take advantage of the revolutionary situation and press for the most radical government. As the guarantee of success the Bolsheviks relied on the support of the international revolution which, they confidently expected, would be set off by their example. "All over the world the storm signals are flying," proclaimed the party congress that met in August 1917. Bukharin, at the time one of the most hot-headed of the Bolshevik leaders, declared on the same occasion, "We will wage a holy war in the name of the interests of all the proletariat. . . . We will light the fire of world socialist revolution."

On the eve of his successful seizure of power, Lenin gave full rein to his imagination and penned a series of utopian sketches outlining the character of the new regime. Most famous of these documents is the book, *State and Revolution,* a monument to Lenin's un-Leninist fancies of the revolutionary year 1917 and highly misleading as an illustration of its author's basic philosophy. (It is, unfortunately, commonly cited for just this pur-

* "Old style," by the Julian calendar, which was thirteen days behind the Western Gregorian calendar. Because of the traditional nomenclature of events the old style of dates is observed here respecting events in Russia up to the calendar reform of February 1918.

pose.) Lenin went back to draw anew from Marx, and particularly from the model of the Paris Commune. It was the task of the revolutionaries, Lenin now argued, to "smash the bourgeois state," abolish all the repressive institutions and distinctions of rank associated with the old order, and make a fresh start by instituting the dictatorship of the proletariat based on "the armed people": "The workers, having conquered political power, will break up the old bureaucratic apparatus, they will shatter it to its very foundations, until not one stone is left upon another; and they will replace it with a new one consisting of these same workers and employees, *against* whose transformation into bureaucrats measures will at once be undertaken, as pointed out in detail by Marx and Engels: (1) not only electiveness, but also instant recall; (2) payment no higher than that of ordinary workers; (3) immediate transition to a state of things when *all* fulfill the functions of control and superintendence, so that *all* become 'bureaucrats' for a time, and *no one,* therefore, can become a 'bureaucrat.'" The task of the dictatorship of the proletariat was to suppress the resistance of the "exploiting" classes, expropriate the instruments of production, and initiate the organization of a socialist economy. With the success of international revolution, the elimination of the class struggle, and the spontaneous execution of administrative tasks by the masses, the exercise of political power would become superfluous, and the state—i.e., the proletarian dictatorship created to carry out the tasks of revolution—would "wither away."

This was, to say the least, a sanguine vision, particularly out of keeping with the abysmal cultural level of the Russian masses. As we shall see, the Communists' underestimation of the intricacies

of modern governmental and industrial administration opened the way for an unanticipated but
overwhelming impact of these problems upon the
movement. The very nature of the Communist program was radically transformed as a result. The
existing bureaucracies, governmental and industrial, were never really "smashed" but only refash-
ioned and restaffed. Beginning as the most radical
attack on bureaucratic relationships and political
compulsion, Communism eventually became the
most elaborately entrenched system of hierarchical
organization and dictatorial violence.

In October 1917, the Bolsheviks swept into
power on the crest of a wave of elemental revolutionary emotion among the populace. Much as
Trotsky had envisioned it, the new regime, based
on the urban minority, found itself driven to measures progressively more dictatorial and more socialistic. While civil war raged, the Communists *
endeavored in the so-called period of "War Communism" (1918–21) to institute what they believed
to be a thoroughly socialist system, complete with
the nationalization of every little workshop and
the "withering away of money." Meanwhile the
parties opposing the Communists were one by one
outlawed. The "dictatorship of the proletariat" became indistinguishable from the dictatorship of
the Communist Party.

* The party name was changed in 1918 from "Russian Social-Democratic Workers' Party (of Bolsheviks)" to "Russian Communist Party (of Bolsheviks)."
In 1925, after the non-Russian parts of the country
were formally reincorporated into the Union of Soviet
Socialist Republics, it became the "All-Union Communist Party (of Bolsheviks)." In 1952, it was renamed
simply the "Communist Party of the Soviet Union."

All the while, this dictatorship of the "proletarian" party and its bootstrap operation to create a socialist society were maintained in the conviction that international revolution, in the chaotic years following World War I, was imminent. Nevertheless, Lenin took a step almost at the very beginning which belied the party's Marxist conviction that the Russian socialist regime could make sense only in conjunction with European support. This issue was peace with Germany. Bolshevik diehards—the "Left Communists"—pleaded for the proclamation of a "revolutionary war," which they fervently believed would evoke mass upheavals both in Germany and in the Entente countries. Peace with Germany, they felt, would betray the revolutionaries abroad and leave the new Soviet regime open to the corrupting forces of the bourgeoisie, Russian and foreign. To Lenin, by contrast, the defense of the Russian state suddenly became paramount once he was in power. He refused to risk a war that might destroy his new government, and if indulgence in humiliating power politics was the price, he was ready to pay it: the Carthaginian peace of Brest-Litovsk was signed in March 1918. By this act the die was cast: henceforth the security and success of the Soviet government in Russia were to transcend any considerations of revolutionary idealism, at home or abroad.

Lenin could always persuade himself that his policies were the incarnation of Marxian wisdom, though he could flexibly concede his errors, and he remained convinced for a time that world revolution was still just around the corner. By 1921, however, it was clear that things had gone awry, and that capitalism had succeeded in "stabilizing" itself in the rest of the world. Trotsky's second proposition, on which the first (socialism in Russia) intimately depended, had failed to materialize. It would seem that the Communist regime had no foundation for its existence! This was not just a theoretical void. There was an obvious upsurge of popular antagonism against the Bolshevik regime, its experiments, its excesses, and its signal failure to keep the wheels of the economy turning.

At this juncture Lenin displayed his tactical sagacity by suddenly sounding a retreat. Introducing the "New Economic Policy" (NEP), he put an end to the utopian violence of the civil war years, restored private trade to appease the peasants, and set a course of policy described as "state capitalism." Capitalist institutions and practices, complete with money, prices, cost accounting and occasional genuine strikes, were resumed, with one major difference: most large-scale enterprises and the financial and communications systems (the so-called "commanding heights" of the economy) were kept under government ownership. The result, in a sense, conformed to Lenin's old scheme of the "democratic dictatorship of the proletariat and peasantry"—a capitalistic economy run by the revolutionary party, which tried to balance the interests of workers, managers, peasants, and private traders, in anticipation of the time when progress in Russia and/or a resumption of the international revolution would make it possible to proceed toward the socialist goal of collectivist equality. Assurance that such steps would be undertaken when conditions permitted was provided by the allegedly proletarian character of the state. This in turn required, or at least justified, the rigorous enforcement of the Communist Party dictatorship, to prevent "bourgeois elements" from translating their economic recovery into political power. Such was Leninism—the disciplined party wielding po-

litical power in defiance of economic conditions—
when its author breathed his last in 1924.

3 STALINISM—"BUILDING SOCIALISM" IN THE SOVIET UNION

The situation of the Soviet regime in the 1920's,
insofar as its defenders could offer a theoretical
description of it, was that of a "workers' state"
ruling without outside support in a country still
largely backward, which by all the postulates of
Marxism was incapable of sustaining such a government. The "dictatorship of the proletariat" in
fact *preceded* the extensive development of industry and the working class, which were theoretically
the prerequisites for the proletarian revolution.
Postrevolutionary Russia offered the spectacle of
a Marxist regime trying to use its power to create
the economic base which was supposed to be mature before such a Marxist regime could exist. Did
this mean that Marxism was wrong in asserting the
dependence of political systems on the stage of economic development, and in the proposition that industrial abundance was a prerequisite for socialism? Or was the character of the Soviet regime in
fact changing, despite the retention of revolutionary labels, to adjust to the conditions of life in
which it found itself?

At the time, the Russian Communists were quite
aware of these problems and were seriously disturbed by them. A straightforward answer, however, was impeded by the exigencies of partisan
polemics in the factional debates then going on
in the party between the "ins" led by Stalin and
the "outs" under Trotsky. Trotsky and the Left Opposition, in an effort to discredit their rivals,

hinted that the leadership was beginning to pursue unsocialist policies. They charged in particular that the government was favoring the individual peasants too much at the expense of industry and the workers, and that the party and state were becoming excessively bureaucratic. They alleged further that this "deviation" was the natural result of Russian conditions which militated against the collectivist equality of socialism. While they hesitated to say so directly, they strongly implied that the Soviet regime was in grave danger of losing its quality as a "workers' state."

Insinuations of "bureaucratic perversion" or a "Thermidorean degeneration" of the revolution were naturally intolerable to Stalin and his associates in the party leadership, who depended heavily on their sense of Marxian orthodoxy for justification before the public and in their own eyes as well. They responded with a radical innovation in doctrine, significant both as an alteration in the substance of Marxist ideology and as a change in its function for the Communist state. The new idea was the theory of "socialism in one country," propounded by Stalin in December 1924. Based on one quotation from Lenin taken out of context and misinterpreted, Stalin's new proposition held that the new development of socialism could proceed in Russia alone, despite the country's backwardness, and that the prospects for the "workers' state" in Russia did not depend on the fortunes of the international revolution.

The issue between Stalin and Trotsky was not, as is often thought, whether to export revolution or play power politics (both factions talked of the former and supported the latter), but whether, in the absence of revolution abroad, Russia could be considered safe for socialism. The Opposition,

with the preponderance of Marxian reasoning behind it, argued the negative. The group in power
insisted on the unchallengeable correctness of its
position, and undertook to quell its critics both by
force and by the free manipulation of doctrine. It
became unpardonable heresy to speak of Trotsky's
theory of "permanent revolution" or the attendant
notion that Russia could not easily become socialist
on its own. "Trotsky does not appreciate the inherent strength of our revolution," charged Stalin. "Lack of faith in the strength and capabilities
of our revolution, lack of faith in the strength and
capabilities of the Russian proletariat—that is
what lies at the root of the theory of 'permanent
revolution.' "

Thanks to his control of the party organization,
Stalin had little difficulty in destroying the influence of his critics. Trotsky's Left Opposition was
expelled from the party in 1927, and Bukharin's
Right Opposition was condemned in 1929. In the
course of these factional struggles within the party,
the thinking of the victorious Stalinist group took
a radically new turn. Marxist-Leninist doctrine was
reduced to a mere political device. It became subject to reinterpretation without regard for the
spirit of the original, in order to meet the desire
of the party leadership for absolute doctrinal support of any policy which it wished to pursue. If
the peasants were to be conciliated, this had to be
deduced from the scriptures as the only true and
correct course of action; if they were to be coerced,
a new interpretation was required, and the old one
had to be denounced as the fabrication of hidden
counterrevolutionaries. One is tempted to suspect
that the party leaders, especially Stalin, were cyni-
cally manipulating phrases which they had ceased
to take seriously, yet the evidence by and large in-

dicates that they were really persuaded of their
true orthodoxy, and that the flexibility of policy
on which they insisted was enhanced rather than
restricted by the aura of orthodoxy which reinterpretation could confer on each new twist and turn.
Here is the familiar phenomenon of the party line,
with its unexpected zigs and zags so disconcerting
to the membership. Marxist-Leninist doctrine was
harnessed, through reinterpretation, to the task of
rationalizing action after the fact. This made the
doctrine lose all definite and permanent meaning;
it meant only what the leaders said it meant at any
particular time. The effect of this was to denude
the doctrine of all power as a guiding force; it
served no longer to direct action but only to justify
whatever might seem practical and expedient.

There was another serious implication of the
new use to which doctrine was put. Reinterpretation, as the case of "socialism in one country"
showed, often had to be contrived quite artificially
and was subject to embarrassing challenges. For
such doctrinal manipulation to proceed smoothly
and give the leadership the absolute justification
desired, the complete suppression of deviant points
of view was required; only one interpretation of the
scripture, on no matter what subject, could be allowed. The logical conclusion of this was the
thought control imposed in Soviet Russia in the
1930's—the sweeping subjection of every sphere of
expression to the dictates of Stalin and the official
spokesmen of the party.

The full realization of the implications of doctrinal sleight-of-hand and intellectual straitjack-
eting came after Stalin had assumed unchallenged
leadership over the Communist Party and the So-

viet government in 1929. This era witnessed the true establishment of the totalitarian state, and a profound alteration in the real mentality and goals of the Communist regime.

A foretaste of the trend was offered by Stalin very early, when he began elaborating on Lenin's theory of the party (itself a clear departure, in the decisive revolutionary role assigned to it, from the earlier understanding of Marxism). Asserted Stalin, "The proletariat needs the party not only to achieve the dictatorship; it needs it still more to maintain the dictatorship, to consolidate and expand it in order to achieve the complete victory of socialism . . . , imbuing the millions of proletarians with the spirit of discipline and organization . . . , creating among the proletarian masses a cementing force and bulwark against the corrosive influence of petty-bourgeois elements and petty-bourgeois habits . . . , helping the masses of the proletarians to educate themselves as a force capable of abolishing classes and of preparing the conditions for the organization of socialist production." Stalin assigned to the party, in the post-revolutionary era, when it enjoyed the blessings of power, the kind of driving function Lenin had envisaged only for the work of accomplishing the revolution. All of the organizational rules which Lenin had advanced for the success of the movement as an underground conspiracy Stalin now applied to the administration of the state and the conduct of its political life. Thus, the model of the disciplined party, as we shall see in detail later, was of decisive significance in shaping the character of the Soviet regime and the entire Communist movement as we know it today.

With his application of the Leninist party ideal to the postrevolutionary regime, Stalin supplied

himself with the means for solving the dilemma of
a socialist state in the wrong circumstances. The
party would be the instrument for transforming
the economic base of the society and "building socialism" from the top down. Later on Stalin himself acknowledged the late twenties and early thirties as the time of a "revolution from above," and
brought the official conception of the role of government more into line with reality by stressing
"the function of economic organization and cultural education by the state organs," as well as "the
function of protecting socialist property from
thieves and pilferers of the people's property" and
"the detection and punishment of the spies, assas-
sins and wreckers sent into our country by foreign
espionage services." It is not hard to see what this
approach did to the basic principles of Marxism:
historical materialism was cut to shreds. Stalin administered the doctrinal coup de grâce himself in
1934: "There can be no justification for references
to so-called objective conditions. . . . The part
played by so-called objective conditions has been
reduced to a minimum; whereas the part played
by our organizations and their leaders has become
decisive, exceptional. What does this mean? It
means that from now on nine-tenths of the responsibility for the failures and defects in our work
rests, not on 'objective' conditions, but on ourselves,
and on ourselves alone."

Characteristically, these sweeping revisions of
Marxist theory came as responses to practical political needs. The party and its General Secretary
were in fact becoming supreme, and theory was
helplessly dragged in the wake of dictatorial expediency. In 1929, having eliminated his political
rivals and perfected the machinery of political
control through the party, Stalin commenced a

massive effort to transform the country by the use of governmental force. Industrial development was pushed at an astonishing rate; agriculture was completely reorganized, with the forcible collectivization of the peasants; controls and policing ramified without end; the totalitarian state became a reality. In both theory and practice, political organization and personal power became for the Communists the really significant determinants of the course of history. Lenin and Stalin became the heroes (and Lenin remains one) without whom the Communist system could never have come into being.

While Stalin and his apologists never weakened in their professed allegiance to Marxism, expedient reinterpretation and the liquidation of the old school of Communists served to convert the doctrine, in almost every substantial sense, into the opposite of the original. If the state had obviously become the primary force in social development, transcending all limitations of the economic "base," this would be accepted as pure Marxism. Expectations of the "withering away of the state" in the foreseeable future were condemned by Stalin in 1934 as "unhealthy sentiments." Of the political and intellectual "superstructure" of society Stalin wrote in 1950: "The superstructure is a product of the base; but this does not mean that it merely reflects the base, that it is passive, neutral, indifferent to the fate of its base, to the fate of the classes, to the character of the system. On the contrary, no sooner does it arise than it becomes an exceedingly active force." This implied, according to a subsequent official explanation, "the special creative role of the new socialist superstructure and in particular of the socialist state, which represents the principal instrument in the creation of

the economic basis of socialism. . . . Now, in the
period of the gradual transition from socialism to
communism, there comes into view in full power
and energy the role of the Soviet state as the chief
instrument for the building up of communism."

Not only the metaphysics of the Soviet leaders
but their policy norms as well were recast in the
1930's. When the requirements for industrial success in a nation of stolid peasants ran counter to
revolutionary objectives of equalitarianism and individual liberation, Stalin pronounced such goals to
be "reactionary," the "petty-bourgeois prejudices"
of "leftist blockheads." The task, he declared in
1931, was "to do away with wage equalization . . . ,
to put an end to lack of personal responsibility . . . , to change our attitude towards the engineers and technicians of the old school . . . , to
introduce and reinforce business accounting." Progressive education and compassionate criminology
went by the boards. A wholesale shift took place
in the implicit social philosophy of the Soviet regime: instead of economic conditions being held
responsible for the defects in human beings, human beings were to be held responsible for the defects in economic conditions. Instead of being
liberated, man needed to be disciplined.

Simultaneously with the industrialization drive
and these changes in social policy, stringent party
controls were imposed in almost every field of cultural and intellectual activity, ranging from music
to psychology. Once these controls were in force,
drastic changes of line could be effected—though
always under the artificial label of Marxian orthodoxy. In almost every field of thought and social
action—history, literature, education, law, industrial organization, even the mores of sex and patriotism—the Soviet regime turned in practice, and

in its revised theory as well, to the model of the
most conservative fashions of a century past. All
this became "progressive," while what the revolutionaries had thought they were fighting for was
now styled "bourgeois degeneracy" or worse. Old-
fashioned notions of historical accuracy were dismissed by Stalin as "rotten liberalism," as he proceeded to rewrite the past to prove his own
undeviating orthodoxy and never-failing genius.
Every obstacle, every difficulty, every failure of the
"socialist" state was soon attributed to nothing but
the individual malevolence of "wreckers," spies,
and "Trotsky-Bukharin fiends," until the entire
country was convulsed in the later 1930's in an orgy
of purge and confession.

The achievement of "socialism" was proclaimed
in 1935, and incarnated in a new constitution in
1936. "Classes" were declared to be a thing of the
past, even if "survivals of capitalism in the consciousness of the masses"—i.e., graft and black-
marketeering—continued to prove troublesome.
Now only distinctions of "strata" were admitted,
though they soon came to involve all the differences of income and status that prevailed in "bourgeois" societies. Not only in the manner of its
development and in its modes of dictatorial operation, but even in the goals and values which it
finally settled on, the Soviet regime came close to
complete negation of the doctrine which inspired
its establishment.

4 THE LEGACY OF
MARXIAN SOCIALISM

It is often pointed out that Marx erred in pre-
dicting that the proletarian revolution would be
initiated in the advanced countries of the West,

and that the success of the Communists in Russia
and then in Asia is proof of this error. Would it not,
however, be equally valid to contend that self-
styled Marxist revolutions under the wrong conditions were really not at all the kind of movement
which Marx had in mind? We must distinguish
between revolution caused by the forces which
Marx analyzed, and revolutionaries who are or
claim to be inspired by Marx's revolutionary
program. Only in the latter sense was the Russian
Revolution Marxist. Communism's claim to Marxist
legitimacy has nothing to do with the real understanding of historical forces—it is only a pretense,
anxiously imposed and self-deceiving.

To illuminate this state of affairs we need only
recall the Marxian notion of "ideology" as a system
of "false consciousness" embraced for the greater
glory and justification of a given social order or
movement. Applying this concept of ideology to the
Communist movement in power, we find indeed
that claims are made by the powers-that-be which
have little, if any, relation to political and social
reality. They need not have—their function is to
provide the regime with the sense of righteousness
and legitimacy which it desires. We can thus
understand the "dictatorship of the proletariat"
and the "classless society" not as actual policies
or intentions but as the window dressing for a
social system whose reality is vastly different.

While the Communist social system neither fits
nor follows from the Marxian philosophy of history
and society, we must not lose sight of certain
features of Communism which are either derived
from its Marxist heritage or from the general background of nineteenth-century socialism. Modern

Communism, despite all its differences from Marx, is still a particular form of socialism, if we define socialism simply as any system of public control over economic life. Of course, Communism is not the only genuine form of socialism, as the Communists claim. Other forms of socialism can and do have completely different political, ethical, and economic characteristics, and are entirely independent of the Communist movement, both historically and presently. Communism has nonetheless been outstandingly successful in capitalizing upon the socialist tradition. The socialist principles embodied in Communism still exercise a powerful emotional influence, not only in attracting outsiders to the movement and sustaining the belief of the rank and file, but even in the innermost self-justifying convictions of the Communist leaders.

The basic socialist feature of Communism, which the Communists have always held as a primary axiom, is the principle of the nationalization and public ownership of industry. In Marxism the dispossession of the capitalists is the essence of the proletarian revolution, and the liquidation of the private ownership of industry has been a consistent Communist aim everywhere from the very beginning. Nationalization has been pursued by the Communists to the maximum that their political security would permit, regardless of economic losses that might ensue. We see this at various times—the irrational centralization of industry in the hands of the Soviet state during the period of War Communism; Stalin's violent collectivization of the peasants and expropriation of private traders after 1928; the drives against private peasants and businesses in Eastern Europe after the Communists took over; the Chinese drive for a

completely communal economic organization in
1958 after some years of cautious coöperation with
individual business and farming. The ideal of public ownership is so strong in Communism that the
theoretically private coöperative nature of the Soviet collective farms has repeatedly bothered Communist theorists as an impurity in the system.
Theft of socialist property is an affront to the
whole system and is treated as one of the most
heinous of crimes.

The other side of the coin of nationalization is
the intense anticapitalist spirit which has always
characterized Communism, whatever temporary
accommodation with bourgeois forces the Communist leaders may have felt compelled to make.
The Communist has a deep moral antipathy to
capitalism, which to him means "speculation," "the
exploitation of man by man," and "imperialism."

Khrushchev, seeking to recharge this moral
fervor, declared to the Twenty-First Party Congress in 1959, "The spirit of individualism, personal
gain, greed for profits, hostility and confusion—
such is the essence of bourgeois morality. Exploitation of man by man, on which bourgeois society
is built, represents the grossest violation of
morals." Socialism he extolled as the creed of
goodness: "a socialist morality—a morality of collaboration and collectivism, friendship and mutual
help." In Soviet Russia any attempt by an individual to make a profit by reselling even something as trivial as a pair of shoes is speculation, a
moral lapse attributed to "bourgeois ideology," and
ground for criminal prosecution.

The requirements of socialist morality have
never cramped the ruthless realism of Communist
policy-making. Thanks to its dictatorial powers
over thought and communication, the Communist

movement has become the greatest system of organized hypocrisy the world has ever known. Every charge made against the capitalist democracies could be hurled back against the Communists ten times over, but Communism carefully defines all the epithets it uses in terms that are applicable only to capitalism. Communist governments sanctimoniously deny their own glaring transgressions in exploitation and imperialism and continue unabated their fervent denunciation of these sins on the part of capitalism.

The anticapitalist spirit of Communism is, as we shall see, of fundamental importance in understanding the relations between Communism and non-Communist powers and movements. Communist anticapitalism defines the fundamental struggle and feeds the fires of international suspicion with its fuel of moral fervor. In practice anticapitalism has not determined the actual tactics of Communist foreign policy, nor has it prevented temporary alliances between the Communists and non-Communist powers, but it has made the kind of basic accord and trust that prevails among the Western democracies out of the question between the Communist states and the rest of the world.

Communist hostility to capitalism as such has not prevented Communist regimes from borrowing or adapting a great deal of the technological and organizational character of capitalist industry. American capitalist technology and productivity are still the frank envy of the Communists. It is the presumed spirit of capitalism which the Communists reject, while they can readily take over its working details. The power of the socialist ideal under Communism lies in its emotional generalities but not in its particulars, which, as we have already noted, are subject to infinite variation and

were drastically modified by the Communists
themselves after they came to power. Communism
has in effect copied the entire system of modern
concentrated capitalist industry beneath the level
of the institutions of ownership, and has extended
the social logic of the factory to the whole of society. This should not appear too paradoxical if we
cut through the Marxist presuppositions that
Communism represents the postcapitalist dictatorship of the proletariat, and realize that in reality
Communism is not the successor to capitalism but
a parallel alternative form of the industrializing
society. The relation of Communism to the process
of industrialization is fundamental in understanding the movement, and we shall devote an entire
chapter to this subject later on.

Apart from its premises about social organization, which have been greatly modified to fit the
requirements of industrialization, Communism retains from its Marxian background powerful elements of propaganda appeal. Communism clings
firmly to the myth of the "classless society" and
the "workers' state," much as American capitalism
professes to be democratic and equalitarian even
though most Americans are extremely conscious of
the realities of power and status. Myths have a certain power of satisfaction even when there is no
effort to live up to them—or perhaps especially
when there is no effort to live up to them. In addition, the proletarian ideology of Communist Marxism does promote some concern for the masses.
They are at least tightly integrated into the social
system rather than alienated and neglected as in
many of the Latin and Asian countries, even if this
integration means control more than satisfaction.
They are provided with public services—education,
pensions, free medical care—which, though often

limited in quality and quantity, do contribute substantially to popular welfare. Most important, channels are open for upward social mobility through education and loyal effort. The ordinary man is not ignored by the Communist dictatorship, as he is in old-fashioned absolute regimes. He is too useful to be left unorganized. Neither in suffering nor in success can he stand alone.

Our discussion of Marxism would not be complete without considering how Communist reality appears in the light of Marxian theory objectively brought to bear on it. We have already noted how the Communists' retention of Marxist doctrine corresponds to Marx's notion of "ideology" as "false consciousness" to which a ruling class clings. Here we will consider the idea of economic conditioning of social structures and political organizations, and the possibility of human action producing results which, owing to the play of circumstances, are other than what was intended.

In barest outline, the situation which we observe is one where a political movement, calling itself Marxist and aspiring to establish proletarian socialism, but relying primarily on an instrument (the party) which was not derived from Marxism and whose importance contradicts Marxism, succeeded in assuming political power under circumstances far removed from the capitalist maturity which was presumably the anteroom to socialism. Such Communist successes occur in areas which are backward but under the shadow of the industrialized West, and which are beginning to experience the dislocations and frustrations of exceedingly rapid change. This situation actually parallels Marx's "bourgeois" revolution, though

under circumstances which are so different as to
rule out much similarity between the resulting
movements. Marx never took such a situation into
account, and Lenin did not pursue its implications
fully.

Communists have seized power, professing certain objectives, but in situations which make the
results likely to be quite different. Economic conditions—the problems of overcoming backwardness
and the problems of running industry once it is
developed—have a massive effect. The revolution
begins to take an entirely unanticipated course.
Bent on keeping power, and enabled to do so by
the efficacy of the political machinery which the
Leninist concept of the party provides, the Communists introduce one expedient after another.
The revolutionary program is rapidly eroded, and
in its stead rises the structure of the totalitarian
state. The archetype was perfected in Russia in
the 1930's.

To call the result a "workers' state" in a "classless society" becomes an elaborate fiction. It became apparent soon after the establishment of the
Communist dictatorship in Russia that the regime
would not tolerate any independent voice, however
proletarian, that claimed to speak for the workers
and against the party. The workers, according to
Lenin, could not by themselves be "socialist," could
not understand the dictatorship which professed
to represent them, without the educative influence
of the party and its ideology. To attack the party
or the self-styled "proletarian" state was to betray oneself as "petty-bourgeois." In China, the
Communists carried the proletarian fiction a step
further: the revolution did not depend on the
indoctrination of the workers by the party; it
could dispense with the workers altogether, if the

party was strong and ideologically armed with the
correct "proletarian" doctrine.

*Communism is not the outcome of the indus-
trial maturity and the workers' movement analyzed by Marx. It is a product of the accelerated
impact of Western civilization on the rest of the
world. Marxism, a doctrine developed in the West
and for the West, became, by what is strictly
speaking a historical accident, the irrational inspiration of a vast movement distinguished by its
combination of the despotism of the East and the
West's own standards of material accomplishment.
Communism is not caused by Marxism nor is its
character determined by Marxism, except in certain superficial respects. Marxism, appropriately
manipulated and encysted in dogma, is the "ideology," the official faith, of a movement grown as
far apart from its doctrinal antecedents as the
Renaissance Popes from the Twelve Apostles.*

2 Communism and Revolution

Communism is a product of history, as well as of the intentions of its progenitors. The movement as we know it has emerged from the complicated workings of a particular society— Russia—under conditions of great stress. Communism grew out of the Russian Revolution and would never have existed without it. Accordingly, one of the first requirements for understanding the movement is to put it in the context of revolution, as a natural, if perhaps abnormal, historical phenomenon.

1 THE REVOLUTIONARY PROCESS

Revolution, as we understand it here, must be distinguished from minor political overturns, for which the terms "revolt" or "coup d'état" might be reserved. The great revolutions—the English Revolution of the seventeenth century, the French Revolution, the Russian, the German Revolution of 1918–45 and the Chinese Revolution that began in 1911, possibly others as well—were not abrupt events but long-term processes of social upheaval, taking decades to work themselves out. Furthermore, they all appear to be members of a definite class of events, characterized, despite vast dif-

46

ferences of detail, by a certain common pattern.

The course of development to which the major revolutions have tended to conform has often been described metaphorically as a wave or as a fever. The collapse of the old order leads to an upsurge of revolutionary feeling and experimentation, of elemental social conflict and political violence, which in turn is followed by a reaction or recovery back toward more familiar forms of political and social life. Further oscillations back and forth may ensue (depending on the severity of the initial upheaval) until stability is finally attained. The result is usually a compromise, with certain fundamental changes but preserving many of the basic features of the old order.

The beginning of the process is marked by a characteristic revolutionary situation, when social change has produced rising tension and unrest. The government refuses to make the necessary concessions, becomes more and more oppressive though ineffectively so, and alienates virtually everyone. A shock—military or financial—can then bring the whole structure of the *ancien régime* tumbling down, and the moderate revolutionaries—the reformers—are able to take over. This is what occurred in England in 1640–42, in France in 1789, and in the February Revolution of 1917 in Russia. Also analogous are the German Revolution of November 1918, which ushered in the Weimar Republic, and the overthrow of the Chinese Imperial government in 1911.

In every case, it rapidly becomes apparent that the moderate revolution has only opened a Pandora's box of mass disaffection and social conflict. Long pent-up grievances find expression and are translated into action. Compromises like constitutional monarchy break down. The atmosphere

becomes increasingly radical, and the political
groups most in accord with this new spirit are
thrust to the fore. The moderate revolutionaries
and the extremists fall out with one another, and
the extremists take power. In England, this "second revolution" was represented by the army
coup and the establishment of the Commonwealth
in 1648 and 1649; in France it was the upheaval
which gave birth to the First Republic and the
rule of the Jacobins in 1792 and 1793; in Russia,
it was the Bolsheviks' October Revolution which
overthrew the moderate but shaky Provisional
Government. Germany and China are not so obviously comparable, though perhaps the Nazis' accession to power in 1933 corresponds to the radical
seizure of power in the earlier cases.

The second revolution is the signal for the outbreak of the most intense political fanaticism and
violent civil strife. Old and new enmities are given
free rein. The jailed monarch is executed. Utopian
innovations are forced down the nation's throat.
The new revolutionary regime openly resorts to
terror as it endeavors to extirpate its enemies and
enforce what Crane Brinton terms "the Republic
of Virtue." In Russia the extreme of open and protracted civil war was reached. (The English Civil
War, by contrast, was a struggle between the old
regime and all the revolutionaries, until the cleavage among the latter sharpened.)

In time, the revolutionaries overreach themselves. As opposition to their extremism and violence mounts, contrary trends appear and a crisis
is reached. In the case of Russia, analysis of the
developments which occur from this point on is
difficult because the superficial continuity of the
Communist regime obscures deeper changes. We
will reserve treatment of the later phases of the

Russian Revolution for the following section, and consider here the English and French experiences.

One of the typical postrevolutionary changes is the exhaustion of revolutionary emotion, in the face of growing antirevolutionary feeling. The revolutionary wave, after reaching its peak, begins to subside, and life in general begins to return to its normal or more familiar ways. If the revolutionary government refuses to adjust to the new balance of social forces, it is overthrown. Thus we have, in the French Revolution, the coup d'état of the "Ninth Thermidor of the Year II" (the revolutionary equivalent for July 27, 1794), when Robespierre was overthrown, the Terror stopped, and the puritanical regime of the extremists terminated. The effect, socially, was much the same in the English Restoration of 1660, which saw the return of Charles II and the Good Old Days.

The other characteristic development after the peak of revolutionary fervor has been reached is the trend toward individual dictatorship, less fanatic, perhaps, but equally ruthless and more efficient than the initial revolutionary regime. In France this was initiated by the coup d'état of the "Eighteenth Brumaire" (November 9, 1799), which brought Napoleon Bonaparte to power. The English analogue differed in preceding rather than following the "Thermidorean reaction" back to normalcy in social life. Oliver Cromwell assumed virtually absolute power in 1653 and ruled as a military dictator until his death in 1658. War accompanied both regimes; Napoleon's evoked an unprecedented outburst of national energy and aggressive expansion.

In both the English and French cases, the dictatorship came to an end only as a result of a historical accident—the confusion occasioned by the death of the dictator, in the first instance, and in the latter, total military defeat. These upsets provided the opportunity for the actual restoration of the prerevolutionary monarchy, and Charles II and Louis XVIII, respectively, came out of exile to assume the thrones of their ancestors. Ostensibly the whole revolutionary era was to be forgotten.

But despite reaction on the surface, the clock cannot really be set back. Much of the fundamental change brought about by the revolution proves to be enduring, and its principles ultimately have their way. The towering issues of the English Revolution—religious toleration and the supremacy of Parliament over the king—were both ultimately decided in favor of the revolutionary point of view. The French Revolution involved, basically, the concept of individual rights and legal equality, and a government that was centralized and above all rational, the whole being capped by the new mass nationalism which the revolution introduced to all of Europe. All of these elements were preserved, whatever the form of the regimes which followed in France in kaleidoscopic succession.

In large measure the experiments and excesses which appear in the heat of the revolution are repudiated. As often as not these more ephemeral accomplishments of the revolution are liquidated even before the restoration of the old regime. Democracy, for example, as the theoretical right of universal manhood suffrage, endured in France only from 1792 to 1795. Bonaparte, when he made himself Emperor in 1804, went far toward reviving the ancient social and political hierarchy, even if the faces were new, and he restored the Catholic Church to its place of privilege. In France, at least, the restoration was well under way before the Bourbons came back.

It was, of course, the intention of the restored monarchs and their entourages to undo the work of the revolution altogether. But as a new generation harked back to the ideas of the revolution, forces of opposition accumulated which were sufficient to overthrow the absolutists and affirm the compromise of tradition and revolution. The upshot in England was the "Glorious Revolution" of 1688, deposing James II and affirming the constitutional primacy of Parliament. France presents a more complicated picture: the July Revolution of 1830, installing the "bourgeois monarch" Louis Philippe, went part of the way toward a reconciliation with the revolutionary tradition, but whether because of the insufficient liberalism of the new regime or the new stresses of the age of industrialism, or both, the July Monarchy proved unstable. Not until it underwent a whole new series of revolutionary upheavals between 1848 and 1871 did France finally achieve the stability of sorts that was the Third Republic.

To recapitulate, the pattern against which we shall measure the Russian experience is this: accumulation of tension; breakdown of the old monarchical government; moderate revolution; extremist revolution; "Thermidorean" reaction, preceded or followed by a military-like dictatorship; conservative trend, breakdown of the dictatorship, and restoration of the prerevolutionary regime; reaction against the restoration regime, and revival, in moderated form, of the revolutionary tradition.

Historians who are on their guard against any sweeping philosophical interpretations of the past

would contend that the construction of such a
pattern as has here been adduced for the process
of revolution is meaningless. It is true that every
historical situation is unique, the product of myriads of factors which can never recur in the same
combination. Many people therefore argue that
apparent similarities in history are a matter of
accidental analogy and that no prediction of the
future course of events can be made. The pattern
of revolution—and here we must indeed endorse
the point clearly—is not a "law" that somehow
asserts itself mysteriously to make events conform to the standard.

There is, nevertheless, a similarity in the course
of events in the revolutions we have discussed
which cannot possibly be dismissed as accidental.
Despite the vast differences of detail and person-
alties in the various situations, the revolutions do
have something in common: they reflect a recurring kind of political crisis—acute political
breakdown in a tense society—and a recurring pattern of response to such a crisis. The natural result
is the characteristic sequence of swings in the
political pendulum. The forces for change which
are set off, and the reactions to such changes, are
such that no matter how different the situations
and the intentions of the people involved, the revolutionary process in one form or another has to be
worked out. It is important to distinguish between
the essentials of the process, and the details and
timing which can vary from case to case. Such a
distinction will prove critical in discerning the full
revolutionary cycle in Soviet Russia.

There remain several practical objections to the
use of a pattern of revolution. The process as set
forth here or in any other version is just one interpretation of a vast and complicated record of

events. It is at best a hypothesis, a mere guess as to the essential forces at work. Its validity is limited because there are so few examples of great revolutions from which to generalize; it is difficult to distinguish essence from accident with any degree of certainty. Furthermore, even to the extent that the revolutionary pattern does seem valid, one can never be sure, when applying it to a new and incomplete revolution, just where the recent events fit. The meaning of the present is always obscure until it has been claimed by the past and can no longer be affected by human efforts. In the wisdom of hindsight there is the assurance of futility.

2 THE PROCESS OF REVOLUTION IN RUSSIA

Communism cannot be divorced from the Russian Revolution. It is a product of the revolution in Russia, and at least some of its fundamental features can be ascribed to the natural operation of the revolutionary process, although this by no means can account completely for the movement and its characteristics. The Russian Revolution must therefore be understood in some detail, both as a manifestation of the recurring phenomenon of social revolution, and in its particular aspects as well.

The revolutionary situation in Russia was the product of a long period of ferment and accumulating tension. Many decades before the monarchy and the serf-based feudal society of Russia began to experience serious dislocation, currents of protest and of revolutionary hope were arising under the stimulus of the liberal and socialist thought which burgeoned in Europe during the second half of the eighteenth century and the first half of the nineteenth. The Russian revolutionary movement, harking back to the abortive "Decembrist" coup of 1825, was peculiarly a movement of disaffected members of the educated upper (and later on middle) class, while the revolution itself was unique in the degree to which it was consciously hoped for and planned.

During the third quarter of the nineteenth century the absolute monarchy in Russia had shown a disposition to modernize itself, but after the assassination of Tsar Alexander II by revolutionary terrorists in 1881, the government set its face steadfastly against the slightest relaxation or diminution of its absolute power. This, coupled with the repressive incompetence of the last tsar and most of his ministers, made a revolutionary explosion more likely both to occur and to succeed. The explosive material was meanwhile being manufactured rapidly in the last decade of the nineteenth century and the first years of the twentieth, as Russia at last began to experience the impact of the industrial revolution and the new social tensions which characteristically accompanied it.

The revolutionaries found their cause invigorated under these circumstances. They began to get significant mass support, and real political parties representing the workers (Social Democrats), the peasants (Socialist Revolutionaries) and the liberal middle class (Constitutional Democrats) were organized. When the government got itself involved in war with Japan in 1904 and 1905, and was staggering under its defeats in the Far East, the accumulation of discontent burst forth. A wave of riots, demonstrations, and mutinies was capped by a general strike and an abortive insurrection in

Moscow—the so-called "Revolution of 1905." This was but the curtain raiser to the real affair. The government made timely concessions, proclaimed a constitutional regime which proved to be very limited, and restored order.

While the revolutionary movement was thus set back, the industrial development of the country went on apace. Some writers have contended that this trend toward modernization could have brought with it gradual political reform, and that the upheaval of revolution could have been avoided—but the question is entirely hypothetical. The intrusion of an external strain—involvement in World War I—threw an unbearable burden on the Russian economy and put the cumbersome and addle-pated tsarist regime to a test which it could not pass. Every stratum of society was alienated by the government's fumbling and its bloody military defeats. When food riots gave the signal for mass demonstrations in the capital, Petrograd (now Leningrad), late in February 1917, the government of Nicholas II went to pieces, literally overnight.

The Russian monarchy, being in an advanced stage of decomposition, was swept away much more quickly than the French, while in England the royalists held out through almost five years of civil war. Generally speaking, the events in each stage of the revolution in Russia were more extreme than in the corresponding phases of the earlier revolutions. In the confusion following the collapse of the tsarist regime, there were actually two new governing authorities set up. One, assuming sovereignty officially, was the Provisional Government, composed chiefly of representatives of the upper and middle classes, who dominated the Duma (the limited parliamentary body set up

after 1905). The other was a new creation, the
Petrograd Soviet (in Russian, *sovet,* "council")
of Workers' and Soldiers' Deputies, which, with its
counterparts in other cities and regions, exercised
from the start considerable *de facto* power.

The February Revolution was the signal for a
tremendous outpouring of centuries-old grievances. Almost all authority and all restraints dissolved in an upsurge of primeval anarchism among
the Russian masses. The war-weary soldiers de-
serted the trenches; the peasants seized the
estates; the workers threw the industrialists out of
their factories. Clutching at any support, the Provisional Government drew in the leaders of the
soviets, until, with Kerensky's assumption of the
premiership in July 1917, the government became
largely a soviet affair. But in the meantime the
original leaders of the soviets—Menshevik Social
Democrats and Socialist Revolutionaries—had
failed to keep abreast of the growing spirit of
radicalism. By the fall of 1917 they were losing
control of the soviets to a newly powerful group of
extremists—Lenin's Bolsheviks. Taking for their
own the aspirations of the newly liberated lower
classes, the Bolsheviks proclaimed their goal of
"bread, land, and peace," and demanded "all power
to the soviets"—implying, of course, all power to
the Bolsheviks.

The actual assumption of power by the extremists was comparatively easy. The soviets were already as much a governing authority as Kerensky's
ministry, and a show of force on October 25 (November 7), 1917, sufficed to put an end to the Provisional Government. With the endorsement of the
soviets, a new cabinet headed by Lenin—the
"Council of People's Commissars"—was set up, and

the "Soviet" regime which has formally endured ever since came into being.

Inasmuch as the Communists have never been overthrown, some observers have been led to conclude that the Russian Revolution, reaching its peak in October 1917, has never left that point, and that Soviet totalitarianism is simply the revolution perpetuated in all its intensity. It can be shown quite easily, however, that beneath the surface continuity of the Soviet regime and its professed doctrine, fundamental changes continued to take place. Developments which follow the pattern of revolution outlined above can indeed be discerned in Soviet Russia. Overt and violent changes of government at each stage of the revolutionary process, while likely, are details which can vary from case to case and are not essential to the process itself. The basic emotional fluctuations of radicalism, conservatism, and authoritarianism, which constitute the essence of the revolutionary process, have made themselves powerfully felt in the changes which the Soviet regime has experienced in the course of its history.

When the Bolsheviks took power, the most extreme point in the Russian Revolution was yet to come. Initially the Bolsheviks coöperated with or tolerated the other socialist parties in the soviets, and moderated their plans for the socialistic reordering of the economy. Lenin called this the policy of "one foot in socialism." The most radical phase of the revolution began in the summer of 1918, when the Civil War broke out between the Soviet government and its opponents, the "Whites" (who ranged from moderate socialists through

middle-class liberals to arch-reactionaries and
proto-fascists). Terror commenced on both sides;
fanaticism mounted; non-Communist political
groups were outlawed in Soviet territory; violent
"requisitioning" of the peasants' food stocks commenced; and an effort was launched to establish
a completely socialized economy. This was the period of War Communism, lasting from 1918 to 1921,
when the Whites were being overcome. So far, the
parallel with the English Puritans and with the
Jacobins in France is dramatically apparent.

In 1921, the Communists found themselves in
a desperate state. Their utopianism and excesses
were alienating more and more of the population,
including many of the people who had originally
supported the October Revolution. The nation was
growing tired of revolution, while the chaos of civil
war and class strife had brought the economy almost to a standstill. On the other hand, the most
extreme and idealistic of the Communists were
themselves becoming disaffected over the expediencies which the Soviet regime had adopted in its
struggle to survive—especially its reliance on centralized bureaucratic authority and its failure to
realize absolute equality of all citizens. The "Workers' Opposition," on the far left of the Communist
Party, corresponded to the left-wing Hebertist
faction among the Jacobins, or to the socialistic
sects such as the Diggers and the Levellers in
revolutionary England. The growing currents of
opposition, both radical and conservative, combined to erupt in an armed challenge to the Soviet
regime. Peasant guerrilla forces took to the field,
and the naval base at Kronstadt (near Petrograd)
revolted in the name of the October Revolution
against the "commissarocracy."

Lenin's master stroke at this point, viewed in

the perspective of revolutionary history, was to
carry out his own "Thermidor." He proclaimed the
New Economic Policy, and with it an end to the
effort to reconstruct Russian society overnight.
Primary attention was given to meeting the basic
material needs of the population, even if this required broad concessions to the spirit of capitalism,
and life for the average man began to return to
normal. Revolutionary emotions were exhausted;
relief was the general feeling, even among most
Communists. The Republic of Virtue was at an
end.

Such a shift to the right created the problem
of disposing of the die-hard revolutionary extremists. They had to be curbed and purged, and Lenin
set the wheels of his party machinery into motion
to accomplish just this. The Workers' Opposition
was denounced as a "petty-bourgeois anarchist
deviation," condemned and broken up; it shared
the fate of earlier idealist hold-outs, like Babeuf
in France and Lilburne in England.

Suppression of critics on the left was particularly necessary for the Communist leadership
if it was to continue to represent itself as the exclusively correct "proletarian" regime. Thus began the period when Marxism was fundamentally
transformed, both in its meaning and in its use:
it lost the power to guide, and was relegated to the
role of justifying every governmental act after the
fact, while for the rank and file it became a matter
of obligatory faith. Viewed in the context of the
revolutionary process, this change in the significance of doctrine was quite natural. If the revolutionary extremists were to hold power during
the ebb tide of the next phase without repudiating
their own creed, they would be compelled to resort
to such casuistry, and to suppress the criticism

which might expose their rationalizations. Engels once wrote of the revolutionary leader whose movement does not enjoy propitious circumstances, "He is compelled to represent not his party or his class, but the class for whom conditions are ripe for domination. In the interest of the movement itself, he is compelled to defend the interests of an alien class, and to feed his own class with phrases and promises."

The NEP was a period of bold pretension but cautious action. The Trotskyists, after they had fallen out with the rest of the Communist leadership in 1923 (when Lenin was already on his death bed), actually began to compare Soviet developments to the Thermidorean reaction in France after 1794. Such was the situation which prompted Lenin's successors in the party leadership—Zinoviev, Stalin, Bukharin—to begin the process of doctrinal reconstruction. Anxious or ambitious, these men would shield themselves with the cover of orthodoxy no matter where practical considerations might lead them.

It was only logical to proceed from the idea of Thermidor and look for a rising Bonaparte. Both factions actually began to do this; Trotsky's enemies could point out that as a popular military leader he represented such a threat, while the Left Opposition soon perceived the menace of Stalin. Zinoviev's partner Kamenev warned in 1925, after they had broken with Stalin and were at the point of joining Trotsky, "Comrade Stalin cannot fulfill the role of unifier of the Bolshevik staff. We are against the theory of one-man rule, we are against creating a 'Duce.' "

The Opposition's alarm was justified but futile.

Stalin used his control of the party's organizational machinery to build an irresistible political machine, and then by adroit political maneuvering he eliminated all his rivals at the top level of the party. Simultaneously he put an end to the NEP and energetically launched his new policies of forced industrialization, collectivization of agriculture, and totalitarian control. The Thermidorean relaxation of the NEP had come to an end, as the new dictator applied the lash to evoke from the country an unprecedented effort toward the goal of industrial power.

The differences between Stalin and Bonaparte are obvious, but the analogy is nonetheless remarkable. Both imposed themselves on their respective nations at corresponding stages of the revolutionary process; both demanded and got the release of tremendous national energy. They differed, of course, in that France's violence was aimed outward in military expansion, while Russia's at this stage was directed inward. In the basis of their power the two dictatorships differed outwardly but were essentially akin: Bonaparte's prominence as a military leader and Stalin's success as boss of the party organization brought to power in both cases the man backed by the best organized group in the country. By the time of Stalin's triumph the Communist Party was permeated with military thinking and organization, and if it is viewed in its own terms as an army for waging class war, Stalin's regime can indeed be classed with the earlier cases of postrevolutionary military dictatorship.

From this point on the changes in the Soviet regime were much more subtle. The continuity of the leadership and its policies, at least until Stalin's death in 1953, makes it difficult to demonstrate

any further stages in the revolutionary process.
How could there have been anything, indeed, corresponding to the English and French restora-
tions? A strong case can be made for the argument
that Soviet Russia has never left the "Bonapartist"
phase of dictatorship.

Rather than rest with such an exception, however, it would be preferable to revise our conception of the revolutionary pattern, to cover both
the Russian and English-French cases as variants.
What is common to both types in the last phases
of the process? In no case was the Restoration
complete except on the surface, while in the Soviet
instance superficial continuity concealed an extensive shift toward prerevolutionary and antirevolutionary policies and ideas, both in the government and in the standards which it imposed
on society at large. In every revolution at this stage
there appears to be a strong tendency back to
tradition, traditional values, and strong authority.
Whether the postrevolutionary dictatorship is
overthrown in the process is a matter of accident,
and immaterial.

After the tumult of the First Five-Year Plan,
the Soviet government under Stalin made its peace
with tradition. In a series of steps taken between
1932 and 1936—i.e., after Stalin had consolidated
his personal rule and had clamped tight party control on all spheres of social and intellectual life—
the Communist regime turned its back on almost
all of its heritage of revolutionary ideas and ideals.
We have noted this trend already as it appeared
in the development of Stalinist ideology. In one
field after another, as practical problems arose,
Stalin ordered the repudiation of the revolutionary
norm and its replacement by conservative standards. Most observers, both sympathetic and criti-

cal, were thrown off the track by Stalin's insistence that the new line was correct Marxism, while earlier revolutionary ideas in practically every field were condemned as the reactionary outpourings of "bourgeois degenerates" and "counterrevolutionary wreckers." But such talk, as we have noted, was only the propaganda device whereby Stalin screened his maneuvers and sustained his self-righteousness.

We have seen at length how the Marxian theory of the state and its role in the historical process was turned upside down by Stalin, thus reversing the rectification of Hegel which Marx said he made. Soviet theory, like Soviet political practice, was brought into line with nineteenth-century conservatism, according to which the state, its continuity, and its leadership were decisive. In consonance with this shift the whole array of revolutionary expectations about the "withering away" of traditionally restrictive or disciplinary institutions—the state, law, school, family—was explained away or rejected outright.

Social relationships finally settled down in the thirties in a conservative mold. Social stratification rapidly became marked again. The government did not merely apologize for this, but welcomed it and actively encouraged it. Stalin asserted in 1934, "Every Leninist knows (that is, if he is a real Leninist) that equality in the sphere of requirements and individual life is a piece of reactionary petty-bourgeois absurdity worthy of a primitive sect of ascetics, but not of a socialist society organized on Marxian lines. . . . Equalization . . . , levelling the requirements and the individual lives of the members of society . . . , has nothing in common with Marxism, with Leninism."

Without much stretch of the imagination, the

new ideas and policies of Stalinism can readily be
viewed as aspects of a "restoration." Outworn revolutionary causes such as the persecution of the
Church ceased to be pursued seriously; the final accommodation of Orthodox Church and Soviet State
came during World War II. The virtues of patriotism and nationalist history were rediscovered,
while the cultural autonomy of the non-Russian
nationalities yielded before a stepped-up Russification. Modernism and revolutionary experiments in
all the arts were suddenly assailed as works of the
bourgeois devil; the field was left to the Victorian
styles of "socialist realism." The bourgeois ameni-
ties returned—for those who could afford them. In
place of the old class-warfare talk, legalistic and
constitutional window dressing was set up on an
elaborate scale, with the "Stalin Constitution" of
1936. The political priority of the working class for
admission to the party and to higher education
came to an end soon afterward.

While the "restoration" in Russia took place under Stalin's firm control, there was nevertheless a
political upheaval to mark the transition: the
Great Purge of 1936–38. The old anti-Stalin oppositionists, with Zinoviev and Bukharin heading the
list, were tried and executed, but this was only the
most publicized aspect of the purge. Simultaneously, most of the military hierarchy, the leading
officials of the non-Russian republics of the USSR,
and myriads of lesser functionaries were arrested
on charges ranging from "wrecking" to treason.
The number of people executed or sentenced to labor camps on trumped-up political charges in the
"Yezhovshchina"—the campaign by Interior Commissar Yezhov before he himself was secretly dis-
posed of—probably approached one million.

The climax of the purge came with the liquidation of almost the entire Stalinist party machine. The stalwarts who had come all the way with Stalin, excepting only a handful at the very top, were suddenly arrested, tortured, and executed. The operation was carried out late in 1937 and early in 1938 with the utmost secrecy, and the names of the victims, instead of being vilified like the Trotskyists, were simply cast into oblivion. As far as the rewritten history of the party was concerned, these men never existed.

The reasons for the purge of the Stalinists, as for the sweeping arrests among the officialdom at large, are still shrouded in mystery. Suggested explanations include such varied points as the need of a totalitarian government to keep its bureaucracy from feeling too secure, the secret police system running away with itself, and the personal paranoic madness of Stalin. For one reason or another, a deep cleavage had appeared between Stalin and the "Old Bolsheviks" around him. Historical perspective suggests (though direct evidence is lacking) that the split between Stalin and most of his prominent followers was connected with the basic change which occurred midway in Stalin's rule, from the earlier line affirming revolutionary goals though stressing the lengthy period and violent effort necessary to prepare for them, to an implicit contention that the goals were wrong all along. Stalin's oppressive, reactionary totalitarianism had reached the diametric opposite of the revolutionary dream.

Nonetheless, there were sources of strength in the Soviet "restoration," though unrest simmered and the labor camps swelled. The Second World War was a desperate test which Stalin's government passed, though it nearly went under in the first months of the German onslaught. Had this happened, the restoration would have proceeded from the change in substance to the change in form as well. But summoning the utmost in a disciplined patriotic effort, Stalin brought his country through the war far more successfully than anyone had anticipated; at the end Russia was stronger than ever. Only at this point, as war left power vacuums both to the west and to the east, did the export of revolution commence on a serious scale. But inasmuch as the revolution had run its course in its original Russian setting, its international extension proved to be more the reaching out of aggressive nationalism and suspicious *Realpolitik* than the proselyting urge of a militant faith.

If Soviet Russia has indeed followed the pattern of the earlier revolutions to the extent of arriving at a "restoration" in the nature of the political authority and in the substance of much of its policy, it would be logical to look further for developments corresponding to the last phase—the revival, in moderation, of the ideas of the revolution. Events since the death of Stalin in 1953 strongly suggest some such basic change, despite the limits in its scope. While the shift is once again beclouded by the continuity of the regime and its professed doctrine, there is reason to believe that Russia under Khrushchev has undergone a development analogous to the revolutions of 1688 in England and of 1830 and after in France.

In both France and England the significance of this last stage of revolution was to confirm the basic ideas and accomplishments of the revolution, to halt efforts to turn the clock back unnaturally, and to repudiate the excesses both of the revolution and of the restoration. Some of the revolutionary developments, such as the centralized and efficiently administered state in France, were of course never undone, and in Russia the state-owned planned economy and the Communist Party political monopoly clearly fall into this category. The significant changes in the final stage of revolution naturally bear on the most backward-looking aspects of the restoration regime. In Russia, these were the personal and capricious dictatorship of Stalin, his police terror, his xenophobia, and his conservative social and cultural norms.

Stalin's death brought the first of these aberrations to an end, and the reforms immediately instituted by his successors tempered the second. With the explicit attack on Stalinism made in 1956, the Soviet regime set its face at least formally against the most violent and autocratic aspects of Stalin's rule, although his record up to 1934—i.e., before the "restoration" trend and the purges—continued to be endorsed. The few surviving victims of the purge of Stalinists in the late thirties were amnestied, and the others posthumously rehabilitated. Most of Stalin's oldest and closest collaborators were dropped and condemned by the successor leadership—Beria in 1953, and the Molotov-Malenkov-Kaganovich group in 1957. Khrushchev claims to have dissolved the whole system of forced labor camps, and the Soviet citizen now enjoys reasonable security against arbitrary arrest.

In certain areas of doctrine and policy the Khrushchev regime has returned to older revolutionary norms. For the first time in three decades, it took steps to reduce economic inequality, by raising minimum wages and pensions, and gave increased attention to the main problem of mass consumption, the food supply. Particularly important was the reversal of the educational inequality encouraged by Stalin; tuition fees were once again abolished and the polytechnic ideal of combined mental and manual training was restored to favor. These steps were accompanied by a pronounced ideological shift, with emphasis on the role of the masses in history, and renewed stress on the future transition to the "communist" society.

In some respects the Soviet regime is not returning to the revolutionary spirit at all. For the most part, these are matters concerning the stability of society and the stability of international relations. The social stratification and bourgeois morality which are upheld in the USSR show no signs of losing governmental endorsement, while hypersensitive nationalism and the aggressive pursuit of national interest remain the rule in Soviet foreign relations. Both at home and abroad the Soviet regime is far more conservative than revolutionary. Domestic legality and international coexistence are professed as absolute virtues. All this still goes by the name of Leninism. The manipulation of doctrine to suit the convenience of political practice goes on as before.

Any effort to analyze Soviet Russia on the basis of a theory of revolution must, of course, be quite tentative. But as best we can tell from the sequence of policy changes and what we know of present social forces in the country, Soviet Russia has probably reached the end of its revolutionary journey. The political and social forms now established in the USSR are likely to prevail for decades. Communism in the dynamic phase of its revolution is now to be found only outside Russia.

3 COMMUNIST REVOLUTION OUTSIDE RUSSIA

Complex as its development has been inside the Soviet Union, the Communist movement in the rest

of the world has an even more tangled and paradoxical history. So wide are the variations of times,
situations, and personalities that a satisfactory
general description of the international Communist movement is extremely difficult to arrive at.
Certain points, of course, we can make without
qualification. Communism is undeniably an international movement. The Marxian doctrine that
"the workers have no fatherland" contributes to
this, but is not the primary reason. Communism is
international primarily because it is revolutionary.

It seems usual (though not inevitable) for a
major revolution to become an international affair.
While it has its start in a political breakdown in a
particular country, the tensions and antagonisms
producing such a crisis have their analogues elsewhere, especially in areas which are similar in culture, economic development, and political organization. Revolution in one country, as example and
inspiration, and often through the exertion of national power, can set off ripening revolutionary
conflicts elsewhere; the ripples of revolt proceed
with diminishing intensity to the farthest shores.
England is not a good example here, though its
revolution did meet with some response in the
Netherlands. France provides a spectacular instance of international revolution radiating from a
national base. Communism, similarly, represents in
every corner of the globe an eruption of social antagonism and revolutionary emotion touched off by
the example and assistance of Soviet Russia. The
Communist parties throughout Europe and in
many parts of Asia and the Americas were founded
within three or four years of the Russian Revolution, as pro-Russian groups split off from the exist-

ing socialist or radical movements. Even Fascist
Italy and Nazi Germany inspired an international
movement of extreme right-wing sympathizers.

The fortunes of revolution as it moves abroad
can vary widely. No other area is as ripe for revolution as the country in which the movement origi-
nates, and while foreign example and aid can still
bring local revolutionaries to power, their regimes
are likely to be artificial and insecure. The satellite
regimes which the French, the Nazis, and the Russians set up are remarkably similar in this respect.

There are significant sources of tension and
conflict within the international revolutionary
movement. The original revolutionary power and
its foreign sympathizers are likely to find that their
interests and aims diverge. Serious friction can
arise when the revolution in its initial locale moves
on to the later phase of dictatorship and conservatism, while the movement abroad is still animated
by the earlier radical fervor. This has been an endemic source of discord between Moscow and foreign Communists.

Even more serious is the contradiction between
the cosmopolitanism of the original revolutionary
appeal, and the nationalism which the original or
dominant revolutionary power invariably espouses.
The experience of revolution and the international
antagonism which stems from the clash of revolutionary and antirevolutionary ideas have a powerful effect in welding a nation more tightly together
and heightening its national pride and ambition.
The principal revolutionary state aspires to dominate the international revolutionary movement
and all the countries to which it extends, while on
the other hand revolutionary ideas and experience
generate more nationalism than ever in these subsidiary areas. Napoleonic France, Nazi Germany,
and Stalinist Russia were all impaled on this di-

lemma. The international revolutionary movement contains active seeds of its own disintegration.

When the Communists came to power in Russia, most of their foreign sympathy was to be found in Western Europe. Here, in line with Marx's predictions, the Communists expected the decisive battles of the world revolution to be fought. But while the Communists made much political headway in the West in the years following World War I and again after World War II, they never reached a position from which they were prepared to strike for power. In the advanced industrial countries where the proletarian revolution was supposed to occur first, it has confuted Marxism by failing to materialize at all.

In part this failure of proletarian revolution in the West can be attributed to the very success of the Marxists and other socialist groups in the last decades of the nineteenth century and the first quarter of the twentieth. Through trade unions and democratic political organization, taking advantage of or compelling the adoption of universal suffrage, the Western European socialists were able in some cases to score such successes in social reform and redistribution of wealth that the revolutionary conditions observed by Marx were actually eradicated. Lenin was correct in arguing that reform would make revolution less likely; but for Lenin the revolution was an end in itself, while the reformists in some countries went far toward the realization of their substantive goals. If we judge by the measures outlined in the Communist Manifesto, Great Britain and Scandinavia have almost completely realized the objectives of the proletarian revolution.

Where reform was less successful or where gov-

ernments were seriously disrupted by the course of
events, the Communists have been more fortunate.
Thanks to the social dislocations and political ferment that followed World War I, the Communists
attracted substantial support everywhere in Central and Southern Europe as long as democratic
opportunities were available, especially in France,
Italy, Germany, and Czechoslovakia. But nowhere
was the situation bad enough to produce real revolution and a Communist seizure of power. (Hungary was the sole exception, where the Communists
under Bela Kun came to power in 1919, largely by
default, and were near the point of collapse when
they were unseated by Allied intervention.)

The likeliest prospect for revolution was Germany. Germany, after the fall of the Kaiser and
the end of World War I, was indeed in a revolutionary situation. During the five years of chaos which
followed, left- and right-wing extremists battled
with each other and with the democratic adherents
of the Weimar Republic. The German Communist
movement grew rapidly (it attracted some fifteen
percent of the vote at its peak), but it lacked the
power and the firmness of leadership necessary for
the seizure of power, while the government and the
military acted with determination to hold their
ground. After four abortive uprisings, in 1919, 1920,
1921, and 1923, the German Communists resigned
themselves to the role of an obstreperous but essentially nonrevolutionary opposition party. The situation was simply not ripe for Communist revolution.
If the German Revolution did go into an extreme
phase, it was under the banner of the Ultra-Right
—the Nazis. The Nazi movement was certainly
revolutionary, and unlike Communism it was in
accord with the actual revolutionary situation in
Germany, which was psychological more than eco-

nomic. If "proletariat" is slightly redefined, to indicate the uprooted and the demoralized generally,
the Nazis represented the true proletarian revolution, the real rebellion of the disaffected of all
classes against modern civilization.

It is remarkable that, despite two devastating
wars and the agony of the Great Depression, Communism has made no more headway in Europe
than it has. Fascism, until its obliteration in World
War II, was considerably more dynamic and successful in the West as a whole. This suggests that
Fascism is the characteristic revolutionary tendency for advanced industrial countries, if they must
experience revolution at all, while Communism, despite the claims of its doctrine, is much more at
home in the more backward areas of the globe. In
the West Communism has remained a strong force
only in France and Italy, where the working class
has failed to win a fair position either socially or
economically. In both these cases, Communism has
for all practical purposes ceased to be revolutionary; it is but another uncompromising pressure
group, distinguished by its Muscovite control.

Latin America is exceptional; some countries in
the region are particularly sensitive in the face of
Communism. There the combination of backwardness and change in countries whose cultures are at
least semi-Western can lead to a revolutionary situation paralleling that of Russia in 1917. Communism has considerable influence among Latin
American intellectuals, trade unions, and prole-
tarianized peasants, and has already shown itself
to be a serious contender for power where revolutionary conditions—as in Guatemala up to 1954
and in Cuba since 1959—have given the extremists
an opportunity. The Castro regime in Cuba offers
the singular spectacle of revolutionaries being won

over to close coöperation with, and copying of,
Communism *after* their acquisition of power. It remains to be seen, however, whether Communism
can permanently capture the native revolutionary
process in any Latin American country as it has in
China.

In Eastern Europe the initial response to the
Russian Revolution was a strong one. In Hungary,
Bulgaria, and Yugoslavia, as in Mussolini's Italy,
left-wing revolutionaries were kept in check between the wars only by right-wing dictatorships.
Czechoslovakia, which remained democratic until
Hitler annexed the country in 1939, had one of the
largest of all Communist parties, though a relatively nonrevolutionary one. Nowhere in Europe did
the Communists simultaneously have both the will
and the strength to take power, until World War II
radically altered the balance of international
forces.

The decisive international expansion of Communism had to await Russia's readiness to back up
the revolution. In the case of the French Revolution, expansion began almost immediately. France
was the most powerful nation in Europe at the
time, and the French Republic followed up its defeat of the initial attempt at monarchist intervention with offensives to carry the revolution abroad.
By contrast, Russia, despite its size, was the weak-
est of the major powers at the time of the revolution, and the country suffered grievously during the
Civil War. The Soviet government had all it could
do to overcome its internal enemies and Allied intervention, and was in no position to use force to
expand the revolution abroad. The Hungarian
Communists were crushed while Russia stood help-

lessly at a distance. Only when Poland launched a
backfiring attack on Soviet Russia in 1920 did Moscow entertain the idea of exporting revolution by
means of the Red Army, and military defeat quickly
put an end to such hopes.

Between the wars, Eastern Europe was an open
field for the revolution of the Right. The fear of
Communism or simply of social change, together
with the example and encouragement of Italy and
Germany, brought Fascist or semi-Fascist dictatorships to power in every East European country save
Czechoslovakia, which finally fell to German annexation. The fortunes of World War II brought to
the area the domination of a different power—Soviet Russia—and the German satellite dictatorships were replaced with a new set, no more democratic. During the last year of the war, between the
spring of 1944 and the spring of 1945, Soviet forces
moved into Eastern Europe as far as Belgrade, Vienna, and Berlin, and brought with them Moscow-
trained East European Communist exiles to form
the nuclei of new regimes. The former German satellites Rumania and Bulgaria were forced to accept
increasing Communist influence in their governments, until the Communists were able to eliminate
all opposition in 1946. In Poland an entirely new
Communist-controlled government was created,
and by 1947 it had dictatorial power. Yugoslavia
and Albania were taken over by Communist-domi-
nated resistance movements when Germany collapsed, and Greece would no doubt have gone the
same way had it not been for British intervention
on the side of the Greek government-in-exile in
1944, followed by Anglo-American support to the
government in the civil war that dragged on until
1949. In Hungary the Communists maneuvered
themselves into power in 1947, and in Czechoslova-

kia they stepped from paramount strength to exclusive dictatorship in the coup of February 1948.
Finally, in 1949, the Soviet occupation zone in East
Germany was organized as yet another Communist
dictatorship, the "German Democratic Republic."

The East European Communist revolutions
were by and large artificial, the result of Soviet efforts to guarantee Russian control of the region. In
such cases, where revolution is imposed by a foreign power, it cannot go through the natural process. In the Soviet satellites, aspects of every phase
of the Russian Revolution have been mixed up and
applied contemporaneously—radicalism and authoritarianism, force and conciliation, nationalism
and internationalism. The result has been a kaleidoscopic jumble of violent experiments and policy
changes, bitterly resented by most of the populations concerned.

One issue has persistently recurred in East European Communism—the question of national autonomy versus Russian domination. Both the inter-
nationalist ideal of Communism and the national
sensitivities of the people concerned have been violated by heavy-handed Soviet control. The consequence of this has been serious cleavages and
bloody purges in the Communist parties of practically every Soviet satellite. In Yugoslavia alone the
nationalists under Tito's leadership got the upper
hand, and the result was a complete rupture and
a period of open hostility between Yugoslavia and
the Soviet bloc. There were definite reasons for this
defiance occurring in Yugoslavia, apart from the
country's location and the accidents of leadership.
Other East European nations shared the Yugoslavs'
fierce nationalism and left-wing tendencies. In Yugoslavia (and Albania), however, the Communists
had come to power largely without Russian aid;

something approaching the true revolutionary
process was transpiring in Yugoslavia. It appears,
curiously enough, that the most ardently revolutionary Communists in Yugoslavia were the source
of pro-Russian sentiment, while Tito's break from
the Soviet bloc in 1948 was the sign for a moderation in his regime that might pass for a Yugoslav
Thermidor. In any case, the Yugoslav Communist
leadership could count on enough active popular
support to be able to dispense with Russian backing.

China, in contrast to Eastern Europe, but like
Russia and Germany, had already entered into a
revolutionary upheaval when Communism made its
entrance on the political stage. The Empire had
given way in 1911, though the reformers' hopes
were disappointed by the succeeding era of war-
lordism and imperialist incursions (mainly Japanese). The revolutionary movement was revived in
the early 1920's in the form of the Kuomintang
(Chinese Nationalist Party) of Sun Yat-sen and
Chiang Kai-shek, vaguely democratic and socialist
in its professions, ardently nationalist, and inclined
to authoritarianism in practice. Allying himself
with the newly formed Communist Party, and ob-
taining valuable Soviet backing and advice, Chiang
waged a vigorous and successful campaign against
the Peking government and the warlords. Purging
his Communist allies along the way, Chiang was by
1928, to one degree or another, the ruler of most of
China.
The Kuomintang revolution is hard to place in
the scheme of Western revolutions. It seems more
like a fusion of the moderate and Bonapartist
phases than the extremist movement to which it

corresponds in time sequence. Once in power, and beset by tremendous difficulties both in ruling the country and in fighting Japanese imperialism, the Kuomintang began to decay, and its democratic revolutionary slogans became hardly more than window dressing for something on the order of a Thermidorean oligarchy.

Meanwhile, the Chinese Communist movement, while still hesitant to challenge the central government, had the unique advantage of being able to set up a functioning regime at Yenan in northwest China, where it enjoyed the *de facto* independence of any provincial warlord. Through long years of gestation the Communist regime, led by Mao Tse-tung, underwent substantial evolution: it tempered its program to the needs of the peasant population, built a disciplined army and administration, and incorporated the new Marxist dogmatism of the Stalinist sort. Most important of all, a new social base was found for the movement. Chinese Communism after the early 1930's was only by the flimsiest fiction (still maintained today) a "proletarian" movement. Essentially it became a bureaucratic machine drawing its nurture from, and guiding the destinies of, a peasant population. As such, Chinese Communism accommodated itself to the pattern of Chinese history: the dynastic cycle was taking one more turn.

Insofar as the Western-type swings of radical and conservative emotion were operative in Chinese Communism, they had mostly run their course before the Communists took power in the civil war of 1947–49. While much of the country at large was in a revolutionary mood at this time, the Communists already represented a tightly disciplined post-revolutionary type of dictatorship, and one of their earliest concerns after taking power was to instill such discipline in their unstable revolutionary sympathizers. The real choice for China was between exhausted dictatorship and one with full vitality and ruthless fervor. Mao's system was pre-formed when it went into effect, and has ruled stably ever since.

In contrast to Eastern Europe, the Chinese Revolution is clearly an independent affair. China was in upheaval before Russia became Communist. The Chinese Communist Party came to power without appreciable Russian aid, thanks largely to its own vigor and the disintegration of its opponents. Communist China is linked to Soviet Russia, according to the best informed opinion, only voluntarily, by a common faith—the Stalinist reading of Marxism which Mao adopted. Such connections are notoriously weak; let differences of interpretation and of doctrinal authority produce disharmony, and sympathy can change into bitter hostility.

Russia and China differ, moreover, in the historical context of their revolutions and in the problems which the revolutionaries are called upon to solve. The Chinese Communists seem to have come to power in a more traditional way, and their accession to power has probably caused less shock and dislocation than the extremes and reversals of the Soviet experiment in Russia. On the other hand, the magnitude of the economic problems which the Chinese regime aspires to solve is unequaled. Beneath these differences, the Communist system has a certain common relevance for both countries. Communism has come to power and taken form in both countries as a movement of rebellion against the West; it is not a "proletarian" revolution nor yet a movement of colonial peons, but the upsurge of nations which have felt the impact of the West and wish to defeat the West at its own game.

4 REVOLUTION AND THE CLASS STRUGGLE

According to Marxism, revolution is a natural phase in the evolution of society. As new conditions of production promote the rise of new social groups, tension accumulates until, as the dialectic states it, quantitative changes turn into qualitative ones, a new class seizes political power, and the institutions of society are reorganized to conform to the interests of the newly dominant group. Actually, Marxism exaggerates the role of revolution, making it appear to be the normal manner of historical development, when in fact it is quite rare.

By and large the Marxian conception of revolution is that of a simple overturn, followed by whatever forceful consolidation is necessary; little allowance is made for the oscillation of political emotions which is in fact so apparent in revolution. Of the danger of backsliding, Marx and Engels were aware; Engels warned pointedly in 1891 against a "transformation of the state and the organs of the state from servants of society into masters of society," and advised that the "working class must . . . *safeguard itself against its own deputies and officials* by declaring them all, without any exception, subject to recall at any moment." The political means was to be kept from becoming an end in itself. Yet this was precisely what happened in Russia. There is no clearer instance of a government standing above all classes, as the master of society, than the Soviet Union.

The tie between revolutions and particular classes is one of the fundamental propositions of Marxism, and one of the most mythological. Nothing reveals this more clearly than the history of Communist revolution. At every stage, efforts by Communist leaders to describe their revolutions

and their governments as "proletarian" have been
conspicuously unconvincing. The workers, to be
sure, played an important part in the initial Communist success in Russia, but very soon the Soviet
government found that it had to disregard the interests and wishes of the proletarians in order to
achieve political and economic success. By 1920,
equalitarianism was suspended; group decision-
making in military and industrial life was abolished; individual authority and responsibility were
stressed; and the bourgeois "specialists"—i.e., the
technically competent in every field—were cajoled
or coerced into working for the Soviet government.

Much was written in the early years of the Soviet regime to explain and justify this need to rely
on and appease the "technical intelligentsia." This
circumstance has not changed; the difference under Stalin was only to make a virtue of necessity.
If "ruling class" be defined as that group to which
the government must give most deference in the interest of its own political success, the "technical
intelligentsia" became and remains the Soviet ruling class. It is without question in a preferred position socially and economically, thanks to the need
(present in any modern state or industry) for a
technically competent officialdom. Soviet Russia
indeed bears out James Burnham's thesis of the
"managerial revolution": quite independently of
what anyone intended, the conditions of establishing and maintaining an industrial society were
pressing for the dominance of the "technocracy."
Similar trends can be observed, of course, throughout most of the world; why they assumed the form
of revolution in Russia, of all places, is a question
which will bear further inquiry.

While the idea of "technical intelligentsia" as

the dominant class, or the concept of the "managerial revolution," contributes some insight into the Soviet system, it does not by any means account fully either for the revolution in Russia or for the nature of the regime which issued from it. For the analysis of revolution the strictly class and economic approach is not adequate. (It is least unsatisfactory as applied to France, since it was primarily the French experience that went into the theory of historical materialism.) All kinds of exceptions to the class analysis are found in Russia: the revolutionary movement was based on the upper-class intelligentsia, not the downtrodden masses; the new regime was not controlled by any class and was not dependent on any one class, not even on the workers; workers who became disaffected were condemned as unproletarian, "petty-bourgeois." Under Stalin, every facet of the genuinely revolutionary spirit was dismissed as "petty-bourgeois," a threat to the "dictatorship of the proletariat." In China, Mao Tse-tung could (and did) dispense with the working class altogether, as long as his party preserved its "proletarian" ideology, i.e., its Marxist-Leninist orthodoxy and its organizational discipline. It is these qualities that make Communism, not any social class.

The inadequacy of the class approach to revolution impels us to attempt a different kind of general explanation. Revolutions can better be viewed as moral movements, gathering converts, crusades of the faithful, to realize certain social and ethical ideals. As such, revolutions bear a close relationship to religious movements, as we shall see at length later on. It is not by chance that every great revolution has involved an orgy of puritanism and a severe conflict with the established religious system: in England, the Presbyterians and Independents against the Episcopalians; in France, the devotees of Gallicanism and the Goddess of Reason against the Church of Rome; in Russia, the familiar campaign to impose Marxist atheism. It is essentially a matter of rival faiths.

Revolutions can also be viewed as struggles over certain principles of social life and organization. In every case, the initial impetus to revolution comes from hostility to a system of hierarchical authority, which is rejected not on class lines but by rebellious people on all social levels of the hierarchy, in favor of relationships of equality. Whatever their subsequent resort to dictatorial violence, revolutions can never entirely live down their antiauthoritarian origins, and this, no doubt, is a decisive factor in the last phase of moderate revolutionary revival. It is graphically illustrated in the Soviet repudiation of the "cult of personality."

More specifically, each revolution can be characterized as a struggle over a certain set of social ideals, which, though they may be betrayed or distorted, never cease to exert their influence. Such are the basic ideas of each revolution: religious toleration and parliamentary government in England, legal equality and the centralized national state in France, the socialist economy in Russia. The question is not which class can rule, but what kind of system will be set up to rule all classes.

5 CHANGE AND CONTINUITY THROUGH REVOLUTION

Revolution is the consequence of strains which overload the fabric of society and rip it apart. Change then proceeds with a rapidity unequalled in other situations; the revolutionary society is in a state of flux, and adapts readily to whatever pres-

sures are brought to bear. The revolution creates its
own agents and follows its own laws, independently
of what even the revolutionaries intend. Some of
their general principles, of course, particularly
those first formulated and most in accord with the
trend of the times, may be realized institutionally
or endure as inspiring ideals. But most of the radical experiment is likely to be swept away in the
later phases when tradition reasserts itself. The
society which issues from the process of revolution
is, in its actual practices and standards (as distinguished from doctrinal rationalizations of
them), closer to the old regime than to the revolutionary experiment. Continued revolutionary talk
only buttresses the new conservatism, by disarming
would-be radical critics.

The really significant changes which occurred
in Russia were brought about as the flux of revolution opened the way for influences which beforehand had scarcely been taken account of at all.
Overwhelming in their impact were the problems
of modernizing the country and catching up with
the West both economically and culturally. Moreover, as the country moved toward modernization,
a new set of problems asserted itself—the tasks of
organizing life in the modern industrial community. Thanks to the revolutionary rupture of traditions and inhibitions, Russia has been able to adapt
more extensively than any other society to the social and political logic of industrialism. In subsequent chapters we shall inquire in detail into these
social and economic roots of Communist totalitarianism. A more immediate requirement, however, is
a realistic understanding of the unique political institution that distinguishes the Communist movement—the system of individual power and bureaucratic hierarchy represented by the Communist
Party.

3　The Communist Party

There is some justification in the Communist hagiography that attributes almost superhuman influence to a few prophets and leaders of the movement. The doctrinal foundations of Marxism were provided by two men, not a school of thinkers or a variety of currents of thought. The organized Communist movement was launched by one man. The full-blown Communist dictatorship was constructed by yet another single individual. While the official history is an exaggeration—it counts as devils practically all of the many remarkable individuals who helped Lenin set up the Soviet Republic and the Communist International—Communism is nonetheless unusual in the extent to which it is the creation and expression of a few personalities. Only in some of the great religions can a parallel be found.

The impress which Lenin and Stalin had on the Communist movement hinged on their development and use of a singular political institution —the intricate, militarily organized machine of control known as the Communist Party. The Communist Party as we know the institution the world over is largely the creature of these two men—conceived and set in motion by Lenin, forged into its ultimate form and compass by Stalin. It became a

political force sufficiently powerful to guide the
raging tumult of revolution in Russia and to constitute the backbone of a unique new totalitarian
society.

1 LENIN'S PARTY AND
THE BOLSHEVIK SPIRIT

Lenin conceived of the party as an instrument
for making revolution occur; he had little faith in
the laws of history unaided by human will. Discounting the spontaneous political development of
the masses, he placed his reliance on a dedicated
elite who would steel themselves for the struggle
and organize their following into a victorious revolutionary movement. For Lenin, the party and the
strength of its organization were decisive.

Lenin's emphasis on the party and his dicta on
its proper organization were his distinctive contributions to the theory of revolution. Marxism had
never made much of the party in theory, and by the
turn of the century the Marxist parties in the West
were increasingly inclined to be democratic mass
organizations. Furthermore, Lenin's concept of the
party's role as the motive force of revolution implied a radical break with historical materialism as
it previously had been understood. Most Marxists,
including Lenin's Menshevik rivals in Russia, in-
dignantly rejected his conspiratorial model of organization.

Lenin's scheme of party organization followed
logically from his assessment of the political situation in Russia. "In its struggle for power the proletariat has no other weapon but organization,"
Lenin wrote in 1903. Only thus could police repression and the masses' lack of revolutionary vigor be
overcome: "The proletariat can become, and in-

evitably will become, an invincible force only when its ideological unification by the principles of Marxism is consolidated by the material unity of an organization which will weld millions of toilers into an army of the working class."

This military analogy permeated Lenin's thinking. The party was the "vanguard," or the "general staff of revolution"; it was to be a professional officers' corps, sharply distinguished from the mass of followers. "I assert," said Lenin, "1) that no revolutionary movement can endure without a stable organization of leaders that maintains continuity; 2) that the wider the masses spontaneously drawn into the struggle, forming the basis of the movement and participating in it, the more urgent the need of such an organization, and the more solid this organization must be (for it is much easier for demagogues to sidetrack the more backward sections of the masses); 3) that such an organization must consist chiefly of people professionally engaged in revolutionary activity; 4) that in an autocratic state, the more we *confine* the membership of such an organization to people who are professionally trained in the art of combating the political police, the more difficult will it be to wipe out such an organization, and 5) the *greater* will be the number of people of the working class and of the other classes of society who will be able to join the movement and perform active work in it."

Such were the principles of the disciplined revolutionary elite which caused most of the original leaders of Russian Marxism to break with Lenin. In their eyes he was a bureaucrat and a militarist, devoid of faith in the revolutionary masses; his system seemed to be the reversed image of the very evil of tsarist police repression which it was designed to combat. The implications of Lenin's idea of the party were prophetically drawn forth by a future Communist, none other than Leon Trotsky: "These methods lead, as we shall yet see, to this: the party organization is substituted for the party, the Central Committee is substituted for the party organization, and finally a 'dictator' is substituted for the Central Committee."

Lenin did not, to be sure, set himself openly against the principles of democracy, and the strength of this ideal is attested by the unceasing insistence of the Soviet dictatorship that it is really the most democratic of all governments. In practice, however, Lenin would not be constrained by democratic scruples; "democratic centralism," implicitly far more centralism than democratic, was his formula for combining the ideal and the practical. "The principle of democratic centralism," he explained in 1906, "means specifically *freedom of criticism* . . . , as long as this does not disrupt the unity of *action already decided upon*—and the intolerability of any criticism undermining or obstructing the *unity* of action decided on by the party."

The idea of the revolutionary party as a disciplined, conspiratorial elite was not, of course, solely Lenin's invention. Lenin's critics found it easy to demonstrate his affinity with conspiratorial ideas both of the West and of Russia. The Jacobins, with their network of clubs that covered France, provided the organizational model of a hierarchy of committees and cells. The French revolutionist Blanqui (1805–81) and the Russian "Decembrist" Pestel (1793–1826) had both argued the importance of a conspiracy to seize power and establish a revolutionary dictatorship. Lenin did not explicitly reach this conclusion until he was in the very act of taking over. His party was then transformed, from an engine to start the train of revolutionary events, into the actual machine of revolutionary government.

For the form of the party Lenin found his model in the history of Russian revolutionary conspiracy that dated back to the 1860's. The student groups of the 1860's, the extensive "Land and Liberty" organization of the 1870's, and the terrorist "People's Will" organization, which assassinated Tsar Alexander II in 1881, provided the tradition of a disciplined movement of dedicated professional revolutionaries, and Lenin was happy to acknowledge his debt to these people. The Bolshevik Party moreover incorporated the spirit of complete personal devotion to the revolutionary cause which characterized the earlier Russian revolutionaries. A full explanation of these traits of the party must await our general discussion of the Russian background of Communism; it is enough to note here that Lenin's combination of the native Russian revolutionary psychology and organization with the Marxist doctrine of the proletarian revolution proved to be a strong attraction to the more fervently revolutionary elements in Russian society.

Unique to the Bolshevik movement was the state of mind which grew up within it. The Bolshevik outlook was the joint product of the Russian revolutionary spirit, the organizational logic of the party, Lenin's personality, and the Marxian doctrine which served to give expression and justification to the movement. Lenin accepted the Marxian idea of the proletarian revolution. He took it, however, not as something inevitable, but as the goal for which the party *ought* to strive. Revolution for Lenin was a moral imperative, not an event that was bound to occur anyway.

The revolutionaries who joined the party in its

mission did so not because of any particular social
origin, but simply because they had dedicated
themselves to the revolutionary ideal. In noting
this, Lenin was realistically expressing the Russian
situation. However, to Lenin the only guarantee of
this dedication, the only assurance that the revolutionary effort would persist in the right direction,
was correct revolutionary doctrine—i.e., Marxism
as interpreted by Lenin. People who disagreed with
Lenin convicted themselves, in his mind, of bourgeois deviation, and had to be expelled from the organization. Long before the revolution Lenin welcomed splits and purges as devices to temper the
hard core of the movement and solidify his control
over it. "The Bolsheviks have cleansed the ground
for party spirit by their relentless struggle against
anti-party elements," he declared in 1909 after the
first major purge of the Bolshevik ranks.

Lenin was a singular individual, as any ac-
quaintance with his writings, let alone the weight
of his whole career, can testify. Like most outstanding revolutionary leaders he was aggressive,
dynamic, and utterly single-minded. He was as assured of his own righteousness and the depravity
of his opponents as were the prophets of old. He
completely identified political virtue with his own
leadership, and displayed amazing force in imposing his own will on dissident or faint-hearted followers. These was something un-Russian about
Lenin's emphasis on discipline, but this alien quality was the secret of success in Russian revolutionary politics. In all revolutions and among most
revolutionaries there appears to be a factor of ado-
lescent revolt against all symbols of authority, accompanied by the creation of a new authority and
violent and compulsive efforts at self-justification
in the name of the latter. Whatever the reasons for

this behavior, it is clear that Lenin set up the standards for his movement to reflect his own bent. He selected and purged his followers to keep the movement headed in the same psychological direction. The only major exception to this rule occurred when Trotsky and many other independent-minded radicals joined the Bolshevik Party in 1917. Though these new people played very active roles in the early years of the Soviet Republic, they never fully assimilated Lenin's disciplinarian and dogmatic thinking. The consequence was the series of intraparty struggles between Leninists and Left Oppositionists that ended only in 1927, when Stalin expelled the latter from the party altogether.

Dogmatism, intolerance, and the frantic rejection of all free criticism have distinguished the Communist movement ever since the founding of the Bolshevik Party. The Communists have directed their most bitter hatred not against avowed counterrevolutionaries but against their nearest rivals and their former comrades within the revolutionary ranks. They cannot tolerate any challenge to their organizational principles or their claim to sole revolutionary virtue. Lenin and his successors fought the democratic socialist parties tooth and nail, in Russia and abroad, before, during, and after the revolution. Change in this respect came only when the Russian Revolution had reached the phase of conservative reaction: in the mid-1930's it became possible for Stalin's government to put its ideological antipathies aside and promote the "Popular Front" with foreign socialists, as a matter of national interest in building a coalition against Nazi Germany. On the other hand, the Communist International continued to harry the Trotskyist deviators from Communist orthodoxy wherever they could be found. After World

War II, when the socialists rallied to the forces opposing Soviet imperialism, Russian interests dictated to the Communists a more uncompromising
line, and the non-Communist left was once again
denounced as an adjunct of capitalistic reaction
and imperialism. With the post-Stalin moderation
in Russia, there have been occasional attempts to
woo European and Asian socialists, but the Communists' sense of exclusive Leninist righteousness
persists. Even the Yugoslav Communists, since they
reject Russian dictation and claim ideological autonomy, remain outside the fold.

Accompanying the dogmatic assurance which
marked Bolshevism from the start was the conviction that the revolution was a life-or-death struggle, in which any and every means whatsoever had
to be employed. Violence, deceit, demagogy, and betrayal became political virtues; humanitarian
scruple was cast to the winds. This is not to say
that the Communists abandoned the objectives of
human welfare and social justice; they thought
themselves devoted to these ends, but in an abstract fashion which did not preclude present
violations of the ideal in the name of the future.
"Morality," Lenin declared in 1920, "for us is subordinated to the interests of the class struggle of
the proletariat." Everything hung on the success
of the revolution; once it succeeded, it would supposedly guarantee the kingdom of righteousness
on earth.

In reality, the revolution became an end in itself, while its ostensible goals tended to become
mere justifications for the seizure and consolidation of political power. We can readily observe the
actual process whereby the methods and organiza-

tional precepts of Bolshevism became the ultimate standards for the Soviet state. The grisly outcome, Stalinism, followed logically from the fundamental moral deficiency of Bolshevism, which in turn was made possible by a crucial inconsistency in the Bolshevik interpretation of Marxism. Every means, however evil, had to be employed to accomplish the objective of revolution. Marxist inevitability had guaranteed that the revolution would usher in the new order of classless virtue, untainted by the bloody spectacle of its birth. But the Bolsheviks' very insistence on such violent midwifery implied that historical inevitability could not be counted on. If the revolution was not inevitable, neither could the particular form which it would take if successful be predicted with assurance. Hence there could be no guarantee of the goodness of the coming society—it would be what its progenitors and their tactics made it. The violence, deceit, and authoritarianism employed to bring the revolution about had an epochal effect. The new order was indelibly stamped with the methods of its begetting: the Bolsheviks reaped as they had sown.

2 THE ORGANIZATIONAL PRINCIPLE—DISCIPLINED MILITANCY

Lenin's model of the party organization had nothing but the name in common with the political parties of Western Europe and America. It was not an opinion-expressing group with a mass enrollment, as the Mensheviks in Russia would have had it, but a restricted group of dedicated revolutionaries, convinced of the necessity of impelling and manipulating the masses toward the

moral imperative of revolution. With good reason
the Bolshevik-type party has been likened both to
a military staff and to a priesthood. It is a community of the elect, bound by the strictest discipline and consecrated to the objective of seizing
and holding exclusive political power.

The basic principles of the party organization
were not unique, though their Russian application
was new. The party was a form of the military-
bureaucratic system of organization, which has
occurred in many places and at various points in
history. In all essential features the party conformed to this familiar pattern—the hierarchy,
with authority at the top; and responsibility at all
lower levels to the overall interest as decided by
the top authority; the chain of command; allocation of functions to subordinates on a presumably
rational basis; and the dependence of individual
status and authority on one's office in the hierarchy rather than on family or wealth. This pattern can easily be grasped when it is contrasted
with other organizational types which have prevailed either in the present or the past: the
familial-feudal, for example, where each individual is linked only to immediate superiors and
inferiors and enjoys his status by hereditary right,
and the democratic collective pattern, where members of a group participate as equals in the man-
agement of their common affairs.

It is easy to see, of course, that elements of all
these patterns, and perhaps others which could
be established, occur widely and in infinitely varied
combinations. The bureaucratic pattern, far from
being an exclusively Communist mode of operation, is familiar in modern Western society as the
typical structure of corporate enterprise, armies,
governmental administration, many churches, and

all kinds of private organizations which are nominally supposed to conform to other principles. There is, however, a crucial difference between the "open societies" of the West and Communist or other totalitarianism, in the limits which are placed on the bureaucratic pattern. In the West, the bureaucratic principle does not apply at the top political level, where democratic relationships prevail, but in Communist societies it is the absolute rule for the body politic as a whole. One will prevails, and it is the duty of every citizen, in his appointed place, to execute that will as he is directed.

The success of Lenin's bureaucratic organizational idea in Russia, and the totalitarian social structure to which it contributed, were not altogether matters of accident or of momentary violence. Lenin's concept of the party has proved to be of great significance in relation to certain widespread problems of a world in upheaval. The bureaucratic forms of organization and group relationship that are embodied in the Communist Party are particularly (though not exclusively) advantageous for meeting social problems of two sorts: effective organization in modern industrial society, and the rapid accomplishment of the transition from feudal backwardness to industrialism. This close relevance of the Bolshevik organizational pattern to modern economic trends is fundamental in comprehending the present success and power of Communism. We shall return later to this question of how Communism promotes and is itself promoted by the industrial revolution.

The military character of Communism does not stop with the Bolshevik organizational model.

The whole mentality of the Communist movement is pervaded by a spirit of combat. Class struggle is one principle of Marxism which Bolshevism preserved and stressed to the utmost. "To repudiate civil war, or to forget about it," Lenin exclaimed in 1916, "would mean sinking into extreme opportunism and renouncing the socialist revolution.' . . . 'Social' parsons and opportunists are always ready to dream about the future peaceful socialism; but the very thing that distinguishes them from revolutionary Social-Democrats is that they refuse to think about and reflect on the fierce class struggle and class *wars* that are necessary for the achievement of this beautiful future."

For Stalin, struggle was the *sine qua non* of the party's growth and political progress. "In the struggle against deviations from the Leninist line our party grew and gained strength . . . , it forged the *Leninist unity* of its ranks," Stalin asserted in 1930. "The misfortune of the Right deviators is that . . . they do not want those ways and means of struggle without which it is impossible to build socialism. . . . They do not want the uncompromising struggle against the capitalist elements and the sweeping offensive of socialism against capitalism . . . , without which it is impossible to retain the proletarian dictatorship and to build socialism in our country."

The Bolshevik organizational pattern requires the sense of absolute and unending class conflict to justify its disciplinary rigors, while Bolshevik discipline reinforces the members' sense of struggle. Communist statements from Lenin's time to the present read as though struggle were the real end of all existence. Long after the proclaimed defeat of the old ruling classes, the class struggle reflex continued to dominate the thinking of the

Soviet leaders, who professed to see the need for an unremitting campaign against "survivals of capitalism in the consciousness of the masses." But as the Soviet system became more stabilized and relatively conservative in the later 1930's, there was a shift of emphasis from the class struggle to international struggle. The German and Japanese threat served admirably as the external menace which could justify the rigors of the dictatorship. It was invoked especially in connection with the Great Purge. In retrospect it seems inevitable that following World War II the Soviet government should have turned against its erstwhile allies and found in them a new menace to its existence. This mentality has persisted even after the dethronement of the memory of Stalin, with renewed warnings of the machinations of imperialism and the danger of infection by "bourgeois ideology" from abroad.

The sense of crisis in Soviet politics has never been allowed to subside. If real threats do not exist, others are invented. The Soviet regime has apparently been able to justify itself and command sufficiently vigorous support only by maintaining the feeling that catastrophe is imminent. In 1921, when the Soviet government emerged from the fiery test of civil war, the spirit of struggle and the internal discipline of the movement were not relaxed but intensified, in the alleged fear of counterrevolutionary subversion. The same sort of tightening notably followed World War II. Every change in the party line, down to Stalin's death, involved a heightening of the demand for vigilance against bourgeois and traitorous influences. In 1937, in the midst of the Great Purge, Stalin flatly asserted that the closer the Soviet Union came to "socialism," the more bitter would be the struggle against the class enemy. (This proposition proved to be too much for Stalin's successors, and it was repudiated by Khrushchev in 1956.)

The historical experience of the Soviet regime after the revolution to a certain extent can account for the militaristic forms which Communism assumed in the USSR. Particularly severe in its effect was the Civil War of 1918–20, a life-and-death struggle which left its imprint upon the Communist movement at a young and impressionable stage. The Civil War confirmed, and even exaggerated, the Leninist reliance on authoritarian and disciplinarian organizational forms, and imparted a ruthlessness to which the Bolsheviks had never dreamed of bringing themselves. Further, it gave a permanent military cast to Communist political thinking, which has ever since proceeded in terms of war—"campaign," "offensive," "front," "advance," "shock troops," "retreat," "advance guard," "reserves," "officer corps," "general staff," etc.

At times the military spirit has undoubtedly contributed much vigor to the Communist movement. In the long view, however, it has had a stunting effect; in this sense as in many others, the means for revolutionary action have perverted the original ends and have become ends in themselves. Under Stalin, Communism became prejudiced against direct and serious pursuit of the humanitarian objectives originally associated with socialism. With astonishing candor Stalin asked rhetorically in 1926, "What is the economic content and economic basis of socialism? Is it to establish a paradise and universal happiness? No, it is not. This is a petty-bourgeois idea of the economic content of socialism." The Bolshevik virtue of "hardness" will not permit of such soft distractions.

Communist values lean toward the sense of manly
pride in military strength and the thrill of heavy
industries rising above the steppes, while serious
attention to mundane consumers' goods has always been given a low priority. Feudal aristocracies
adhered to a kindred ordering of virtues and
vices.

3 LENIN, THE PARTY, AND THE REVOLUTION

Lenin's Bolshevik movement was ten years in
evolution before it became a distinct political
entity. In 1902 Lenin began to lay down his principles of organization. His first breach with the
other Russian Marxists came in 1903, but it was
not until 1912 that he cut all organizational ties
with non-Bolsheviks. By this time the Bolshevik
Party was entirely Lenin's creature; all of his
original associates who had minds of their own
had quit or had been forced out. Lenin's injunc-
tions on centralized organization, discipline, and
doctrinal orthodoxy became axiomatic for his
party. Narrow-minded as they were, however, the
Bolsheviks had some political success despite
tsarist police repression, and when 1917 came they
had an appreciable body of support among the
workers of the principal Russian cities.

The collapse of the Imperial government in
February 1917 took Lenin completely by surprise,
and his followers in Russia were utterly confused.
They had been taught that their party would
have to take the lead in the "bourgeois" revolution and establish a "democratic dictatorship."
Now that this overturn had been accomplished
without their participation, they could see no
course but grudging support of the Provisional

Government. Lenin, however, was emboldened by
a new vision: returning to Russia from Switzer-
land (crossing Germany in the famous "sealed
train"), he began to demand of his party that it
lead workers' councils—the soviets—in seizing
power and instituting the long-dreamed-of dictatorship of the proletariat. In a feat of personal
leadership rarely equaled anywhere, Lenin revo-
lutionized his own party and impelled it forward
to prepare and accomplish the seizure of power.
This was a triumph of the leader more than of the
organization. The party and its discipline were
diluted with the influx both of new leaders (especially former left-wing Mensheviks like Trotsky)
and of new followers. It was widespread revolutionary fervor and devotion to the cause that
carried the day, rather than slavish military command and obedience. The latter would have its
place in the bleak years ahead.

There was nothing inevitable about the October
Revolution, nor, as far as the Bolsheviks were concerned, was there even a strong likelihood that
they should win and keep power. The spokesmen
of the cautious wing of the party, Zinoviev and
Kamenev, actually argued against the projected
coup on Marxist grounds—it was doomed to failure,
they feared, if isolated in a country unripe for
socialism. "We have no right to stake the whole
future on the card of an armed uprising," they
warned. "We have never said that the Russian
working class *alone,* by its own forces, would be
able to bring the present revolution to a victorious
conclusion. . . . We must not permit ourselves to
be hypnotized. . . . The question is not now or
never. . . . Two tactics are contending here: the
tactic of plot and the tactic of belief in the moving
forces of the Russian Revolution."

Actually, the circumstances of revolutionary upheaval in which Russia found itself at that moment, together with the weakness of the Provisional Government, made a new political overturn very likely. Had not the Bolsheviks struck, other left-wing parties (such as the peasant-oriented radicals, the Left Socialist Revolutionaries) might have taken their place. Possibly a coup by the right-wing militarists, like that attempted in August 1917, by the commander-in-chief, General Kornilov, might have succeeded. Victory at this stage in the revolutionary process would go to him who had the will to power and who commanded the leadership ability and the political organization to translate his will into actuality.

Lenin, emerging triumphant in this fateful competition, was the agent of his own success. His leadership, his determination, his apt coinage of the most effective slogans, his uncanny insight into political situations of the moment, together with the vigorous support of his fervent lieutenants (particularly Trotsky, who as the Bolshevik chairman of the Petrograd Soviet actually directed the preparations for the uprising), brought victory to the Bolshevik cause. Here the impact of personality on the course of history was decisive.

Leadership and organization brought this movement of professed Marxists to power in Russia, all of the prognostications of their theory to the contrary. Leadership and organization kept them in power, with all the consequent paradox of a professedly socialist government trying to create the economic and social prerequisites for its own existence. The success of the Bolshevik revolution is one of the most compelling refutations of the unamended doctrine of historical materialism.

Lenin's unique leadership and his distinctive party principle were furthermore responsible for the great anomaly in the process of revolution in Russia—the fact that after the extremists came to power there were no further breaks in the continuity of the government. Forceful and flexible leadership and the ever-tighter party organization made it possible for the Communist Party to stay in power through all the subsequent phases in the revolutionary process, and to adapt itself successfully at each critical point.

We can now begin to see how the specific traits of the Communist movement were produced by the particular combination of circumstances—doctrinal, organizational, revolutionary—under which the movement arose. Revolution enabled the Bolsheviks to come to power. Organization enabled them to keep power despite the subsequent ebb of the revolution. Doctrine gave them an image of themselves which could be maintained under the conditions of postrevolutionary rule in Russia only by absolute dictatorship.

The Communist idea of the party and its function, as the world now knows it, was not fully developed until after the stress of revolution, civil war, and the responsibilities of exercising governmental power had left their imprint on the movement. Bolshevik theory had previously been vague on the role of the party in the revolutionary seizure of power and in the organization of the new state. Until it was actually organizing the October uprising, the party was thought of only as an instrument for generating a mass revolutionary force which would then solve the problem of power itself. Curious as this may seem, the idea of the one-party dictatorship was never embraced explicitly by the Communists until after they had already established such a regime.

Juridically speaking, the October Revolution was carried out through the soviets, most of which the Bolsheviks controlled by that time. It was not a strictly Bolshevik affair; the Left Socialist Revolutionaries, who had split off from their parent body much as the Bolsheviks had from the Mensheviks, joined forces with Lenin in the overthrow of the Provisional Government. After some negotiation, the Left Socialist Revolutionaries were actually brought into the new Soviet government as partners in a coalition cabinet. The other parties in the soviets—Mensheviks and Right Socialist Revolutionaries—continued to function as an opposition, though their freedom of action was progressively curtailed.

A test of the Bolsheviks' intentions soon came when the democratically elected Constituent Assembly convened in January 1918, with an anti-Bolshevik majority: the Assembly was dispersed and denounced. It was only with the onset of civil war in mid-1918, however, that the dictatorial implications of the Bolsheviks' position emerged fully. Their coalition partners, the Left Socialist Revolutionaries, were suppressed after they rebelled against the Soviet government for coöperating with Germany, and then the other parties were one by one outlawed and broken up. By 1920 the Communists were the sole party, and now they began to claim such a privileged position by doctrinal right. "Marxism teaches," Lenin maintained in 1921, "that only the political party of the working class, i.e., the Communist Party, is in a position to unite, educate, and organize such a vanguard of the proletariat and all the laboring masses as will be able to counteract the inevitable petty-bourgeois wavering of the masses, to counteract tradition and unavoidable relapses of trade-union narrowness or trade-union prejudices within the proletariat, and to direct all sides of the proletarian movement and hence all the working masses. Without this the dictatorship of the proletariat is meaningless."

The experience of revolutionary struggle confirmed Lenin's original feeling that only one movement, one organization, one doctrine, could be correct, good, and successful. Political monotheism was thenceforth an obligatory tenet of Communism—there shall be no other parties but The Party. Coalitions and nonparty organizations, wherever resorted to, inside or outside the USSR, would be only for the purpose of advancing the cause of the one Party. It is a Communist axiom that there can be no sincere coöperation between Communists and other groups—the latter are to be dealt with only insofar as they can be useful, and until they are either swallowed up or destroyed.

4 STALIN AND THE EVOLUTION OF THE PARTY DICTATORSHIP

Like the one-party dictatorship, the establishment of dictatorial control within the Russian Communist Party was a step-by-step process accompanying the successive phases of the revolution. In 1917, the party reached its lowest point in the observance of Lenin's standards of discipline and organizational cohesion. It was torn by controversy both immediately before and immediately after the October Revolution. Among Lenin's most enthusiastic supporters in the drive for power were new Bolshevik Party members like Trotsky who had never subscribed to Lenin's principles of discipline. One of the few people who followed Lenin's every twist and turn without a serious misstep was Stalin.

Throughout the critical period of the Civil War there was wide latitude in the party for criticism and factional controversy, although no one seriously challenged Lenin's leadership after the crisis over the treaty of Brest-Litovsk in 1918. The party did not attempt to enforce true Leninist discipline, in the original sense, until 1921. This step, as it happened, coincided with a critical point in the revolutionary process—the moment in 1921 when Lenin, sensing the balance of political realities, carried out his own "Thermidorean reaction." With this strategic retreat the Communist Party entered upon a situation in which discipline was at a premium, for it was attempting a feat which no extremist revolutionary party had ever managed before—to hold on to power after society had recovered from its revolutionary fever.

As the Kronstadt revolt demonstrated in March 1921, both radical and conservative grievances were eroding the Communists' popular support. Lenin's task was to satisfy the people without giving them power, and keep power for the Communist Party without satisfying its members. He liquidated the last non-Communist opposition, while allowing the nation to relax with the introduction of the NEP. For the Communist Party he revived and rigorously applied his principles of unity and discipline, in order to restrain opposition on the part of those Communists who would not take easily to the Soviet "Thermidor." At Lenin's behest, the Tenth Party Congress, in the critical month of March 1921, banned the further

existence of organized factions within the party:
"The unity and solidarity of the ranks . . . are
especially necessary at the present moment, when
a series of circumstances intensifies the wavering among the petty-bourgeois population of the
country . . . It is essential that all conscious
workers clearly realize the harm and intolerability
of any factionalism whatsoever, which unavoida-
bly leads . . . to stronger repeated attempts of
the enemies of the ruling party who attached
themselves to it to deepen the split and utilize it
for the ends of counter-revolution. . . . The Congress prescribes the rapid dispersal of all groups
without exception which have formed themselves
on one platform or another, and orders all party
organizations to deal strictly with any factional
manifestations by prohibiting them. . . . Failure
to execute this decision of the Congress will lead
to immediate and unconditional expulsion from
the Party." The revolutionary party was adjusting
to the ebb of the revolution, and the Communist
leaders were most of all concerned about criticism
from their own previous supporters. To silence
such as these—and any subsequent Communist
criticism of the leadership—the old conspiratorial
organizational pattern was called upon once again.
Now its function was to justify repression and provide the machinery for it. The criteria for an underground conspiracy had finally become the rules
for the political life of the revolutionary republic.

The changed relation between the party and
the underlying forces of revolution was reflected
at once by a dramatic shakeup in the Communist
Party leadership. The Trotskyist left-wingers, who
had stood midway between Lenin and the utopians
in the controversies since 1918, dominated the
Party Secretariat and most of the other important

organizational jobs. They were now summarily ousted, and a new group of reliable Leninists came in to replace them and enforce the new standards of discipline. The dominant figure among these new organization men was Stalin.

During the period between the Tenth Congress shakeup and Lenin's death in January 1924, the organizational structure of the party evolved rapidly toward bureaucratic perfection, rounding out a trend that had begun during the Civil War. The soviets, nominally the organs of local government, lost power to the party. Local organizations, including those in the party, lost authority to central organizations. Large parliamentary bodies lost authority to smaller committees. The result of these three trends was to make the Politburo of the party—composed in 1922 of Lenin, Trotsky, Stalin, Zinoviev, Kamenev, Rykov, and Tomsky, with Bukharin, Molotov, and Kalinin as alternate members—the country's supreme and virtually absolute governing authority.

A further change in the power structure occurred as groups of all sorts lost authority to individuals. In the party this meant the assumption of power at each level in the organization by the party secretary, who was nominally elected by the corresponding party committee. In practice party secretaries were nominated by the central secretariat, to which they accordingly owed their primary allegiance. Finally, the central secretariat was formally placed under the authority of an individual when Lenin had the Central Committee elect Stalin to the new post of General Secretary in 1922.

With this step, Stalin acquired personal and

undivided authority over a rapidly growing hierarchy of party officials who in turn were becoming the key force in Soviet politics. The secretaries ran the local organizations of the party, and now could usually hand-pick delegates to the national party congresses that theoretically had the last word in party affairs. Thus control of the Secretariat conferred upon Stalin the power to manage the party congresses and the Central Committee (elected at the congresses), even though he was only supposed to be their agent. Control of the Central Committee and, through it, of the Politburo meant that Stalin dominated the groups to which he was technically responsible. With no independent sources of power or avenues of expression left to his rivals, Stalin was by the middle twenties well on his way to absolute personal dictatorship.

Before 1922 Stalin had never distinguished himself as a major Communist Party leader, though he had been active in the central organizations of the party ever since Lenin had him co-opted to the Central Committee in 1912. He enjoyed neither intellectual brilliance nor any particular administrative ability, but he was a hard worker and an energetic schemer. The stature Stalin had won by 1922 or 1923 was not based on the exercise of any charismatic personal leadership, in which he was singularly deficient, but on machine politics and his identification with the party organization and its discipline. This remained the source of his power throughout the period of controversy in the 1920's.

Stalin reached the top rank in the party hierarchy thanks mainly to Lenin's favor, and he never ceased to acknowledge Lenin, alive or dead, as the source of all Communist authority and wisdom. He was unswervingly loyal to Lenin in every party controversy, having deviated from Lenin's line only once, in the early months of 1917 when Lenin was not present in Russia to make his views clear. Stalin no doubt appealed to Lenin as a model of Bolshevik discipline, and as a good organizational hatchet-man. However, Stalin was so immersed in the techniques of exercising party power that even Lenin soon expressed reservations about his capacity to lead the movement wisely. In his "Testament" of December 1922-January 1923, Lenin wrote: "Comrade Stalin, having become General Secretary, has concentrated an enormous power in his hands; and I am not sure that he always knows how to use that power with sufficient caution. . . . Stalin is too rude, and this fault . . . becomes insupportable in the office of General Secretary. Therefore, I propose to the comrades to find a way to remove Stalin from that position. . . ." Fortunately for Stalin, Lenin's warning remained unknown to the party until after its author's death in January 1924, by which time Stalin had consolidated his direct control over almost the entire party organization.

Stalin's drive for personal power began as soon as illness had removed Lenin from the political scene. Trotsky, apparently the major threat to the Leninist majority in the Politburo and the Central Committee, was confronted by a coalition of almost all his colleagues. A temporary leadership was unofficially raised to the fore—the "troika" or triumvirate composed of Zinoviev, Kamenev, and Stalin. In the fall of 1923, the forces of opposition within the Communist Party crystallized. The Trotskyists and Democratic Centralists, who had been defeated in 1921, took alarm over economic policy and the bureaucratic trend in the party organization, and rallied behind Trotsky to carry their challenge before the party membership. This was the decisive test between the organization and the quasi-democratic opposition of the left wing. Thanks to Stalin's control over the party organization and the press, the leftists were completely crushed. They were condemned as a "petty-bourgeois deviation" on the grounds that they had become a faction and had violated the principle of unity. During the year that followed, Trotsky's alleged heresies were repeatedly attacked (though he kept his government and party jobs). In the course of these campaigns the doctrinal orthodoxy of "Leninism" was hammered into shape.

Led by Stalin, Bukharin, Zinoviev, and Kamenev, the party was meanwhile proceeding on the cautious policy tack characteristic of the NEP. Alarmed by Stalin's growing power, Zinoviev and Kamenev broke with him in 1925 and attempted— unsuccessfully—to challenge his leadership. They were humbled, as Trotsky had been, and Stalin took the opportunity to begin moving his own creatures—Molotov, Kalinin, and Voroshilov—into the Politburo. In 1926 Zinoviev and Kamenev made an alliance with their former enemy Trotsky, and these three, with their followers, carried on a spectacular but fruitless campaign against the leadership of Stalin and Bukharin for almost two years more. In the fall of 1927 the Left Opposition was expelled from the party *en masse*.

After he had crushed the Communist Left, Stalin moved swiftly in 1928–29 to dispose of his own former allies on the Right, the cautious Communists Bukharin, Rykov, and Tomsky. To force the right-wing leaders into opposition, he suddenly adopted the Trotskyists' speeded-up industrialization program and combined this with a call for the

rapid collectivization of agriculture. Then he
moved with his invincible organizational machinery to eliminate all who dared stand up against
him. The Right Opposition tried to compromise on
the economic issue. Stalin simply made his program all the more extreme, and called for a tempo
of industrialization and collectivization far beyond
what the Left Opposition had ever anticipated.
Bukharin and his supporters had to capitulate
with hardly a fight. Meanwhile Stalin had committed himself to a new revolution.

The revolution of 1929 was not deliberately
planned, though it was the work of an individual
with a small group of his followers. Stalin does not
seem to have had any clear advance notion of the
totalitarian solution to Russia's problems which
he was about to work out. He was concerned with
the pursuit of immediate political advantage
against the Left and Right Oppositions, and with
this pragmatic end in view he adapted himself
freely to the totalitarian logic of the situation.
Stalin's success, in retrospect, is the success of the
man who hitched his wagon to the totalitarian
trends present in postrevolutionary Russia. All his
rivals balked at totalitarianism at one point or
another. Stalin, thanks to the political accident of
his acquiring the key organizational position, was
the one man who had no cause to resist totalitarianism.

The revolution of 1929, though it was a "revolution from above," meant almost as radical a change
in the fabric of Russian life as the revolution of
1917. Autocracy was reëstablished, as Stalin asserted his unchallenged individual dominance over
the party and thus over the Soviet state (though
he did not assume the government post of premier
until 1941). Stalin's dictatorship was much more

complete than Lenin's, and it steadily worsened. No opposition, no criticism, no idea of any sort that did not accord with the dictator's preferences was tolerated. Official adulation of the dictator commenced, and soon reached heights scarcely equaled even under the tsars. Finally came the purges of 1936–38, when all of Stalin's former critics, and most of his ostensibly loyal supporters as well, were ruthlessly liquidated. In the economic sphere Stalinism meant remorseless belt-tightening (unequally apportioned) and the subordination of all human needs to the requirements of the state. For the peasants, collectivization was the great change, more than undoing their gains of 1917. Finally, in the realm of thought and culture not directly impinging on the political, Stalin's revolution meant the end of individual freedom and the imposition of party control and party standards on every channel of expression. Stalin's revolution was the second and decisive stage in the erection of a totalitarian society in Russia.

The period of Stalin's struggle with the various opposition groups witnessed fundamental and lasting changes in the Communist Party. The military, monolithic qualities of the party organization were extended to its topmost level, as all opportunity for genuine discussion and debate was eliminated in favor of the single will of the dictator. Not only were opposition factions and public controversy eliminated for good, but the strong element of collective leadership and the recognizable existence of genuine individual opinions among the men around Lenin were finally terminated. So strong did the custom of official unanimity become under Stalin that even after his death, when real collective leadership resumed temporarily, public controversy continued to be tabooed. All that reaches the public now is the victor's condemnation of the vanquished—as in the case of Beria and Malenkov—after the fight has already been won behind the scenes.

Together with the perfection of monolithic control over the party, the period of Stalin's rise also saw the great changes in the party's manner of apprehending its doctrine, to which we have already referred. Under Stalin, theory ceased to represent a goal or a guide, and was reduced to the status of a mere instrument of power. Stalin was no theoretician, but he could wield doctrine as a weapon of debate well enough to make his opponents appear in the wrong. He was adept at puncturing pompous nonsense with a little common sense, and his one-two-three, down-to-earth argumentation could only have come as a welcome relief to audiences surfeited with the hours of cloudy discourse in which Stalin's associates of the 1920's were accustomed to indulge. Stalin effectively used Lenin's principles of discipline and ideological purity to condemn all criticism. On a multitude of issues, ranging from collaboration by the Comintern with non-Communists, and appeasement of the peasants at home, to the question of democracy or boss rule in the party, he was able to provoke the oppositionists into criticizing formal decisions of the party, and then, adroitly recalling their records of deviation both before and after the revolution, he was able to indict them as inherently un-Leninist and un-Bolshevik. With equal ease he broke the Trotskyist Left Opposition by taking a moderate line, and smoked out the Bukharinist Right Opposition by switching to an ultra-radical line. Faith, party unity, and the

defeat of the Opposition were all that Stalin demanded as the conditions of socialist success. But
the term "socialism" was coming to be so defined
as to mean whatever the Soviet government did,
and nothing else. Stalin reserved full freedom of
action to himself; he was dogmatic without being
doctrinaire. While he was making doctrine sacro-
sanct and immune to questioning, he was sub-
ordinating it to political expediency. By reinterpretation, more self-righteous than cynical, Stalin
manipulated doctrine to give the aura of unquestionable orthodoxy to whatever actual policy he
decided on, whether it was the cautious line of the
NEP or the violent industrialization and collectivization line to which he shifted in 1928–29.

Stalin's thinking and action were profoundly
colored by a narrowly suspicious, either-or attitude. He could brook no reservations concerning
his own power, could endure no rival among the
living, could concede no truth not promulgated
by himself. His reactions were all-or-none—all of
this policy up to a point, then all of that one, as
in the case of his shift in economic policy in 1928.
He could see only one problem, one danger, one
necessity, one avenue of endeavor at a time. This
is a trait which the Georgian Stalin shared with
the typical Russian; bursts of energy in one direction at the expense of others appear to be a common personality characteristic in the Russian culture. Whatever its cause, Soviet administrative
practices still suffer from the habit of emphasizing
one objective or one method at a time, while letting other needs or resources go unheeded.

Like Lenin and most of the Bolsheviks, Stalin
saw political life as an unremitting struggle—the
Party against all others. Between "We" and "They"
there was no middle ground and no possibility of

compromise. It was always a primary Bolshevik assumption that whoever is not with us is against us. This political dualism was intensified by the ideal of unity in the Communist camp. Whoever violated the norms of party unity or deviated by questioning the leadership was subject to the charge of joining the counterrevolution. Thus it was with Stalin's defeated rivals in the Opposition. Dissent became synonymous with treachery.

In the later twenties, Stalin made use of the Opposition groups as an outlawed internal enemy. In the course of combating and condemning them Stalin was able to cement his control and authority over the party. The Opposition was the excuse for bringing the mentality of struggle to a permanent high pitch and for perfecting the machinery of totalitarian control. The struggle within the party also sorted out the natural disciplinarians to whom Stalin's way of unrelenting struggle in an either-or world was congenial.

The mentality of Stalinism, which by attraction and selection became the prevailing mentality of Communism, can be aptly described in terms of the psychology of the "authoritarian personality." This applicability of the theory of the authoritarian personality to Communism is particularly interesting because the theory was formulated with no specific reference to Communism but rather in the study of right-wing movements in the West. Viewed in the light of the concept of the authoritarian personality, Stalin's behavior and policies become much more comprehensible. We see an anxious, rigid, compulsive, combative mind, imposing a disciplined militancy on himself and on all the members of his movement. He demands absolute authority—the authority of the prophets and their doctrine, to which he can subordinate

himself, and his own political authority, to which
the entire movement must be subordinated in
turn. He imposes a characteristic set of social
values, embodying discipline, tradition, struggle
with the enemy, and the supremacy of the state
over the individual. These preferences and values,
which Stalin legislated into the Communist movement, have little to do with the earlier socialist
tradition, but they are markedly similar to the
policies pursued by the recent totalitarian movements in the West.

Certain aspects of Stalin's rule require more
basic reference to abnormal psychology. This question is not without historical antecedents. There
have been many cases of despotic regimes headed
by individuals whose minds were partially or
totally deranged. There is good reason for be-
lieving that Stalin himself suffered from some
form of paranoiac psychosis.

The presumption of Stalin's insanity arises
principally from one episode—the fantastic purge
of 1937–38. In this blood bath not only were the
old oppositionists tried and condemned, but the
Stalinist party leadership was almost annihilated,
not to mention the hundreds of thousands of people in every sort of technical, managerial, or administrative post who were tortured and im-
prisoned. The record was too horrible for Stalin's
successors to keep silent about it, and in his secret
speech at the Twentieth Party Congress in February 1956, Khrushchev confirmed to the Communist
Party of the Soviet Union the story that the outside world had long since pieced together.

Khrushchev's long and detailed indictment is
the most telling evidence of Stalin's psychopathy

in the Great Purge. "Fabrication of cases against
Communists, false accusations, glaring abuses of
Socialist legality . . . ," and charges that were
"absurd, wild and contrary to common sense,"
were the basis of Stalin's sweeping action against
anyone denounced as an "enemy of the people."
The whole affair was totally irrational. Asserted
Khrushchev, "There is . . . no doubt that our
march forward toward socialism and toward the
preparation of the country's defense would have
been much more successful were it not for the
tremendous loss in the cadres suffered as a result
of the baseless and false mass repressions in 1937–
1938." There was only one explanation—the insane
abuse of absolute personal power: "Stalin was a
very distrustful man, sickly suspicious. . . . The
sickly suspicion created in him a general distrust
even toward eminent party workers whom he had
known for years. Everywhere and in everything he
saw 'enemies,' 'two-facers' and 'spies.' Possessing
unlimited power, he indulged in great willfulness
and choked a person morally and physically."
Stalin's mania for personal vindication was revealed, Khrushchev declared, when one of his
wartime decisions was criticized: "You should have
seen Stalin's fury! How could it be admitted that
he, Stalin, had not been right! He is after all a
'genius,' and a genius cannot help but be right!
Everyone can err, but Stalin considered that he
never erred, that he was always right." With this
megalomania went a world of self-delusion. Khrushchev placed Stalin unequivocally within the
terms of the definition of psychosis: "You see to
what Stalin's mania for greatness led. He had completely lost consciousness of reality. . . ."

Neither Khrushchev nor any other contemporary Soviet figure has explained the development

of Stalin's psychosis or assessed its more subtle
and lasting effects on the Communist movement.
Nevertheless, Stalin's career presents a consistent
picture of psychopathic development. The pattern
of his action and thought in the 1920's (about
which there is considerably more documentation)
reveals the passion for power and self-justification from which his delusions of grandeur and
conspiracy of the 1930's grew. Both drives were
self-reinforcing: the more power over his rivals
and subordinates, and the more elaborate his self-
glorification, the more important became both
considerations in order to sustain the autocrat in
his pose.

Dictatorial power itself can account for the
transformation of the dictator's minor personality
aberrations into a major psychosis. Control, falsi-
fication, and repression generate heightened opposition and resentment, which the dictator not
only welcomes but exaggerates as the excuse for
intensifying the machinery of dictatorial rule, terror, and propaganda. Such was the course Stalin's
mind took during his contest with the Communist
Opposition in the 1920's and the purges of the
1930's. When some of the Stalinist party leaders
expressed uneasiness about the spread of the purge
in 1937, Stalin made them his next victims. Since
the dictator has power over everything, he is responsible for everything. Any opposition or criticism will naturally be directed at him. The temp-
tation to use repression in order to silence criticism
and crush opposition is usually irresistible. Even
humor is banned: the dictator cannot tolerate being laughed at. Where opposition does not actually
exist, the despot can easily suspect it in potential
form, and the line between vigilance and paranoia
fades from view.

Stalin ruled as a personal despot in an atmosphere of adulation and terror from the time of the purges until his death in 1953. The party, with its upper levels decimated by the purge, ceased to be the central ruling institution; it was only one of a number of control levers, together with the police and the military, which Stalin kept at his finger tips to assure the abject subservience of the whole apparatus of power in the Soviet Union. Purging continued intermittently after World War II; the "Leningrad Affair" of 1949 claimed victims all the way up to the Politburo (in the person of the economist Voznesensky), and the "Doctors' Plot" of early 1953 appears to have been the prologue to another substantial purge which was kept from materializing only by Stalin's death.

The events of 1953, corroborated by the evidence of Khrushchev's attack on Stalin in 1956, indicate that Stalin's lieutenants lived in the shadow of fear and were determined to undo his system of personal power immediately. The day after Stalin's death his personal secretary disappeared without a trace; laments for the deceased stopped as soon as he was laid to rest in the tomb with Lenin; and his arrangements to make Malenkov the successor to his own undivided power were quickly rescinded. Governmental and party leadership were divided between Malenkov and Khrushchev; the police were curbed and their head, Beria, was liquidated; the members of the party Presidium (as the Politburo was restyled) evidently became a truly collective policy-making group. This situation was not destined to last long, for the man in control of the party organization— Khrushchev—was in the same strategic position in which Stalin had been in the 1920's.

The adjustments of 1953 accounted for most

of the substantive modification in Stalin's system. There remained the reappraisal of what had gone before. This was undertaken by Khrushchev, who had been made First Secretary of the Party in 1953, and was by 1956 the leading individual in the collective leadership of the USSR. Apart from its significance as an acknowledgment of the historical record, Khrushchev's condemnation of the "cult of personality" was important as a statement of what aspects of Stalin's system would endure and what would not. Terror, baseless purges, and physical liquidation of deviant Communists were condemned. Glorification of an individual dictator and control of all thought to this end were rejected—though with qualifications when the memory of Lenin was in question. Stalin's record as Soviet dictator was subjected to sweeping condemnation, but with a significant cut-off date. Only his actions since 1934—the beginning of the purge period—were censured. Most of his work of the previous years—all the time in which he was building his power and accomplishing his most significant acts of leadership—was emphatically endorsed. While the man was severely attacked, the implications of his system were not deeply reexamined.

Khrushchev's rise to personal dominance between 1953 and 1957 closely paralleled Stalin's success a generation before. In a series of factional struggles (this time entirely behind the scenes and not involving matters of principle) Khrushchev eliminated most of his colleagues from positions of power and packed the top Soviet leadership with his own supporters from the party apparatus. Thus, as Leonard Schapiro has demonstrated, the party as an institution regained the all-powerful position in the Soviet power structure

which it had had in the late 1920's and early
1930's. There is every indication that Khrushchev
will not climb above the party to reëstablish the
kind of personal despotism which Stalin achieved.
He is too old; his country is stable and does not
afford the opportunity for ruthless changes in
which Stalin asserted himself; there is too much
apprehension about a repetition of the evolution
from the party dictatorship to a personal one;
the evils of the personal dictatorship have been
explicitly acknowledged by Khrushchev himself.
On the other hand, the party dictatorship remains
in full force and rigor, and no sector of Soviet life
is immune from its controls. The party dictatorship appears to be more secure than ever. Lenin's
organizational philosophy, together with his mentality of pseudo-orthodox pragmatism, is permanently institutionalized in the Communist system.

5 THE PARTY IN
COMMUNIST SOCIETY

The distinguishing feature of government in
the Soviet Union, as in the other Communist states
which have been set up on the Soviet model, is the
application of Lenin's party concept—the militant,
disciplined organization of fervent activists—to
the running of society *after* the revolutionaries
have taken over. Stalin personified this system.
In his mind, party organization was the highest
revolutionary virtue, and he could not conceive of
political life except in the militant conspiratorial
pattern laid down by Lenin before the revolution.
Stalin explicitly maintained that the military hierarchy and discipline of the underground party
were all the more important for the Soviet state.
We need only recall his assertion, "The proletariat

needs the party not only to achieve the dictatorship; it *needs it still more to maintain* the dictatorship; to consolidate and expand it in order to
achieve the complete victory of socialism." For
Lenin, the revolution would not occur spontaneously; for Stalin, the new order would not stay
revolutionary of its own accord; for both, the party
was the indispensable force to drive and keep the
course of history *out* of its natural channel.

In the Soviet Union the key position of the
Communist Party has been given constitutional
sanction. The Communists are recognized as the
only legal "party," and the whole elaborate façade
of election and legislation serves only to register
the decisions made by the party. The party's decisions, in turn, by virtue of the organizational pattern mapped out by Lenin and brought to its
logical perfection by Stalin, are the decisions
made by the top party leaders or leader. The party
controls the government directly (though much
is made of their formal separation), by the simple
fact that the top governmental officials—the premier (Chairman of the Council of Ministers, formerly People's Commissars) and most of the
deputy premiers—are members of the supreme
decision-making body of the party, the Presidium
of the Central Committee. From 1941 until his
death Stalin held the offices both of premier and
of General Secretary of the party; by virtue of his
power in the latter capacity he had (through his
appointees) ruled the country as an absolute
dictator after 1929. Khrushchev has combined the
two offices in his person since 1958. With variations
in the degree of individual or collective leadership,
and with the inclusion of non-Communist puppet
parties in false-front coalitions, the same type of
dictatorship prevails in all other Communist coun-

tries. In every case, undisputed power is in the hands of the top Communist Party leaders.

Below the uppermost level in the Communist system the relationship between the party and the government is more complicated. All government officials and community leaders of any importance are members of the party, and subject to party discipline. The directives of the party leadership reach them through two separate channels— they go to the top governmental offices and down through the regular bureaucratic hierarchy; and they proceed down through the party organization and over to the official or agency in question. This situation makes it possible for the party organization—as distinct from the membership—to play a unique role in Communist society.

The party in a Communist country does not control merely the government—it controls everything. This is so partly because of the government's broad economic power, but even nominally nongovernmental organizations are under close party control. The trade unions are the most important of these; others are the Communist youth organizations, coöperatives, educational and cultural organizations, etc. These, together with the army and the local soviets in the governmental structure, Lenin termed "transmission belts"—the agencies whereby the will of the party was to be transmitted to the nonparty masses. Party control of these organizations is guaranteed in the same fashion as in the government itself—by the concerted action of the minority who are party members (the party "fraction"), who are bound by party discipline to transmit the instructions of the party leadership, and whose dominance over the nonparty rank and file is assured because any attempt to organize competing leadership would be illegal, an invitation to intervention by the secret police.

Communist Party organization still keeps to the form established in the prerevolutionary Russian underground and during the early years of the Soviet regime. Nominally the leaders are chosen and decisions made by the elected representatives of the membership, while unconditional discipline is demanded in the execution of policies once decided upon. Officially the sovereign party institution is the congress, which in the Soviet Union is presently supposed to meet every four years. The party congress elects the Central Committee—the executive body wielding full power between congresses—and the Central Committee in turn elects bodies to carry on its day-to-day business. In Russia from 1919 to 1952 these were the Politburo, the Orgburo (Organization Bureau), and the Secretariat. In 1952 the Orgburo was eliminated and the Politburo was redesignated the Presidium of the Central Committee, under which name it still functions.

The reality of Communist Party power relationships has, as the result of a decade's evolution after the Russian Revolution, become the precise opposite of the formal flow of authority. The Politburo, then Stalin as General Secretary, then the Presidium, now Khrushchev as First Secretary, make policy. The party congress rubber-stamps it, and the membership obediently carries it out. The key men in the actual operation of the party organization are the regional and local party secretaries, who are theoretically elected by the representatives of the local membership, but in fact appointed from the center. The secretarial hierarchy, together with its full-time employees, makes up the backbone of the party—the "apparatus," in which the military-bureaucratic organizational pattern reaches near-perfection.

There is a sharp distinction between the party apparatus and the membership. The apparatus alone embodies the specific controlling functions exercised by the party. The party membership at large has in Russia become nothing more than a duty-bound status group, an association embracing and controlling almost everyone who has responsibility or influence of any kind. The proletarian flavor and the preference for admitting workers (who never did become a majority in the party) were discarded in the course of the conservative shift of the middle and later 1930's. The party now represents not the class struggle but the new technocracy. Similar adjustments are to be expected everywhere Communist parties are in power. In China, where since the 1920's proletarian participation in the Communist movement has been conspicuous for its weakness, the party has enlisted anyone—including the so-called "national bourgeoisie"—who will submit to its organizational discipline and its ideological "remolding." The party struggles not against any particular class but against everyone who resists its total authority.

The function of party membership in a Communist country is to bring all important people in the country under the control, discipline and indoctrination of the party. This explains the great stress which the Communists still place on ideological instruction, despite its lack of real meaning for them. Indoctrination is a procedure for establishing and maintaining mental discipline, aimed primarily at the educated classes. The cultivation of positive enthusiasm is not as important as the development of unquestioning respect for

authority. The average Russian now accepts the
government and believes what he is told, though
often with disinterest and practically never with
any fervor except when patriotism comes into play.
The newer Communist states are ideologically less
placid, for they must still battle the protests of
disillusioned Communists and make their control demands clear for individuals who still try to
think for themselves. The most intensive efforts to
enforce ideological discipline have been made in
China, in a series of "thought-reform" movements
culminating in the so-called "rectification" campaign of 1957–58. In Eastern Europe the intensity
of indoctrination has varied, with a notable low
pressure zone in Poland after 1956. As the Hungarian uprising of 1956 demonstrates, the efficacy
of Communist indoctrination efforts in the European satellites should not be overrated.

The duties of the party apparatus in a Communist country are infinitely broad—they encompass all the work of control, checking and pushing,
supervising and executing, making sure that every
other organization and responsible individual in
the society is performing according to the desires
and dictates of the top party and governmental
leadership. The party apparatus is the instrument
of control superimposed on and controlling all
other instruments of control; it supplies the basic
drive to keep the wheels of the social system turning. As such, the party is well adapted to counter
the aimlessness, irresponsibility, and anarchic
wrangling which usually distinguished the Russian character.

On closer examination of the relation between
Communism and the Russian historical heritage,
we shall see how closely the party idea is related
to the problems posed by the cultural background

of the country. Communism has to contend with some of the same problems that tsarism did—though it deals with them far more efficiently. In the measure that Communism represents a reaction to the Russian background, it is relevant to the problems of any country which finds itself in similar circumstances—halfway between backwardness and progress, and confronted with the difficulties of rapid change. The party idea, as we shall see, can have major significance as a program for ruthlessly reorganizing and reëducating a nation to prepare it for industrialism.

The party idea and the party apparatus constitute the core of totalitarianism as practiced under Communist governments. The party, by its direct or indirect controls, exercises a monopoly over all forms of organized social life. (Only the churches are to some degree exempt, but except in Poland since 1956 they have been so constricted in their activity as to be a negligible factor.) The party stands above all, a pillar of bureaucratic perfection, acting with one mind (though not without friction at the joints) to impose its purposes on the society. Everything is political; everything must be in deadly earnest—frivolity is bourgeois. No one, no activity, no thought is exempt from the authority of the party and its overriding drive to heighten the industrial and military might of the Communist state and its tributaries.

6 THE COMMUNIST PARTIES OUTSIDE RUSSIA

The Communist Party—a form of organization which developed in Russia through the fusion of Lenin's theory and revolutionary practice—is the institution which unites all segments of the international Communist movement. Internationally, Communism represents the triumph of a specifically Russian pattern, exported and grafted upon indigenous revolutionary movements both in the West and in the East. The development was not a natural one, and was resisted by most of the foreign revolutionary leaders. It was thanks only to the fact that revolution happened to occur in Russia, and to the vigorous efforts of the Russian Communist leaders to build an international movement under their control, that international Communism as we know it came into being.

The Communist parties in the West originated in much the same fashion as the Russian Bolsheviks, through splits in the existing socialist movements. In most cases the precipitating factors were the First World War and the Russian Revolution: the radical wings of most socialist parties opposed the prosecution of the war and gave their sympathies to the Bolsheviks when the latter took power. In 1919 the Soviet leaders decided to bring these groups into a new revolutionary organization, and proclaimed the establishment of the "Third International" (Communist International or "Comintern") in opposition to the Second or "Labor and Socialist International," which had taken the course of patriotism and democratic reform. (The First International was Marx's "International Workingmen's Association," of 1864–76.)

Most of the original adherents of the Comintern were small splinter groups of left-wing socialists, but in 1920, notwithstanding the problems of attracting mass support, the Russian leaders laid down stringent rules for member parties of the Comintern. These were embodied in the so-called "Twenty-One Conditions," a true catechism of Bolshevik organization and militancy, to which all

who would affiliate with the Comintern had to
subscribe. An uncompromising struggle with all
non-Communist elements was demanded, and "a
complete and absolute break with reformism."
"Democratic centralism" was to be the rule, though
in the foreign Communist parties, as in Russia, it
quickly became centralism without qualification.
Periodic purges and underground organizations to
prepare for revolution were required; "unconditional support to any Soviet Republic" was demanded; and unquestioning obedience to the decisions of the Comintern leadership was enjoined
on members everywhere, on pain of expulsion from
the movement.

The enforcement of these Bolshevik principles
set the tone for the future development of the
Communist parties. The mass socialist parties
which the Comintern had attracted were either
repelled, like the Italian and Norwegian, or seriously split, like the French and the Czech. It was
characteristic of the Soviet leaders, however, to
prefer the small but hardened and obedient party
to the loose mass organization infected with independent thinking. Throughout the 1920's the
foreign Communist parties were wracked periodi-
cally by splits and purges, as the Russian leaders
who controlled the Comintern bore down to
tighten their authority and eliminate local Communist leaders who had minds of their own. The
party struggles in Russia, between the leadership
and the Trotskyist Left Opposition, and then between Stalin and Bukharin's Right Opposition,
facilitated this process of "Bolshevization" in the
Comintern, as the foreign Communist leaders who
chanced to side with either of the defeated Russian factions were themselves expelled. By the
early 1930's pliant tools of Moscow were ensconced

in the positions of power in every Communist Party save the Chinese. These new leaders, some of whom are still on the scene (Togliatti in Italy, Thorez in France), owed their tenure to continued Russian favor, which could be earned only by unquestioning subservience. Hardly any of the original founders of the foreign Communist parties survived in the movement.

It is remarkable, in the light of this history, that the Communist movement grew and consolidated itself outside of Russia. Much of the success of the Communists, however, is to be attributed to the fact that from about 1923 until after World War II they did not behave in a really revolutionary fashion. Revolutionary talk, Comintern politics, struggle with the socialists, and the maintenance of discipline among their followers consumed most of the Communists' energy. A further shift occurred in the mid-1930's, when even the revolutionary talk was given up. This was the time of the "Popular Front," as Communists everywhere proclaimed the intention of supporting their former archenemies, the liberals and socialists, to promote social reform and combat the menace of Fascism. The motive for the shift can readily be understood: the Soviet government under Stalin, entering its conservative phase, was alarmed by its international isolation and the German-Japanese threat, and therefore decided to forsake revolutionary purity in the interest of national defense. Accordingly, the Communists everywhere ceased to be revolutionaries in fact or in word, and behaved simply as reformists—in defiance of the whole Leninist tradition.

Tactically the Popular Front was an eminently successful idea, though it failed to achieve a coalition that could prevent war. By playing down the revolutionary theme, the Communists greatly increased their appeal, especially in countries like Great Britain and the United States where their influence had previously been negligible. The new popularity, however, was not as a revolutionary party but as a reformist one, and it was less a specifically proletarian appeal than a general one to frustrated political idealism. But all the while the Bolshevik organizational pattern of centralization and discipline was retained, and with it the unquestioning subordination to Russian orders which the Soviet leaders had put into effect during the previous decade.

As in Russia, the pattern of the organizational system imposed on the foreign Communist parties is that of the military pyramid. The Communist parties of each country are nominally governed by elected congresses and central committees, with a formally democratic structure extending down to the local level. Actually, the parties are firmly controlled by their top leaders, through the same sort of secretarial hierarchy that prevails in the USSR. The national leaders, in turn, are almost always people who have derived their positions *de facto* by appointment from Moscow. Behind the facade of national autonomy stands the pyramid of international authority. Discipline is absolute: the member who questions an order or the "party line" is subject to expulsion forthwith. The cleavage between the professional leadership and the rank and file, so distinct in Russia, is paralleled in the foreign parties. Conspiratorial secrecy is the rule in party activities and decision-making, especially at the local level, where the party unit comes in contact with nonparty groups and activities.

Party influence in non-Communist countries is exerted and enhanced in much the same fashion as in countries where the party is in power. The Communist Party members (constituting the so-called "party fraction") in any other organization, be it political, economic, or social, are bound by party discipline to express and carry out the wishes of the party, and to act as a solid, though secret, bloc to influence or control the organization in question. If the organization can be effectively controlled, it becomes a "Communist front," nominally non-Communist and often having a majority of non-Communist members, but steered toward the accomplishment of some specific Communist objective.

In most cases the Communist Party has a dual personality, as both an open political movement and an underground conspiracy. Democratic forms and the Bolshevik substance of organization operate in combination. Direction for the movement comes from above, and cannot be questioned; the voice of Moscow is infallible, except when a change of line is too abrupt, as in the deflation of the Stalin myth in 1956. It is the conspiratorial character of the Communist movement—its discipline, secrecy, tactical treachery, and ulterior motives—far more than any revolutionary features or intentions which the Communist parties may have, that makes it so risky for non-Communists to cooperate with them toward any objective whatsoever.

While its organizational forms, firmly set in the 1920's according to the Russian model, have remained solidly fixed, the Communist movement has evolved considerably with respect to its original goal of revolution. In the West, revolution has been progressively played down, in some cases with a corresponding increase in the popular support which Communist parties can command. In some countries, such as France and Italy, this has given the movement a vested interest in moderation. On the other hand, wherever or to the extent that revolution is still a goal, the party approach to it is entirely different from that of the revolutionaries from Marx to Lenin who boldly proclaimed their objective of taking power and overturning the social order in the name of the working class. Since Stalin's time, dissimulation has been the rule. The Communist leaders have tried to conceal their totalitarian intentions, and work for them only covertly. Even the Communists' own followers, for the most part now attracted to the movement by visions of peace, reform, democracy, and national independence, rather than violence, revolution, dictatorship, and Russian hegemony, have to be kept in the dark or very gingerly enlightened about the movement's real principles and objectives.

Like the modified Communist appeal, the path to power followed by recently successful Communist parties has been far different from the experience in Russia. The Communist victories since 1945 both in Eastern Europe and in the Far East have all come in the wake of war and enemy occupation. Nowhere have the Communists come to power except where the way was paved for them by enemy conquest and the consequent destruction or serious impairment of the existing political structure. Participation in the war effort against the Axis powers was for the Communists a major stepping

stone to power (or toward strong political influence
in areas where they fell short of the ultimate objective).

In defeated or occupied countries the distinctive organizational features of the Communist
movement—its discipline, militancy, and conspiratorial experience—gave the Communists an immense advantage, and everywhere they came to
the forefront of national underground movements.
As a result of this role in the resistance movements
and in the conduct of guerrilla warfare, the Communists won unprecedented popularity and prestige, particularly in Western Europe, Yugoslavia,
and China. In the latter two cases, to be sure,
guerrilla warfare against the invader was simultaneously civil war and revolutionary struggle
against the representatives of the old regime, but
even here it was the opportunity to play a decisive
role in the national struggle which brought revolutionary victory within the Communists' grasp.

In the countries of Eastern Europe other than
Yugoslavia and Albania, the Communists' final
acquisition of power was accomplished in quite a
different fashion. Here it was revolution behind
the scenes, through political intrigue and maneuver with the backing of the Soviet occupation
forces. Communists got control of the police forces
(at Soviet insistence), and then it was only a matter of time until their coalition partners were
eliminated or reduced to the role of helpless puppets. A new elaboration of the Communist conspiratorial technique was to infiltrate the non-
Communist parties with secret Communists, who
would swing sympathy and influence to the Communist side at critical moments, while contributing to the illusion of a democratic government.
Only in Czechoslovakia (with the greatest in-

digenous Communist strength in Eastern Europe)
does there appear to have been extensive working-
class support of the Communist seizure of power—
the coup which came in February 1948. We can
place the Czech case midway between the police
revolutions elsewhere in Eastern Europe and the
genuine insurrection in Russia.

International Communism is by and large a
movement created by Russian prompting and
pressure out of the political materials at hand. It
represents the shaping of natural revolutionary
tendencies to the Russian mold, and their subordination—with the notable exceptions of Yugoslavia
and China—to the interests of the Soviet Union.
Two factors, broadly speaking, have been responsible for the successes of the movement. One is
negative—the weaknesses or injustices or national
frustration or humiliation in any particular foreign area. The other is the presence or immediate
backing of Soviet (or other Communist) military
power, which was the decisive element in Eastern
Europe and in the northern portions of the partitioned Far Eastern republics, Korea and Vietnam.
Perspicacious Russian leadership hardly deserves
the credit; the notion of a Soviet "master plan" is
an illusion of outsiders who take Communist ideology too seriously. Soviet conduct of the affairs of
the Communist International has been characterized by one short-sighted policy after another,
invariably misfiring except where Communist resistance leadership or Soviet military power was
present in the power vacuum left by the Second
World War. It is despite Soviet guidance, not
thanks to it, that the international Communist
movement has the strength which it now enjoys.

Where Communists have come to power, problems have arisen for Moscow in keeping the movement under its firm control. Non-Russian Communists as officials of a foreign government have a much firmer base for independent action, even if they originally owed their places in the movement to Moscow's favor. Tito's Yugoslavia is the case especially in point. Moscow has not been eager to see foreign Communist parties come to power in areas not immediately subject to Soviet military pressure. The Soviet policy toward China, in particular, just after World War II, was to discount the Communist revolution and treat with the Nationalist government, while pressing for the maximum in imperialist concessions. The power, security, and direct influence of the Russian state appear to have been the real concerns of Soviet policy. Where the foreign revolution can be bent to these objectives, well and good; where there is conflict, the revolution is likely to be sacrificed.

The acid test came when foreign Communist parties took power and then found that their interests as sovereign governments clashed with Russia's interests or policy preferences. As far as Eastern Europe was concerned, the Russians demanded, in the name of "proletarian internationalism," absolute agreement with, and subordination to, the policies of the Soviet Union. This claim they were able to enforce through the channels of control and discipline over the foreign Communist movements which they had built up over the previous two decades, supplemented by direct infiltration of the satellite armies and police forces. When local leaders ventured to resist Soviet demands or assert that they could follow separate routes in the construction of a socialist society, they were shelved or liquidated, and replaced with more pliant tools of Moscow. Characteristically, it was the leaders who had fought in the local resistance (like Gomulka in Poland), suffered in Nazi concentration camps (like Rajk in Hungary), or lived in exile in the West (like Clementis in Czechoslovakia), who committed the "national Communist" deviation, while the men Moscow could rely upon were those who had been residing in Russia. In one case the Russians were unable to make their authority prevail against the "national Communists"; this was Yugoslavia, where, thanks to the independent acquisition of power by Tito's Communist Partisans, and the advantages of geography, the native Communist regime was able to defy Moscow in 1948 and denounce the Russians themselves as the real "deviators." Yugoslavia has rejected not only Moscow's control but the whole idea of international revolution, and pursues its independent neutralist foreign policy. Within Yugoslavia the Communist Party dictatorship has been significantly ameliorated and decentralized. It is as different from Stalinism as the latter is from the Bolshevism of 1917.

A grave shock to Muscovite discipline in the international Communist movement was occasioned by Khrushchev's gestures of reform and his repudiation of Stalin in 1956. The party line which had been asserted for years was exposed as myth and fraud, while the enemies against whom the Communists had endeavored to defend the reputation of the Soviet dictator were proved right. Moscow had destroyed its own infallibility and much of its doctrinal authority. Where Communists ruled outside Russia, reform was expected, and with it the relaxation of Russian control.

The crisis of 1956 owed its severity to the basic contradiction in the Communist movement between the claims of international revolutionary coöperation and the reality of Soviet power interests. In Poland, anti-Stalin Communists determined to take advantage of the new climate to eliminate Stalinist features in their own regime and appease the populace in the manner of Bukharin's Right Opposition. In October 1956, Gomulka returned to power in defiance of Khrushchev, though he was sagacious enough to keep party controls intact and pledge his support of Soviet foreign policy. The real "revisionists" in the Polish Communist Party, who would drastically curb the party's powers of control and reexamine the doctrinal foundations of Marxism, were confined to the status of an intellectual underground.

In Hungary, both the anti-Russian movement and the Soviet response took far more extreme forms than in Poland. As in Russia in February 1917, demonstration turned into revolution in Hungary late in October 1956, and the government's authority dissolved overnight. The short-lived national Communist regime of Imre Nagy could be compared with the Provisional Government in Russia—essentially conservative, but compelled to go along with the revolutionaries. The makeup of the Hungarian revolutionary forces, ironically, came close to the Communist ideal— workers and peasants, sparked by students. Even "soviets" were formed—sovereign workers' councils in the factories and in some entire cities. Such a movement, directed against the reality of Communist rule, could hope for no mercy from the Soviet government, which could afford neither the exposure of its own counterrevolutionary nature nor the loss of Hungary (and possibly more) from its military security system. Naked intervention (recalling 1849), overthrow of the national Communists, and remorseless repression of the revolutionaries put an end to this defiance of Moscow's authority.

Hungary was dynamite in Communist ranks the world over. It looked to them, as to many others, as though the Russians were indulging again in the Stalinist brutality which they had just repudiated. Communist leaders everywhere were thrown into consternation, if not in a crisis of their own consciences, then at least in a quandary over accounting for the Soviet action and assuaging the indignation of their supporters. Some serious splits occurred. Generally speaking, the reaction away from Moscow and the disorganization of the movement were more serious in democratic countries where the Communist movement was already weak—Britain, the United States, Scandinavia. Elsewhere in Europe, while Communist Party ranks held fairly firm, sympathizers and allies fell away in droves. The most serious of such defections was Nenni's Socialist Party in Italy, which practically terminated its alliance with the Communists and moved toward coöperation with the anti-Communist Social Democrats. By contrast, in the Near and Far East the Communist parties experienced very little embarrassment, thanks to the anti-imperialist emotion that was stirred up simultaneously by the Suez crisis.

A major exception to the typical pattern of relations between the Soviet Union and the foreign Communist parties is the case of China. The

Chinese Communists under Mao had been relatively independent of Moscow since the early
1930's. They had come to power largely on their
own, and were treated with far more circumspec-
tion by the Russians. In certain respects, the
Chinese Communist Revolution was more Stalinist
than Stalin himself. It was exclusively the work
of the party: the party did not lead a revolutionary
class, but created it; it did not seize control of the
old government, but created a new one; it did not
have to perfect its discipline and extend its controls after coming to power—the Stalinist pattern
of complete discipline and total ideological commitment was borrowed and made ready beforehand. Taking the Russian revision of Marxism as
their starting point, the Chinese Communists were
able to push to Leninist and Stalinist changes of
doctrine and practice even further, and contrive
a distinctly Chinese revolutionary movement.

Since the crisis of 1956 the Chinese Communists have not been content to take their ideological cues from the Russians; they have translated
their organizational independence more and more
into the realm of policy and theory. Mao Tse-tung
began to be credited by his party as a major theoretician of Marxism, superior to any other living
Communist. The Russians and Chinese divided
over policy toward the Western powers and toward
neutrals, and began to vie for influence among
other Communist parties. By 1960 strong in-
nuendoes of "revisionism" and "dogmatism" were
being traded by the Chinese and Russians respectively, and it took extended negotiations at the
Moscow Communist "forum" of November 1960 to
work out the appearances of a compromise.

The international Communist movement is
now clearly a two-headed affair, and this raises

questions not only as to how long it can remain
united, but as to a possible new freedom of maneuver for the smaller Communist parties between
the Russian and Chinese positions. On the international plane, the Communist movement has recovered some of the variety, disagreement, and
debate which were snuffed out in Russia after the
controversies of the 1920's. It remains to be seen
whether this new experience of controversy within
the movement will infect the various Communist
parties internally and undermine the monolithic
discipline which they have maintained since the
1920's. It is unlikely that such a ferment can be
prevented in all cases.

4 Communism as a Strategy of Struggle

Communism is an international move-ment devoted to the acquisition of political power. At the present time Communism in its international aspect is the all-absorbing problem on the world scene. For a decade and a half it has been the subject of vast speculation and alarm in the non-Communist world. But the international behavior and impact of Communism, as we shall see, are far from fully determined by Marxist doctrine or the Communist Party. While Communism is a party to fundamental new divisions and conflicts around the globe, these are largely the consequence of changes in the international power structure, especially with the polarization of international relations into the sharply opposed Communist and democratic camps. Viewed in the international perspective, Communism, like every ambitious force in prior ages, is fighting primarily for success as an end in itself, in a black-and-white world where all outside forces are enemies. We must consider to what extent the characteristics of the Communist movement follow from

142

this power struggle, as a system of strategy and tactics for the waging of political war.

1 KTO-KOVO

Ever since the Bolshevik seizure of power in 1917 the Communists have regarded themselves as a unique world-wide force battling in the name of the Marxist ideal against all the forces of the old order. Marx and Engels had drawn the lines in theory between the virtue of the proletariat and the evil of the bourgeoisie, and the Communist International was brought into being amid cries for international civil war between these two irreconcilable classes. The expansion of Communist power after World War II only accentuated this sense of conflict by dividing the world into two bitterly hostile sides or "camps," Communist and anti-Communist. In 1927 Stalin sketched out such a perspective of the future: "Two centers of world-wide scope will take shape: the socialist [i.e., Communist] center, drawing to itself the countries which gravitate toward socialism, and the capitalist center, drawing to itself the countries which gravitate toward capitalism. The struggle of these two camps will decide the fate of capitalism and socialism all over the world." The Communist movement has always viewed the world as the arena for unremitting conflict between these two forces, which can only end eventually with the total liquidation of the capitalist enemy.

Communist writings have been permeated since Lenin's day with the sense of struggle between the two tightly drawn antagonists. Communists have constantly approached politics as a contest of black and white that can never end in a settlement. One side or the other must triumph and destroy its adversary. Who defeats whom has been the basic question in the Communist mind, or in the Russian formula which they have occasionally employed, *"kto-kovo"*: "Who-whom," "Who beats whom."

Marxist doctrine has played the major role in defining the sides in this struggle and in making war to the death axiomatic. Marxism posits the opposing forces of the bourgeoisie and capitalism versus the proletariat and socialism. The class struggle thesis of Marxism requires that these two sides be viewed as locked in an unremitting, though not always violent, struggle. Finally, Marxism predicts the inevitable victory of the proletariat, although the Communists have not always regarded this success as a certainty. Lenin declared in 1920, for example, "As long as capitalism and socialism exist, we cannot live in peace; in the end, one or the other will triumph—a funeral dirge will be sung either over the Soviet Republic or over world capitalism." In practice, the Communists have regarded their own victory only as a probability, always threatened by the machinations of the imperialists, and requiring the utmost vigilance and exertion to guarantee its success.

The reverse side of the Communists' commitment to the view of international class war is their conviction that the non-Communist world has constantly been plotting attack against them. This strongly suggests the psychological device known as projection—imagining that someone else harbors aggressive impulses or designs similar to those in one's own subconscious. Committed as they are to fight capitalism, the Communists cannot imagine that the non-Communist world could ever really accept their existence; they persuade themselves of the need for an active defense of the gains of the revolution; the defense looks like offense to the threatened anti-Communists, who take the logical countermeasures; the Communists see their adversaries arm and adduce this as proof of their initial assumption about the belligerence of the "imperialists."

The principle of irreconcilable struggle between the old international order and the new revolutionary forces lay at the very core of Lenin's political thought and action. As a personality, Lenin was addicted to struggle: he could think and act in no other terms. Lenin's real passion was not the proletariat as a human group, but the cause that he could fight for, the movement that would recognize him as its master strategist. To paraphrase the famous Prussian strategist Karl von Clausewitz, Lenin approached politics as the continuation of war by other means. For Lenin the political struggle was an absolute; the highest value, in his mind, was the violent prosecution of a victorious class war. "Major questions in the life of nations are settled only by force," Lenin wrote in 1905. This relapse into the approbation of violence he shared with certain other twentieth-century figures—Mussolini, for example. We will consider this parallel later when we treat Communism as a manifestation of the general phenomenon of totalitarianism.

As we have seen, the thinking of Lenin and his followers in the Communist movement was cast in characteristically military terms. The basic fact of history, in this view, is the state of war between classes or between states controlled by antagonistic classes. Politics is an unending series of military campaigns. The proletariat is an army. The party is ideally a military organization whose mission is to win the class war. Marxist-Leninist theory is the corpus of strategy and tactics which the party employs and elaborates in the course of combat. The leader is the commander-in-chief, on whose inspired strategic intuition the outcome of each battle depends.

2 THE MEANING OF STRATEGY

Strategy is the science of winning. As such, strategy is by no means confined to military operations, but extends to the whole range of politics, economics, and contests of all kinds. Strategy comes into play in any situation of direct competition or conflict among a limited number of individuals or units, be it a game like chess or football, economic rivalry between competing firms, an election campaign, diplomacy among national states, or warfare between opposing armies. Strategy is no less appropriate in guiding the efforts of a world-wide revolutionary movement or the bearers of a militant faith.

While strategy has been a persistent concern of political thinkers ever since Machiavelli's day, its scope is not unlimited. As a guide to political action strategy is subject to two kinds of restrictions, imposed on the one hand by the higher purposes which it is intended to serve and on the other by the values and interests which the various powers wish to preserve above the conflict. Apart from sheer self-preservation, strategy does not establish anyone's ultimate objective or explain what the contest is all about. In the terms of the "game theory" which some American social scientists have recently applied to politics, the "pay-off" and the "players" who compete for it must be determined beforehand; strategy merely guides the effort to achieve the goal. Accordingly, strategy alone cannot account for the existence of the Communist movement, or its objectives, or its commitment to a world-view of inevitable struggle. The basic nature of the movement must still be sought through historical and social analysis. On the other hand, the strategic approach can explain a great deal about the behavior of the movement in the pursuit of its presumed goals, and will clear the ground for subsequent deeper inquiry.

In most kinds of contests the operation of strategy is limited by certain "rules" of the game. The existence of rules means that the players have jointly agreed on certain non-strategic conditions or values which they wish to keep outside the arena of struggle. In some situations there is an authority to compel observance of the rules —the referee in sports or the government in business competition. In international relations, since there is no effective referee to enforce the rules established by custom or treaty, there is always the possibility that one player will see it to his momentary interest to cheat and surprise an opponent with an advantageous violation of the rules—undeclared war, for example. In such cases the only recourse for other players is to retaliate or threaten retaliation in the same or equivalent ways. Sometimes international relations and conflicts may be conducted entirely without rules apart from the physical facts of life. In such cases any expedient means may be employed to win victory over the opponent. Occasionally one player may feel that his own moral standards require unilateral self-restraint in the choice of means of struggle. This would mean that the players have different values and different aims—i.e., different "pay-off" prospects. It is possible to conceive of a player whose aims and values are such that in a certain conflict situation he will experience a net loss no matter what happens.

The classic exposition of the meaning of strategy is represented by the work of Clausewitz. Probably the most important thing to be learned from Clausewitz's treatise on military strategy is that no strategic idea or device should be regarded as an end in itself. Clausewitz harps on the importance of the "single view" encompassing the whole military and diplomatic contest. This means simply that every move and every instrument must be judged according to the overall objective of success. The essence of strategy is that it is a means to an end, not the ultimate interest. Thus, war is but "the pursuit of politics by other means." Exclusive devotion to winning a war is shortsighted, because it diverts attention from the long-run political objectives which the war ought to serve. From this standpoint the use of force is not subject to judgments of virtue or wickedness, but only of effectiveness or ineffectiveness. Where moral opposition to force or a moral commitment to military victory enters the picture the scope of strategy is correspondingly restricted, and the prospects of continuing political success are accordingly sacrificed.

Modern history has witnessed pronounced long-term changes in the scope of strategy in international relations. In the era of the religious wars in Europe in the sixteenth and early seventeenth centuries strategy was circumscribed—

with some notable exceptions—by the overriding emotional commitment to one religious cause or the other. From the middle of the seventeenth century until the end of the nineteenth, with the exception of the period of the French Revolution, European politics were singularly free of any religious or ideological motives competing with the pure pursuit of national power. This allowed the scope of purely strategic considerations to become much broader.

The fact that the ways of international conflict were relatively restrained during this period does not contradict the foregoing, but is explained by it. Each nation, finding itself within a constellation of hostile forces, saw its interest in playing a relatively cautious game for limited stakes. There was a common international interest in agreeing on a system of international rules—international law, the customs of diplomacy, and relatively restrained warfare. Thus, the long-term diminution in emotional objectives, which tended to enlarge the scope of strategy, was offset by a notable constriction of the prevailing rules of the international game, which tended to curtail the scope of strategy. It became the custom among all civilized states to live up to treaty obligations, to declare war before attacking, to respect neutrals, etc. The Hague Conventions of 1899 and 1907 were international agreements to desist from particularly barbarous forms of combat such as poison gas; the Geneva Convention regulates the treatment of war prisoners and the protection of medical services in great detail. The ultimate in rule-making was the Kellogg-Briand Pact of 1928, whose signatories—including all the major powers —abjured "recourse to war as an instrument of national policy." This utopian sentiment was ef-

fective for only three years, until the Japanese
militarists found it to their interest to flout the
treaty and embark on aggression in Manchuria.

The trend toward international rule-making
was supported by the pacifism and anti-militarism
which accompanied the growth of democratic
movements in the nineteenth century. This sentiment culminated in the creation of the League
of Nations. On the other hand, increased mass
political participation had the dangerous effect
of making international rivalries more emotional;
it caused the ideological factors of emotional
nationalism or political creeds to be injected into
national policy-making. The result was clear after
World War I: strategy, with its simple criterion
of success, was enlisted in the service of other
goals—national glory or the triumph of a revolutionary idea. Once subordinated to such compelling objectives, strategy no longer pointed toward limited forms of struggle, but to a fight to
the finish, total war, a campaign of extermination.

World War I began more or less in the old way
—complicated, to be sure, with the Germans'
infamous rule-breaking in Belgium which provoked fateful British retaliation. By the time the
war ended it was a struggle for absolute national
triumph—nothing else explains the four-year
madness of bloody attrition without serious attempts to negotiate a settlement. The war had
meanwhile given birth to the first of the recent
totalitarian revolutionary movements, launched
by the Russian Revolution, and it set the stage for
others in Italy and Germany. The consequence of
totalitarianism was World War II and the full
elaboration of the new type of struggle to the

death, in the course of which all the painfully written rules of warfare and national conduct were swept away. For the democracies, the price of victory was to reply in kind, with the latest weapons of mass destruction. Strategy was freed of rules, only to be subordinated more and more to the objectives of insane nationalism, revolutionary fanaticism, and "unconditional surrender."

3 THE SCOPE OF STRATEGY IN COMMUNISM

A common error among both pro-Communists and anti-Communists is to assume that the Communist movement has never changed its nature and its goals. Many critics of the movement feel that this assumption is borne out by the continuity they observe in the devices of Communist strategy and tactics. However, we have already seen clearly that the Communist movement has undergone fundamental changes in the course of its history, and such change has particularly affected the limits and purposes of strategy under Communism.

In its doctrinal and revolutionary sources Communism represents a system of impassioned ideals, a fanatic onslaught against everything represented by the "bourgeoisie," "exploitation," and "imperialism." Nevertheless, Lenin began to assert considerations of strategy against the dictates of pure idealism from a very early date. Lenin's original concept of the disciplined party organization, with all its totalitarian implications, was initially a strategic device, vehemently opposed by many Russian Marxists and most of the non-Marxist revolutionaries because it violated their democratic or humanist values. The very existence of Bolshevism was a revolutionary adaptation to strategy.

Between 1905 and 1914 Lenin had to carry on a running fight with left-wing deviationists in his own Bolshevik faction who were carried away by revolutionary idealism and insurrectionary romanticism. People driven by such impulses could not tolerate the political compromises which Lenin demanded in the name of strategy, and he finally had to drive them out of his organization. Lenin's notorious opposition to the economic interest of the workers as an end in itself was strategic: he properly reasoned that they would be more inclined to support his strategy of winning power if their immediate desires were frustrated. The essence of Lenin's political contribution to the Russian revolutionary movement was to broaden the scope of strategic considerations—which under the circumstances then prevailing pointed to the conspiratorial party with tight organizational discipline. The fact that the Bolshevik Party was far more open than its rivals to considerations of strategy—i.e., that it was more "unscrupulous"—was one of the keys to its successful seizure of power in October 1917.

The initial impact of Communism on the world scene after 1917 was extremely upsetting to most of the established powers and forces, though not because of actual Communist strength. Russia's position among the major powers was seriously weakened by the upheaval of revolution and was not made up until the 1930's, while most of the early Communist movements elsewhere in the world were relatively ineffectual. The great international disturbance caused by Communism was due to its upsetting all the conditions of the old political game, both within and between countries, and radically altering the scope of strategy. The Communists abruptly extended the sphere of strategy by repudiating all the old rules and customs of political conflict. At the same time they reoriented strategy by injecting into the arena of world politics the radically new revolutionary objectives and lines of ideological cleavage represented by the international class struggle between what was supposed to be the proletariat and the so-called bourgeoisie. Thanks to the challenge of Communism, the units of world political rivalry were complicated by an international revolutionary loyalty that cut into the unity of almost every state. National power competition had to share the scene with a new contest of rival international faiths. Thus, the advent of Communism sharply intensified the twentieth-century shift toward superimposing ideological struggle upon considerations of national strategy.

By the same token, the old rules and customs of politics, which were the reflection of common agreement on certain ends and norms of conduct, ceased to have much value when the revolutionary challenge of Communism raised the overall stakes. This is the meaning of Lenin's treatment of morality, which swept aside all ethical compunctions that might interfere with the success of the revolution on the national or international scale. The Bolsheviks were, in a word, unscrupulous, and this characteristic gave them a major advantage over rival parties and governments which did not quickly abandon the old "bourgeois" norms of political conduct. As a result, the Communists' lack of scruple has often forced their opponents to abandon such restraints themselves.

Within the sphere accorded it, strategy erodes

all other norms and values, and if not carefully
circumscribed it tends in time to enlarge its own
scope like water cutting a canyon. The side which
is less rule-bound has an obvious advantage. If
the other side has to choose between eternal principle and present survival, it will almost always
do what is expedient for survival and simply
hope for the best as far as the future of the principle is concerned. From the moral standpoint,
any conflict tends to proceed according to the
lowest common denominator of the rival forces.

In a bitter ideological struggle the broadened
scope of strategy occasioned by the clash over
fundamentals is particularly apparent. At the
same time this rule-breaking effect may exercise
a reverse influence upon the basic aims and issues
that have brought on the struggle. Once certain
principles have brought a movement into being,
victory or survival inevitably become to a certain
extent ends in themselves, and it is then possible
for the dictates of strategy to call into question
the presumably basic objectives of the movement.
The history of Soviet Russia since 1918 could
well be written as a series of contests between
emotions and revolutionary ideals on the one hand
and the progressively revealed dictates of political
strategy on the other. Invariably the strategic
considerations of practical political success have
prevailed; hence the general drift of the Soviet
political mentality toward the strategic means as
an end in itself. Strategy has more and more come
to govern the realm of policy, and the result has
been a consistent pattern of change in which
revolutionary norms and practices have been
abandoned in favor of practical ones.

The first dramatic conflict between ideology
and strategy came in the realm of foreign policy,
with the Brest-Litovsk controversy of early 1918.
The Left Communists represented total ideological
commitment, ready to stake everything on a
"revolutionary war." The Leninists yielded to the
dictates of strategy: don't do anything that is
likely to throw you out of the game. The strategy
of protecting the Russian base of the revolution
prevailed. Underlying this shift was an implicit
redefinition of the struggle. For the ideologists of
1918 it was a disembodied conflict of principles
whose future outcome would be jeopardized more
by the compromise of ideals than by the defeat of
a particular revolutionary government. For Lenin
and the strategists the world proletarian revolution was already identified with the power of the
Russian state which they controlled. The two
factions operated with different definitions of
fundamentals and hence with different standards
of what could be sacrificed and what would constitute a total loss. By making the integrity of the
Soviet state his prime practical concern, Lenin
abruptly brought the Communist revolutionary
challenge within the arena of traditional power
politics. Power was given precedence over program.

Parallel changes came almost simultaneously
in Soviet internal policies. In the spring of 1918
Lenin violently attacked the anarchistic and
syndicalist presumptions which had animated the
Bolshevik Party and much of the Russian working
class in 1917. The revolutionary expectations were
for decentralization of the economy under peasant
communes and workers' councils, decentralization
of the army under soldiers' councils, decentralization of political power under the local soviets,

and elimination of all bureaucratic authority both
in the government and in the economy, while the
state "withered away." Lenin, as a master revolutionary strategist, had encouraged and utilized
such sentiment to help his party get power. Undoubtedly he believed in the long-term justness
of these sentiments, but the point is that a strategist like Lenin is not influenced very much by the
long-run justness of anything. Whenever ideals
got in Lenin's way he put them off to the future
and concentrated on the requirements of present
political success. These included the Brest-Litovsk
peace to save the Soviet state, and the reëstablish-
ment of central authority and discipline in the
government, the army, and industry, in order to
repair the sinews of political power. While these
moves were explained as temporary expedients for
the "transitional period," they represented in fact
the permanent rejection of revolutionary democracy and equality in Soviet political and economic
life. By the end of the Civil War period the actual
forms of Soviet social and political organization
were not radically different from those which were
coming to prevail in the advanced industrial countries. In domestic as in foreign affairs practical
considerations very quickly impelled the Russian
revolutionaries to give up much of what distinguished them from the old order they were attacking.

Subsequent changes in Soviet foreign and internal policies were almost entirely dictated by
strategic considerations. In internal affairs Stalin's
basic strategic shift was from the more or less
conventional institutions which Lenin had bequeathed, to a system of total mobilization of the
population. This is the significance of Stalin's
industrialization drive and the enduring priority

for heavy industrial development to which Communism remains committed. It is also the rationale for the totalitarian organization perfected under Stalin—particularly the collectivization of the peasants and the imposition of all-embracing thought control. Stalin was not averse to any expedient calculated to enhance the power of the state, whether it was the acceptance of traditional rank distinctions in industry and the army, or the revival of the nationalist propaganda that had been repudiated with the tsars.

In foreign policy the Soviet leaders soon adjusted to the fact that they held power in one large state surrounded by suspicious or hostile powers. During the interwar period they were constrained to play the old diplomatic game, though with new instruments: the revolutionary forces which the Bolshevik example had set in motion were subjected to Russian control and increasingly used as strategic tools in the short-run pursuit of Russian foreign policy objectives. After the failure of the Communist revolutionary gambit in Germany in 1923, the Soviet government adjusted to long-term relations with the "bourgeois" world, and secured recognition by all the major powers (beginning with Great Britain in 1924 and concluding with the United States in 1933).

The threats of German and Japanese aggression which were clear to Stalin by 1934 prompted him to carry out a new revolution in Soviet foreign policy. The USSR embraced the ideal of "collective security," joined the League of Nations after abusing it for a decade and a half, and concluded (in 1935–36) a military alliance with the arch-bourgeois power, France. The Seventh Comintern Congress in 1935 resolved that "the primary duty of the working class and the toilers of the world" was "to help with all their might and by all means to strengthen the USSR and to fight against the enemies of the USSR." World revolution was for all practical purposes called off with the enunciation of the Popular Front line directing foreign Communists to coöperate with anti-fascist moderates. In 1936 the American newspaperman, Roy Howard, asked Stalin, "Has the Soviet Union to any degree abandoned its plans and intentions for bringing about a world revolution?" Stalin calmly replied, "We never had such plans and intentions."

During the Spanish Civil War of 1936–39 the Spanish Communists were expressly ordered to suspend their revolutionary objectives and support the Republican government loyally, in the dual hope that the fascists could be defeated and that democratic sentiment could be aligned with the Soviet position in international affairs. The Spanish Communists actually supported the Republic in putting down revolutionary ventures by the Anarchists and Trotskyists on the left. For Stalin this was a matter of preference as well as tactics, for it corresponded closely with his repudiation of all real revolutionary content in Soviet internal policies. Ever since, the Communist movement has relied on fraudulent appeals to any audience it can find—peasants or intellectuals, democrats or nationalists. Communism cannot speak internationally with its true voice, for that is no longer the voice of bona fide proletarian revolution, but the voice of totalitarian conspiracy and power politics.

In 1939, Stalin's response to the shifting international scene was an orgy of *Realpolitik:* betrayal of his hesitant allies; a deal with the devil—Hitler —to turn him away from the doorstep; and the unabashed use of force and subversion to extend

Soviet defenses in the Baltic region. This entailed the most spectacular sacrifice of international Communism on the altar of Soviet national security. The German-Soviet pact threw the Communist world into utter consternation and probably caused more defections from the Communist movement than any other single event. All such compromises were explained away as steps necessary in the long-run interest of the international proletariat, whose fortunes allegedly depended on the strength and security of the revolutionary citadel, the "workers' fatherland," Soviet Russia. The adjustment of Soviet behavior to the dictates of strategy was now complete: revolution and ideology were reduced to instruments of power, to be utilized, revised, discarded, or revived as the strategic occasion required.

Even though strategic utility had now become Stalin's primary criterion in policy-making, his actual decisions were far from infallible. Thanks to his deal with Hitler in 1939, he had to face the German attack in 1941 without an ally intact anywhere on the continent of Europe. Incapable either of delegating authority or of recognizing his own mistakes, Stalin caused the Red Army what appears to have been considerable unnecessary difficulty and losses in the Second World War. Two astute moves that he did make during the war were in line with the traditionalist bent he had already shown—his closer embrace of Russian nationalism and his accommodation with the Russian Orthodox Church.

The emergence of severe tension and conflict between the Communists and the anti-Communist powers after World War II does not necessarily contradict the thesis that Communism tends to become less truly ideological and more purely strategic, if we bear in mind the readiness of Communism to violate the conventional rules and use unconventional methods. The main thing to understand is that the basic presumptions of strategy are in effect: opposing units—the Communist and anti-Communist "camps" exist—and conflict between them (violent or nonviolent) is inescapable. The great change in Communist behavior after World War II—a wave of aggressive expansion—is easily explained in strategic terms as a response to the new postwar situation. The war had two drastic consequences for the world distribution of power. First, and most important, it removed from the ranks of the great powers with potentially independent foreign policies all states save two—the super-powers, the United States and the USSR. This enormously simplified the world strategic situation. Very little scope was left for diplomatic maneuver and alliance-making; there were only two units which counted in this new "bi-polar" situation; each knew (or ought to have known) that the other was its enemy and that no strategic devices or restraints would affect the fundamental rivalry between the two camps. As a result, strategic reasons for being scrupulous disappeared, and it was up to each side to press for its own advantage wherever and in whatever way was thought strategically expedient.

To make this analysis fully realistic, we must add the human factor. In 1945 the shape of world affairs for decades to come was dictated by Stalin's paranoiac suspicion. Though the opportunity lay before him, after the collapse of Germany and Japan, of participating with the United States and Britain in an enterprise of great-power collaboration without precedent since the Congress of Vienna, Stalin could see only the hostile spectacle of conspiring capitalists. He seized the opportunity of the power vacuum in Eastern Europe to launch an aggressively defensive policy interlarded with nationalist obstinacy, which brought him only the Cold War and the alerted enmity of almost every power in the world whom he could not control. Communism, having by this time lost its genuine revolutionary spirit, did not have to face the rest of the world with intransigent hostility. There was no longer any real issue of "proletarian revolution" to fight over. Nevertheless, Stalin committed the Communist power structure to unending conflict on doctrinal lines. He made irrational dogmatic belief and belligerence permanent characteristics of the Communist movement in its relations with the rest of the world.

The stark and bitter opposition of the USA and the USSR appeared simultaneously with a secondary effect of World War II—the legacy of chaotic power vacuums in the areas of Europe and Asia where the recently defeated Axis powers had held sway. Strategy prescribed to both the American and Soviet camps a maximum effort to gain control or win influence in these zones; any position of power not secured by one of the rivals would in all likelihood go to the other by default. The only alternative to such a scramble would have been agreement between the super-powers to coöperate to their mutual interest in an international security system. Actually the United States did see its interest in this direction, and was for a time led to believe that the Soviet Union did also. However, Stalin discounted the durability of any such coöperation, and judged it to his interest to double-cross the rival camp with an offensive strategy in the power vacuum zone which might win him much more than coöperation would. Here, in brief, is the strategic explanation of the phase of Communist expansion and small-scale aggression which lasted from 1945 until the last area in the disputed zone—Indochina—was partitioned in 1954. With this last event, the most immediate opportunities for Communist political advance were exhausted.

Another factor, in addition to world bi-polarity, has contributed to the enhancement of the scope of strategy in Communism since World War II. This is the eastward shift of the center of gravity of the movement and its success in Asiatic regions where the doctrinal and class foundations of the movement were all the less relevant. The Chinese Communists came to power by waging twenty years of guerrilla warfare, without any working class base and without any tangible commitment to proletarian class interests. Communism in China as well as in the other Communist guerrilla areas of World War II became primarily a military organization, guided by military thinking, and fighting for military and political victory per se. The thinking of the Chinese Communists in particular, far more than that of the original Communist revolutionaries in Russia, revolved around the purely strategic considerations of victory. In respect to ultimate values there was not much else that they were fighting for. This precedence of strategy in Chinese Communism since its rise to power is reflected in its exaggerated manipulation and mobilization of the population, particulary through the "rectification" campaigns and the commune system, into one mammoth engine of national power.

Around 1954 Communist strategy entered a new phase, distinguished by a certain divergence between the two powers which have shared dominant influence in the Communist sphere since that time. Soviet policy took a sharp turn after the death of Stalin. The successor leadership, taking cognizance of differences within the non-Communist world and the new risks of thermonuclear warfare, shifted its strategic emphasis from the military to the political arena. It then became possible for the Soviet Union to explore the advantages of specific negotiations with the American bloc and limited coöperation with countries in the uncommitted group. Soviet diplomacy had thus returned substantially to the more or less conventional strategy of power politics which the Communists had used in the 1930's. Chinese policy remains more nearly Stalinist, where strategy is constricted by the commitment to unalterable hostility toward the American bloc. Nevertheless, to the extent that Soviet strategy still guides the Communist bloc as a whole, it is recognized that the Communist and anti-Communist camps have a common interest in setting certain broad limits within which their competition may proceed. In other words, the two sides tacitly agree to coöperate by forswearing strategies that may lead to their mutual destruction. Here is the meaning of "peaceful coexistence."

"Peaceful coexistence," understood with the proper qualifications (it is not peace without tensions or without armaments), is the paradoxical outcome of the paramountcy of strategic considerations in actual Communist practice. Communism's repeated defiance of the international etiquette preferred by the satisfied and hence peace-loving democracies has made the world conflict seem increasingly bitter and more dangerous. Nevertheless, the steady diminution of nonstrategic, ideological considerations in the Communist mind has had the ultimate effect of restraint. With its permanent stress on the organization and tactics which political war requires, the Communist movement gradually evolved to such a point that the original goals of the struggle became meaningless.

The Communist movement has exhibited a clear trend toward power and self-preservation as the ultimate ends in human society. The Communist strategists want above all to minimize the risks of losing; they want to stay in the game. "Winning" is a less definite objective, since short of a complete Communist triumph, the contest will go on indefinitely. In terms of game theory this is a "recursive" or endless game, each episode of which only sets the terms for the next one. At any particular moment the overriding consideration is to protect oneself against total defeat, not to drive for total victory at all costs. The strategist must guard himself in the present and let the future take care of itself. This is particularly easy if the strategist has some reason to believe that time is on his side, and that with each successive phase of the game his chances for gains are likely to improve. Here ideology may affect the calculations of the strategist: Marxism comforts the Communists about the virtue of biding their time, whereas the Nazi race mythology inflamed Hitler's regime to stake everything in a war to the death which was actually sought and provoked. Communism has become both unscrupulous and cautious, much as the governments of Europe after the religious wars. As far as we can judge from strategic considerations alone, the indications for the future parallel this shift from the fanaticism of the early seventeenth century to the eighteenth century's pragmatic stability based on restrained tension and limited conflict.

4 STRATEGIC PREMISES AND TACTICAL DEVICES

The most distinctive conclusion from the strategic analysis of Communism is the broad sphere accorded to strategy, first by the Communist definition of profound conflict justifying any means of struggle, and second by the gradual discarding of nonstrategic considerations and values in the Communist movement. The actual details of Communist strategy have not been unusual, since strategy is for the most part a matter of common sense, available to any power which is capable of thinking rationally. However, there are a number of strategic premises upon which circumstances have induced the Communists to place particular emphasis, and a full appreciation of the behavior of the movement requires that these strategies be understood in detail.

Communist leaders have customarily emphasized political and psychological factors in the relations between states and parties. This may in part be due to a Marxian predisposition to seek out the social factors underlying any clash of opposing forces, but such a habit of thinking should not be overestimated. The subordination of Marxism to the requirements of propaganda and self-justification has rendered sophisticated Marxian social analysis by Communists extremely rare. The political emphasis in Communist strategy probably stems largely from the early need to make the best of a difficult situation and seek out factors of strength to compensate for the military

and economic weakness of the young Soviet Republic. Accordingly, calculations of foreign revolutionary sentiment and civil morale were given
unusual prominence in Soviet strategic thinking,
and the habit has remained, even if the actual
calculations are distorted by ideological precon-
ceptions. Whatever their perceptual errors, the
Communists have maintained a very broad view
of the political and social context of strategy, and
have thus come closer than most other contemporary powers to the kind of outlook which
Clausewitz urged.

A major shift of Communist strategic premises
toward the conventional occurred just after the
revolution, with the decision to make peace and
preserve Communist power in Russia. Ever since,
it has been a basic and unchallengeable Communist axiom that the Russian "base" of the world
revolution must be defended, no matter what
sacrifices this entails for the Communist revolutionary movement abroad. This absolute requirement of defending Soviet Russia has led to more
and more devious rationalization to justify the
resort to conventional tactics of power politics.
Two implications follow: avoidance of serious risk
to the Soviet Union, even if revolutionary advantages abroad must be surrendered or post-
poned; and the need for intense propaganda and
thought control to keep foreign Communists loyal
to the Soviet Union despite divergences in their
actual interests.

The subordination of ultimate revolutionary
gains to the immediate interest of the Soviet
Union leads to another principle of Communist
strategy—the use of the international revolutionary movement as an instrument of Soviet
foreign policy. Unlike the priority of defending

Russia, this subordination of the revolutionary
objective is not explicitly acknowledged, but it has
nonetheless been fairly consistently observed in
practice. The ultra-left purism of Communists
who took the movement's ideological goals so
seriously that they could coöperate with no one
or make no compromises to extend the practical
influence of the International was constantly
fought by the Soviet leadership. Time and again
foreign Communists on every continent have been
ordered into action as pressure groups to support
Soviet foreign policy, regardless of the damage
this might do to their revolutionary morale or
their popular appeal. Communists have been compelled to support everything from Soviet oil sales
to Mussolini to the American anti-strike pledge
in World War II, not to mention Soviet economic
exploitation of the East European satellites during
Stalin's last years. Such use of foreign sympathizers is of course not unique to Communism—
it is typical of the marriage of ideology and national ambition which figured in the religious
wars and in the recent totalitarianism of the Right
as well as of the Left.

Reliance on foreign revolutionary sympathy
has conflicted with another strategic emphasis
which has figured repeatedly in Soviet policy since
the early 1920's—namely, the use of alliances with
non-Communist powers or movements who share
a common enemy with the Communists, be it
imperialism, fascism, or whatever. Soviet Russia
has entered into alliances with individual powers,
democratic or fascist (Germany in 1922, France
and Czechoslovakia in 1935, Germany again in
1939); with liberal and socialist parties (British
Labor in the 1920's, the "Popular Front" of 1935–
38, the post-World War II coalition governments

in Europe); and with revolutionary nationalist regimes (Turkey and the Chinese Nationalists in the 1920's, Egypt and Iraq in the 1950's). The only groups with whom the Communists have stead-fastly refused to coöperate are rival left-wing revolutionary groups such as anarchists and Communist deviators such as Trotskyists.

The history of Communist alliance-making has not been distinguished by success. In practically every instance alliances with non-Communist forces have broken up within a few years, when the partners have found that the Communist road diverges from their own, and in most cases the Communists have been left with no residual benefit at all. Only in Eastern Europe after World War II—in Hungary and Czechoslovakia particularly—did political alliances serve the Communists as the road to power, and even here their success was determined by other factors such as the proximity of Soviet force. In theory the Communists have made much of the value of finding, using, and discarding allies; in practice they have had to depend largely on their own strength and the weaknesses of their opponents. (Latin America offers a possible exception to this rule. In Guatemala up to the counter-coup of 1954, and in Cuba under Castro since 1959, the Communists won the confidence of the left-wing nationalist revolutionaries and moved into positions of key influence.)

In retrospect we can see that Communist success has depended heavily on the strategic utilization of a certain kind of situation—world war and postwar chaos. War as a prelude to revolution was recognized and stressed by Lenin even before he had hopes of taking power in Russia. World War I was the blow which brought the tsarist regime crashing down and initiated the revolutionary situation in Russia that gave birth to Communism as a real political force. Antiwar sentiment was a major factor both in Lenin's victory in Russia and in the Socialist splits elsewhere that preceded the creation of the Communist International. Postwar privation and political upheaval helped the new Communist movement to become a serious challenge to the status quo everywhere in Central Europe.

The connection between war and the Communist movement is underscored by the fact that after their first tumultuous entry upon the stage of history the Communists made no further gains of any importance as long as the world remained at peace. The Communists were forced to accept this as an "ebb" in the tide of world revolution. World War II afforded them the opportunity to score sweeping gains. If World War I created the Communist movement, World War II and its aftermath saw it expand to encompass almost half the world's population. Everywhere that political order was disrupted by enemy occupation and guerrilla warfare the Communists made great headway. Mao Tse-tung reflected often during his long years of guerrilla campaigning on the value of such a "protracted conflict" in building Communist political power. In the case of colonial nationalism it is a general rule that the harder the natives had to fight for independence, the stronger was the ultimate Communist influence among them; Communists are now powerful in Indonesia, and in North Vietnam they rule the country.

It is important to note that the war situations of which the Communists have taken such crucial advantage have not been of their own creation. Communism has appeared and spread not by sheer deliberate calculation but by taking advantage of the collapse of world order for which all the major powers were responsible. When the rest of the world has kept the peace—both between the wars and after the post-World War II convulsion of 1945–50—Communism has made no significant gains, nor has it even attempted any, outside of areas like Berlin and Indochina where the situation was still unsettled as a result of the war. The only clear instances of direct military effort to advance the Communist cause were Poland in 1920 (provoked by the Poles themselves) and South Korea in 1950 (which was represented as civil strife within the occupation-divided country).

A major shift in the strategy of building Communist power occurred in the mid-1930's, partly as the logical consequence of defending Russia in a stable but hostile world, and partly as an aspect of the general diminution of the purely ideological motivation in Communism. The classical Marxian image of power being seized by the revolutionary industrial workers in an armed urban uprising such as the Bolsheviks actually staged in Russia was largely abandoned, after the total failure of this line in Germany in the early 1920's and in China in the later twenties. After the inception of the "Popular Front" in 1935 the Communists tried to create a reformist rather than revolutionary image of themselves, and based their propaganda appeal on a wide variety of democratic, pacifist, antifascist, or nationalist themes. Ever since Lenin's instructions of 1920 they had been utilizing democratic opportunities in parliaments, trade unions, or wherever possible, and now they began to profess the whole democratic political perspective. Soviet internal political theory was meanwhile shifting in the same direction, as we have noted, with the constitution of 1936 and the return to conventional standards of law and rights. Such legal conservatism existed on paper only—the Great Purge was simultaneously in full swing—but the old revolutionary ideas could no longer be upheld. Stalin became suspicious of pure revolutionary loyalty; he preferred the submission of the disciplined and the bought, who would object neither to conservative expediencies nor to deceit and violence. The purges and the Hitler-Stalin pact sufficed to drive the last of the old idealists out of the international movement, and no one was left to resist the ever-tightening fetters of party discipline.

Communism's shift in the 1930's away from the direct revolutionary appeal was accompanied by the enhancement of certain of the older strategic characteristics of the movement, particularly in the direction of political deceit and undercover tactics. This was the consequence of eliminating the movement's ideological guideposts or transplanting them to the remote future: the scope of strategy was broadened, and new, more subtle approaches were indicated. Communist-front tactics and ostensibly non-Communist or nonrevolutionary appeals were stepped up. "Crypto-Communists" were used and sometimes actually planted to promote certain Communist interests secretly, though their effectiveness has undoubtedly been exaggerated by anti-Communist alarmists. When World War II and its aftermath afforded an opportunity to take power, the Communists preferred to move not with a workers' uprising but in one of two quite different modes—rural guerrilla warfare, or maneuver inside a coalition government. Guerrilla warfare, based largely on peasant and nationalist support and directed initially against foreign occupation forces, brought the Communists to power in Yugoslavia, Albania, China, and North Vietnam, and kept Greece, Burma, the Philippines, and Malaya in turmoil for years. On the other hand, the Communists came to most of Eastern Europe as camp followers with the Soviet Army, arrogated to themselves the police power in nominally coalition governments, and maneuvered by "salami tactics" to pare down the opposition parties and establish one-party Communist rule. The remnants of a number of other parties, reduced to Communist puppets, survive in the "People's Democracies" as a reminder of the devious road by which the Communists secured power.

5 WORLD DOMINATION?

It is clear from the history of the Communist movement that genuine ideological motives and specific revolutionary objectives have progressively lost ground. What is left as the goal of international Communist action? Is the conflict between the Communist and anti-Communist blocs merely a reflex between states committed to the game of strategic advantage, or is Communist policy guided by an absolute and enduring determination to conquer?

The thesis of the Communist drive for world domination rests on a fusion—or confusion—of strategic analysis and Marxist doctrine. As we have noted, strategy has to presume some purpose, some definition of the struggle, beyond its own limits. Many people assume that Marxism supplies such an ultimate purpose to the Communist strategists, but we cannot accept this explanation, for two major reasons. One lies in the original ambiguity of Marxism between scientific prediction and moral purpose. If the world proletarian revolution is the inevitable outcome of irresistible economic laws, there is no logical need for the revolutionaries in one country to strive and bleed for it—they might as well wait. If they do not feel like waiting—as the Bolsheviks did not feel like waiting inside Russia— this is not due to the doctrine but to some kind of emotional commitment to struggle which must be explained on grounds other than Marxist doctrine. Some writers have actually gone so far as to suggest that the Communists realize the Marxian prediction is not coming true, and that therefore they must plan violent conquest in order to divert the course of history and get it back on the predicted track to which they have an emotional commitment. This would be even more irrational, and require further psychological explanation.

The Communists have never admitted to themselves any fault in the Marxian prediction. They have shown an infinite capacity to rationalize any failure as temporary and any expedient as a virtue. In this quality we find the second great limitation in Marxism as a fulcrum of purpose: thanks to the history of the Communist acceptance of expedients as ultimate virtues, the meaning of the Marxist purpose has lost most of its fixity. There are no beliefs or values permanent throughout the history of Communism which are sufficient to explain the world-wide antagonism of the Communist and anti-Communist camps.

While the ideal of world proletarian revolution fails to explain Communist behavior either in Russia or around the world, non-Communists can hardly be blamed for holding such an assumption about the Communists. Communist propaganda has dwelt from the very beginning on the necessity for international struggle and the inevitability of world-wide Communist victory. "Our task," declared Trotsky in the manifesto which he wrote for the First Comintern Congress in 1919, "is . . . to mobilize the forces of all genuinely revolutionary parties of the world proletariat and thereby facilitate and hasten the victory of the communist revolution throughout the world." The real question, however, is how much and for how long this image reflected the real interests and the everyday operating intentions of the Communist leaders.

While Marx and Engels dreamed of the proletarian revolution as a sweeping world-wide event, Lenin introduced a major modification in the scheme. Even before the Russian Revolution he envisaged the proletarian movement as a series of national revolutions, starting in the most advanced countries (not Russia!). The Russian Communists' eventual formula for coming to terms with their so-called proletarian victory in a less advanced country was Stalin's doctrine of "socialism in one country," which eliminated any theoretical need to risk the Soviet state in pressing for quick world revolution. Soviet thinking since then, while it has been inflated with great hopes at certain moments, has never been committed to any particular timetable of revolution for any particular country. The Communists expect world revolution on the basis of their Marxist analysis of history, but they will ordinarily wait for economic forces to take effect without risking the security of the states which they control in the meantime. Here doctrine coincides neatly with practical caution. While the Communists obviously entertain long-range revolutionary expectations and hopes, their actions in the short run are guided by considerations of strategy and expediency—i.e., the political success and military security of the Communist bloc. In practice, the overall course of Communist policy is not set by long-term goals (whether or not

these are contained in the doctrine), but is the re-
sultant of a series of short-term responses to immediate situations. Khrushchev boasts about inevitable victory over capitalism, but as he spells
this out it appears to be merely competitive economic progress and largesse. International relations in the 1960's are pointed toward the spectacle
of the Indian potlatch ceremony of British Columbia—the tribe's big men compete for prestige by
squandering their possessions in an orgy of gift-
giving.

Some writers on the theme of strategy suggest
that Communism's practice of Machiavellian strategic thinking is proof of the movement's devotion
to the goal of world domination and of its determination to use any means whatsoever to reach
that goal sooner or later. This reasoning, as we
have seen, rests on a misunderstanding of the nature of strategy. Strategy does not determine goals,
but only the means of reaching them: it may pre-
scribe either scrupulous or unscrupulous methods,
depending on the circumstances and the foe. The
goals which strategy is to serve may be more or less
definite, more or less immediate, more or less confining. Depending on the nature of the goals, the
scope of strategy may range from zero (for the
pacifist utopian) to infinity (for the cynical prac-
tioner of *Realpolitik*). In the latter case, where
strategy is given no goals external to itself, the
goal simply becomes the maintenance of an opportunity to continue conducting successful strategy
—in other words, to stay in the game. World domination yields to the minimization of risks and the
maximization of security, except in the special
case where the Communists may calculate that a
strike for world domination is the least risky way
to forestall unbearable threats to their own exist-

ence. The man who is bent on annihilating his foe at any cost is not a strategist but a fanatic. Experience has made it reasonably clear that fanaticism of this sort is not what we find in dealing with Communism.

5 Communism
and Russia

With all its international trappings and designs, Communism remains a specifically Russian movement, a product of Russian society, Russian ideas, the Russian Revolution, and Russian power. The strategic perspective has made it clear how fully Communism as a political force is identified with the Russian state. To the Russian background, the Russian revolutionary movement, and the revolutionary crisis in Russia we must attribute not only the birth of Communism as we know it, but a wide range of the specific features of the movement and the emotional drive which has sustained it. Even though the consolidation of Communist rule in China has ended the Russian monopoly of real power in the movement, the movement everywhere is still based on Russian thought and institutions, and cannot escape the impress of its Russian origin. Russia too has been deeply affected by Communist rule, but for better or worse it enjoys an identity with Communism. Communism is native to Russia, while it is a foreign inspiration or intrusion to every other country in which it has come to power, not excepting the national minorities in the Soviet Union.

177

1 RUSSIA AND THE REVOLUTION

From the Marxist point of view the Russian
Revolution was an anomaly—a "proletarian" revolution in a country that was not supposed to have
the material preconditions for such a change.
From our point of view the Russian Revolution was
natural because it occurred, and a theory which
cannot fit it must be rejected. Marxism could be
sustained by the Russian Communists only as an
irrational dogma, to make reality seem to accord
with theory. Actually the Russian Revolution was
not a national instance of a presumed international trend toward proletarian revolution, but a
distinctive national event with consequences which
no theory could have predicted. If the Russian
Revolution corresponds to any type, it is a new type
of totalitarian modernizing revolution of which the
upheaval in Russia was the first instance.

It would be erroneous to assume that the Russian Revolution was made absolutely inevitable by
deep-seated Russian conditions. The defeats and
economic stresses of World War I (a historical accident, as far as the internal development of Russia is concerned) were the precipitating cause of
the revolution, and in their absence it is entirely
possible that Russia could have avoided a revolutionary breakdown and followed a course of gradual
evolution. The difference, for the rest of the world,
would have been immeasurable: the Communist
movement such as we know it would never have
come into existence, though the various revolutionary forces which have plagued the twentieth-
century world would still have had to be reckoned
with. But the fact is that revolution did break out
in Russia under the stress of war, and this in itself

is sufficient evidence of the accumulation of combustible material—revolutionary political and social tension—which was in readiness in Russia by 1917.

Politically the Russian revolutionary situation was unusual in that an articulate movement explicitly devoted to the cause of revolution had long been in existence beforehand. The participants in the revolutionary movement, mostly upper- and middle-class intellectuals or would-be intellectuals, were distinguished by their almost religious commitment to the goal of revolution. The rules of the "People's Will" organization demanded of each member: "Promise to dedicate all your spiritual strength to the revolution, give up for its sake all family ties and personal sympathies, all loves and friendships. If necessary, give up your life. . . ." Uncompromising political extremism and dogmatic attachment to an ideology were typical traits of the Russian revolutionaries which were carried over into the Communist movement with undiluted strength, together with a faith in science, a hostility to religion in the ordinary sense, an aversion to capitalistic profit-seeking, and the subordination of all standards of ethics and aesthetics to the success of the total revolution. In their "Revolutionary Catechism" of 1869 Bakunin and Nechaev wrote, "The only salutary form of revolution is one which destroys the entire state to the roots and exterminates all imperial traditions, the whole social order and all the existing classes in Russia."

A prominent theme among the Russian revolutionaries was the necessity of deliberate and dedicated leadership to prepare the masses for revolu-

tion, "strong personalities," in the words of the
radical critic Chernyshevsky, "who by their superior force impart a correct direction to that chaotic tumult of forces which animate the mass of
the people." Without such inspired leadership, the
revolutionaries assumed, the masses would never
develop the drive or find the right road. There was
indeed substance to this view, for the Russian
masses were notably disorganized and passive most
of the time, and distressingly unreceptive to direct
revolutionary incitements. It followed that to
bridge the gap between the enlightened intelligentsia and the dark masses and to sustain the
revolutionary cause against the government's police repression, a disciplined and conspiratorial organization of revolutionaries was indispensable.
Only through the organizational weapon could the
revolutionary movement act upon the masses and
push them into revolution.

These characteristics of the nineteenth-century Russian revolutionary movement stemmed
from certain distinctive conditions in Russian society—the social gulf between classes, the Westernization of the upper class, and the political
frustration and moral pangs felt by the socially
conscious intelligentsia. The traits of the revolutionary movement to which these circumstances
gave rise in turn became the basic premises of the
Bolshevik Party. The driving role of the party, the
place of professional revolutionaries in it, its discipline and revolutionary single-mindedness were all
well-established Russian revolutionary postulates.
Without the active intervention of the intelligentsia, inspired and guided by the proper revolutionary ethic, Lenin really saw no hope for the Marxist
millennium. It was not Marx speaking through
Lenin's pages, but his Russian forebears.

It has been axiomatic among modern students of politics that revolutionary upheaval is the outcome of profound social change and maladjustments. However, social and economic change did not begin to contribute to the revolutionary situation in Russia until several decades after the beginning of political agitation. Rapid industrialization began only in the 1880's, but this at last produced a sizable, ill-treated, and politically disaffected urban proletariat. The political consequences were quick: in the 1890's the intellectual revolutionaries were finally able to find a significant response among the masses. At the same time the recently emancipated but still impoverished peasantry began to look beyond the horizons of their villages and to see in the preachings of the revolutionaries a new sort of salvation from their woes.

Russian industrialization proceeded rapidly but unevenly. It created a complex set of social conflicts, with middle class and proletariat growing on Western lines, but a landed aristocracy trying to hold its own and clinging to the institutions of monarchy and established church. The revolutionaries faced multiple tasks and could make multiple promises—to gain the benefits of Western society (in the "bourgeois" revolution), and to overcome the abuses of Western society (in the "proletarian" revolution). Frustration whetted ambition; the aspirations of the revolutionaries and of the masses for a free and bounteous future moved far ahead of what the Russian economy could possibly offer, no matter how it might be organized.

A major factor in the rapid industrialization of Russia was foreign industrial experience and investment capital. Russian industry, like that of other areas before or since which have followed

the earlier progress of other countries, could profit
by example. Technology and economic organization did not have to be developed slowly, by trial
and error, but could be taken over ready-made
from the advanced West. Capital accumulation did
not have to proceed slowly, from internal sources
alone: foreign investment funds in large quantities
were ready to take advantage of the new field
which Russian industrialization offered. By 1914,
Russian industry was roughly one-half owned by
foreign investors, and the Russian government itself was heavily in debt to foreign creditors. These
financial ties to the West (particularly the French
and Belgians) were partly responsible for Russia's
fatal involvement in the European international
antagonisms that produced World War I and indirectly triggered the Russian Revolution.

In the broadest perspective, the Russian Revolution was a reaction to the West. It was inspired
by Western ideas, fueled by the social change that
Westernization produced, and animated by a burn-
ing antagonism against the Western capitalist social system which appeared to be taking shape in
Russia. The Russian Revolution was profoundly
anticapitalist. Everyone in Russia save a small
band of sectarian Liberals subscribed to some form
of anticapitalist doctrine. Russian anticapitalism
was an attitude of defiance toward that very force
which was raising the country out of medieval
squalor. Such is frequently the outcome when a society is subjected to the intense experience of acculturation—remorseless change of its way of life
under the impact of a technically and organiza-
tionally superior civilization. The Russians were
being Westernized, and most of them didn't like it,
for one reason or another. The revolutionaries
sought sanction in some of the West's own ideas

for a protest against the Western way. When they found such a doctrine, they announced themselves as the bearers of the new word, to point the way of salvation to the entire globe.

This Messianic defense mechanism in a cultural colony of the West was a fundamental force in the Russian Revolution and the Communist faith. But the Russian upheaval was only the first instance of a much more far-reaching process. The entire globe has been brought under the influence of the West; there is not a single society in the world now not subject to the effects of Western industrialism and the Western way of life. This introduces us to yet another new perspective in which to view the Communist movement—as a particular response of the "East" to all the pressures of Westernization. To this we shall turn in the next chapter.

2 THE SOVIET SYSTEM
AND THE RUSSIAN PAST

Communism has often been denounced as the intrusion of an alien ideology into Russia, but the fact that most Russians have been coerced in the course of Soviet rule does not disprove the basically Russian character of the Communist system. Casual observation shows a broad realm of similarity between the Soviet regime and the tsarist past. We still have the simple fact of autocracy itself, with all authority concentrated at the top of the political pyramid, and no genuine mechanism to enforce the responsibility of the autocrat to the nation. For both past and present regimes opposition has been a crime, and this has justified all the practices of political police, censorship, control of foreign influences, exile to Siberia, and even worse measures of repression. In respect to these tech-

niques and to the duplicity and deviousness of its
official pronouncements and policies, the Soviet regime differs from the tsarist only in the greater severity, tighter control, and broader deceit which it
has practiced.

The correspondence of tsarist past to Soviet
present is to be explained in two ways—by the
common cultural milieu, and by some direct carry-
over of tsarist political habits and assumptions to
the Soviet regime. Russia was susceptible to Communism because it already had an autocratic government, and being used to one kind, could readily
succumb to another based on the same assumptions of statism. Russia's history, as generation
after generation of Russian historians have themselves stressed, was distinguished by the over-
growth of the state and the subordination of everything else to the needs and desires of the state. It is
no surprise that Soviet Russia should have returned to this tsarist pattern, for our analysis of
the revolutionary process has shown the tendency
for a postrevolutionary regime to revert to the
most effective aspects of the prerevolutionary system.

There were compelling precedents in Russia
for such a dictatorial approach to the country's
problems as Communism came to represent. Russia has experienced a recurring pattern of intense
governmental effort to guide and drive the country
and extort from the peasantry the resources which
an iron-willed leader demands for his political
aims. Such has been the impact of Ivan the Terrible in the sixteenth century, Peter the Great in the
eighteenth, and Stalin in the last generation. All
classes of society were reduced to the status of
tools of the state; there was no true "ruling class"
at these moments of autocratic revolution. "Revo-

lution from above" was Stalin's own expression to describe the great postrevolutionary social changes of collectivization and forced industrialization which he had accomplished by governmental command and force. The Russian autocracy was continuously dictatorial in its determination to control everything that went on in the society, to allow no independent action, no private responsibilities, no freedom of thought or communication. It evidently came down to the Bolsheviks and especially to Stalin as an a priori assumption that a real government simply does not allow anything to go on that is not under its control. Applied to the Russian past, the Marxian dictum that the state is the product of the class struggle and a reflection of economic development breaks down altogether; the precise reverse was more nearly true. The state moved everything else in Russia, driving a passive and reluctant populace ahead.

When the Bolsheviks came to power they were not only confronted with the problems and precedents of tsarism. In large measure they had to take over the existing executive machinery of government, and though they gradually restaffed it, they were infected with the bureaucratic attitudes of the old personnel. "Our machinery of state is very largely a survival of the past," Lenin wrote from his sickbed in 1923. "It has only been slightly touched upon the surface, but in all other respects it is a most typical relic of the old state machine." Earlier Bolshevik promises of smashing the old bureaucracy were never carried out, but simply forgotten after the new regime had sufficiently fused with the old one. By the time the revolution had reached its mature phase, the new system more than met the measure of the old in terms of its bureaucratic makeup, and the traditional Russian

relations of *chinovnik* and subject came into effect once again.

The similarity of Stalin's behavior to that of his
early predecessors testifies to the power of the old
tradition. The glorification of the Communist autocrat, and the abject obeisance and servility
which he demanded, exceeded in their Byzantine
ferocity anything ever known in the history of
Western Europe. Stalin's demands for Marxist-
Leninist faith and doctrinal rectitude are not un-
related to the tsars' maintenance of a state church.
Stalin's attitude toward the outside world, and the
suspicion and deceit with which he carried on his
relations with it, have no analogue since the pre-
Petrine tsars, though his passion for hermetically
sealing his subjects off from contamination by foreign influences was matched (if not as successfully realized) by Nicholas I in the second quarter
of the nineteenth century. One must return, again,
to Ivan and Peter for instances of such murderous
vindictiveness as characterized Stalin's rule.

Indirectly the material and cultural conditions
of life did have their influence on the Russian government. The backwardness and poverty of the
population meant that the state would have to use
extraordinary measures of compulsion in order to
extort from the nation the resources which it
needed to compete successfully in the international
arena. Half of the enslaved Russian peasantry
were serfs of the state before the emancipation in
1861, and the other half, privately owned, originally fell into bondage because the state insisted
that its military retainers have assured means of
support. A tradition of inefficiency, irresponsibility,
and passivity, both among the masses and in the
governmental administration, prompted the state
to rely habitually on the maximum use of au-

thority, repression, and retribution in order to get results from its subjects.

The legacy of backwardness constrained the Soviet regime to act with the same disregard of mass freedom and well-being. The state was determined to get from the peasants the resources it needed, and the latter-day state serfdom represented by the collective farms was the result—"a system of military-feudal exploitation of the peasantry," as Stalin's Communist opponents termed it in 1929. For the Soviet regime, however, the problem was compounded. It was not only trying to live with backwardness; it was committed to an intensive effort to overcome it, an effort, moreover, which the regime was determined to make without any help in the form of investments from the hostile capitalist world. Soviet Russia had to train and discipline its citizens, and accumulate capital at the same time by heightened effort and national belt-tightening. Under these conditions, the Russian situation, together with the self-imposed task of changing that situation, exercised a powerful influence in shaping the new Communist regime after it was already in operation. Communism in its ultimate totalitarian form was in this very deep sense the product of the historical situation of Russia, backward, changing, and wracked with revolution.

What becomes of the movement after it has solved the problems that brought it into being? Communism has substantially succeeded in remedying the problem of industrial backwardness in Russia, though noticeable pockets of un-Western inefficiency and sloppiness are still to be observed. Is Communism now eliminating the conditions responsible for its own existence, and thus sowing the seeds of its own demise? Such an expectation

neglects the fact that Communism represents an
adaptation to the inherently totalitarian trends of
modern industrial society, as well as to the problems of creating such a society rapidly. Furthermore, even if the forces which brought a system
into existence are removed, there is no reason why
the system cannot perpetuate itself indefinitely.
The social effects of feudalism were still plaguing
Europe a thousand years after the original military
need for a decentralized warrior aristocracy had
passed away. The Communist dictatorship could
easily muster the strength to control a nation no
matter how anachronistic it became.

Russian conditions begot their own solution, but
something else as well. Russian backwardness plus
Westernization produced the revolution; the revolution, together with the continuing problem of
backwardness, generated Communism as we know
it; Communism has largely solved the original
problem of backwardness; but the movement now
has a crystallized character and an emotional
force of its own. Communism firmly endures in
Russia, with minor adjustments. Abroad, it has
imposed itself on a variety of political tendencies
and situations; it has developed into a dynamic
international political movement that never would
have existed as it does solely on the basis of local
causes. Communism is the Russian revolutionary
movement on a world-wide scale, and cannot escape this character as long as it retains its present
identity.

3 RUSSIA AND THE WORLD
   COMMUNIST MOVEMENT

The character of the international Communist
movement was formed during the fluid, impres-

sionable stage when it was in power only in Russia.
Russian ascendancy in the movement was assured
when the Communists failed to win early victories
beyond the Soviet borders. The non-Russian
branches of the movement were weak, and had to
struggle for their very existence, and in the meantime they were subject to Russian influence, Russian control, and finally to the Russian model, according to which they were permanently shaped.
By the time any of the foreign Communist movements were ready to take power, their Russian
character was firmly established, no matter how
ill-adapted to native circumstances this made
them.

The confinement of the ostensibly international
Communist movement within Russia, as far as political success was concerned, not only subjected
the foreign Communist parties to Russian forms,
but compelled the movement within Russia to
make fundamental adjustments to the nature of
Russian society, adjustments which it had never
contemplated. Shrieking defiance of the entire
world order, the Bolsheviks took power in Russia as
the self-appointed vanguard of an international
movement that was primarily Western in its inspiration. As a Western movement, Communism
was not supposed to depend on Russian society for
its main backing, but between 1917 and 1923 a critical shift occurred. The initial wave of international
Communist revolution was stopped and thrown
back, and the Russian revolutionaries were forced
to fend for themselves on their home ground. They
were compelled to make the most of the Russian
internal situation, to attack its problems, and to
maneuver as required to stay in power. This was
the meaning of Stalin's theory of "socialism in one
country," apart from its significance as a stage in

the doctrinal breakdown of Marxism in Russia. From this time on, Communism was an essentially Russian movement, adapted to Russian necessities. Soviet control over the Communist movement abroad thenceforth meant Russification, progressively more intense as the years went by. After fifteen years' political evolution the Comintern had become an organization of autocratic, bureaucratic, and dogmatic parties, cast in the Russian pattern and totally committed to the Russian cause.

Russification of international Communism was paralleled by a corresponding shift in the Russian Communists' own conception of the movement. Initially the Russians had viewed their own revolutionary effort merely as a part of a much broader international cause apart from which their own revolution made no sense. Very quickly after coming to power, however, the Russian Communists adapted themselves to the *raison d'état* of Russian foreign policy, as we have already observed in the chapter on strategy. Increasingly, the international revolutionary movement was used as a mere auxiliary in power politics.

Certain Bolshevik attitudes facilitated this subordination of the international movement to the Russian political pattern and to Russian national concerns. The Messianic assumptions which the Bolsheviks inherited from some of the nineteenth-century Russian revolutionaries led them to believe that the revolutionary ideas and practices which had yielded success in Russia must be valid for all places and all times. The Leninist organization and the violent revolution, having proved victorious in Russia, would be obligatory for all true revolutionaries elsewhere. In the conditions for a party's admission to the Comintern which he drafted in 1920, Lenin demanded systematic teaching of the dictatorship of the proletariat, and warned that a Communist party "will be able to fulfill its duty only if its organization is as centralized as possible, if iron discipline prevails, and if the party center, upheld by the confidence of the party membership, has strength and authority and is equipped with the most comprehensive powers." The Russians' faith demanded that they impose their Russian ways on all their sympathizers.

Never since the establishment of the Communist International has it been possible for a Communist to resist Russification and still remain a Communist. Where Communists have defied Russian leadership, as in Yugoslavia, they have in effect read themselves out of the Communist movement. Titoism in Yugoslavia and the "revisionist" currents of thought elsewhere are Communist offshoots, but they no more remain part of the movement we are analyzing than the Trotskyists and other Communist deviators of the past. Communist doctrine and the very definition of a loyal Communist are centered on belief in Russia. This helps explain why the nationalistic but highly dogmatic Chinese Communists depended so closely on Moscow's inspiration as long as they did.

4 COMMUNISM AND RUSSIAN NATIONALISM

The history of revolutionary France and Nazi Germany, like that of Soviet Russia, shows that any international ideological movement launched by a national revolution must suffer a deep inconsistency between its doctrinal professions and the impulse toward success as a nation. Communism began with an ultra-internationalist creed, though its origin, core, and base have remained fundamen-

tally Russian. By the time Communist power
spread out beyond the borders of Russia to become
international in fact, the international spirit of the
movement had yielded to the dominance of Russian national power and Russian nationalist sentiments. This has been qualified only since the 1950's
with the upsurge of Chinese Communist power.

The Marxist tradition of internationalism
stands in stark contrast to the actual development
of national power politics under Communism. Until
1914 Marxists always rejected standards of national interest and national defense as a bourgeois
deception. They were antimilitarist and anti-imperialist, and rejected the values of patriotism in
favor of those of the international class struggle.
They expected the proletarian revolution to take
place as a sweeping international event which
would obliterate national boundaries. The chief
national antipathy felt by Marx and Engels was
directed against the very country which was to become the citadel of the Marxist revolution, so-
called; Russian autocracy appeared to them as a
major threat to the fortunes of their revolution.

Most Marxists in Russia, particularly the more
extreme Bolsheviks, were happy to take the antinationalist position as an expression of their hostility to the tsarist government. During both the
Russo-Japanese War and World War I the Bolsheviks frankly hoped for the defeat of the Russian
government, so as to pave the way for revolution.
Lenin alleged in 1914 that "disuniting and nationalist doping of the workers and the extermination
of their vanguard" was one of the main purposes
of the war. He denounced both sides, but maintained that "the lesser evil would be the defeat of
the tsarist monarchy, the most reactionary and
barbarous of governments."

Marxist antinationalism did not eliminate all national pride among the Russian Marxists. The Bolsheviks in particular adhered to the old assumption of the Russian revolutionaries that Russia was much superior to Western Europe in its revolutionary virtue, that Russia could break more cleanly with the past and point the revolutionary path to the rest of the world. Despite Russia's Marxian unripeness Lenin was able to envisage an international revolutionary mission for the Russian workers. "It is the task of the proletariat of Russia," he wrote in 1915, "to carry the bourgeois-democratic revolution through to its end, in order to arouse socialist revolution in Europe." In 1917 the Bolsheviks were carried away with Messianic delusions about the revolutionary and antiwar appeal to the rest of the world which their seizure of power would represent. During the Brest-Litovsk controversy early in 1918 such fantasies still had the left-wing Communists in their grip.

The crisis of making peace in 1918 occasioned a decisive shift in the Communists' international outlook. Before the peace was actually concluded Lenin predicted "a new and genuine patriotic war," and called for a last-ditch defense of the "Socialist Fatherland." Once peace had been bought, the party leaders swung reluctantly into line with Lenin's insistence that Communist political power in Russia was not to be risked in the problematical interest of the international revolution. While by no means abandoning their hopes for the latter, the Russian Communists were thenceforth primarily concerned to hold out in Moscow and let the foreign comrades take care of themselves as best they could.

Until the advent of Stalin's personal dictatorship in 1929 Communist thought and talk contin-

ued in the vein of internationalism. The program
adopted at the Sixth Congress of the Comintern in
1928 hinged frankly on "the program of struggle
for the world proletarian dictatorship, the program of struggle for world communism," while the
USSR was described as "the base of the world
movement of all oppressed classes, the center of
international revolution, the greatest factor in
world history." In their attitude toward the tsarist
past the Soviet leaders upheld the extreme antinationalism of the arch-Marxist Pokrovsky, whose
views dominated Soviet historical writing from the
late 1920's until his death in 1932.

The first hints of adjusting antinationalist doctrine to the real problems of Russian national
power came from Stalin in 1929 and 1930. Having
commenced the intensive industrialization drive of
the First Five-Year Plan in 1929, he sought to give
it a nationalistic justification by recalling the history of Russian military defeats and attributing it
to the country's backwardness: "To slacken the
tempo would mean falling behind. And those who
fall behind get beaten. But we do not want to be
beaten. No, we refuse to be beaten!" In 1934 and
1935 the old Communist antipathy toward nationalism was finally repudiated altogether. Almost
overnight "Soviet patriotism" came to figure
among the highest virtues expected of the Soviet
citizen. "For our fatherland! This call fans the
flame of heroism," a Pravda editorial declared in
June 1934, in announcing the revival of the death
penalty for treason. "He who betrays his country
should be destroyed." This was the turning point:
allegiance to the national state henceforth took
precedence over allegiance to the idea of revolution.

The changing Soviet line on nationalism was

closely related to the German and Japanese threat
of the 1930's, and also reflected Stalin's determination to put national security ahead of international
revolution as an end in itself. At the same time
Russian nationalism became a strong new propaganda line for evoking the support of the Soviet
population. How much the new nationalist orientation was a deliberate maneuver, and how much
the genuine expression of political feelings which
had recently risen to the surface, it is difficult to
say. The change did coincide closely with the general postrevolutionary shift to conservative doctrines and policies, and also reflected the influence
of the Russian milieu, the ossification of the Communist faith, and Stalin's personal preference.

Symptomatic of the revival of nationalism in
the USSR was the sweeping revision of the official
interpretation of the history of tsarist Russia. The
antinationalist attitude current for years under
Pokrovsky was swept aside in 1936 as an "anti-
Marxist perversion." Ivan the Terrible and Peter
the Great became heroes in the new Soviet history.
The exploits of tsarist foreign policy and tsarist
generalship became points of pride instead of vitu-
peration. A series of official Soviet symbols were revised from revolutionary to nationalist forms,
either in the late 1930's or after World War II:
military ranks (from "commander" to "general"),
the national anthem (from the "Internationale"
to "Great Russia"), the name of the army (from
"Red" to "Soviet"), and the designation of top
government officials (from "Commissar" to "Minis-
ter").

During World War II the patriotic appeal
reached its highest pitch, as all the peoples of the
Soviet Union were exhorted to defend the "Soviet
Motherland" against the "bestial Hitler invaders."

According to Stalin the label "nationalist" was too good for the Nazi "imperialists." He proclaimed "a patriotic war, a just war for the liberation of our country," and allowed the class-struggle language of Marxism to lapse almost completely until 1946. Every positive facet of Russian national tradition was invoked to sustain the fervor of the population. In this atmosphere the Soviet government finally came to terms with the Orthodox Church when it permitted the revival of the Patriarchate of Moscow in 1943. Since that time the Russian Orthodox Church has enjoyed *de facto* toleration (which has not always been the good fortune of other sects in the USSR), and has regularly offered up prayers for the success of the Communist state.

In response to the new East-West international cleavage after World War II, Soviet nationalism was both modified and intensified. Marxist doctrinal discipline, which had notably slackened during the war, was abruptly tightened, but not at the expense of nationalism, as was generally thought at the time by outside observers. The assumptions of nationalism were fused with the language of Marxism, so that the national fortunes of Soviet Russia were completely identified with the international progress of the so-called proletarian movement. This amalgam was imposed on the Soviet population as obligatory belief, and offered to the world as the basis for Communism's new uncompromising hostility toward the Western bloc. "America's aspirations to world supremacy encounter an obstacle in the USSR," alleged Stalin's lieutenant Andrei Zhdanov at the founding of the Cominform in 1947, as he went on to claim for the Communists "the special historical task of leading the resistance to the American plan for the enthrallment of Europe."

Inside the USSR Zhdanov commenced a violent campaign in 1946 to enforce Communist orthodoxy and expunge foreign influence in the various fields of Soviet cultural life. "Our Soviet literature lives and should live by the interests of the people, the interests of the Motherland," he asserted in launching a purge of writers. He denounced the Western culture which allegedly influenced them as "putrid and baneful in its moral foundations." The task of literature, according to Zhdanov, was to "assist the party and the people in the education of the young in the spirit of supreme devotion to the Soviet social order, in the spirit of supreme service to the interests of the people."

Zhdanov's purge extended from literature to music and drama, and after his death in 1948, to history and the culture of the religious and national minorities. In 1949 a violent campaign was launched against "nationless cosmopolitans," with ill-concealed anti-Semitic overtones. Between 1949 and 1952 Yiddish-language culture in the USSR was almost completely suppressed, with numerous arrests and executions of Jewish cultural figures.

Beginning in the early 1930's, the age-old subservience of Russia in the face of the superior civilization of the West was the subject for a vigorous nativist reaction, as though in compensation for a national inferiority complex. It became a compulsion, particularly after the post-World War II exacerbation of relations between the USSR and the Western powers, to prove that every invention, every notable scientific discovery and artistic creation, every worth-while idea was anticipated or first put forth by a Russian. While the foreigners Marx and Engels were of course still venerated, in the late 1940's there was a pronounced effort in

this area of sacred origins to emphasize the role
played by Russian revolutionary thinkers (especially Chernyshevsky and Plekhanov) as precur-
sors and contributors to Communist doctrine.

The antibourgeois stance of earlier Soviet doctrinal pronouncements has been subtly refash-
ioned into a general and pervasive antiforeignism.
With the fusion of Marxist terminology and nationalist impulses, particularly as represented by
Zhdanov, "capitalist ideology" and Western
thought were for all practical purposes identified.
Any Soviet scientific or cultural work that betrayed Western influence or acknowledged a debt
to the West was likely to be mercilessly condemned,
and the prohibition against Western contamination was extended with equal rigor to every country that was brought under Communist control.
Blind antiforeignism was curtailed after Stalin's
death, but the sense of Soviet superiority and foreign degeneracy has been maintained. In typical
vein Khrushchev warned in 1957 against "attempts
to insinuate into our literature and art bourgeois
views that are alien to the spirit of the Soviet people." Puerile national pride coincides with the interests of party control to bar any broad and free
acceptance of non-Communist culture.

The ultimate paradox of Soviet nationalism is
that the government has become more nationalistic than the people, to whom the nationalism was
supposedly a concession by Marxist internation-
alists. Soviet nationalism is more manipulative than
genuine. The government tries to whip up nationalism for its own purposes, but on the whole the
Russians' patriotism remains on the purely defensive plane, and they show remarkably little hos-

tility to foreign individuals and influences. Communism uses nationalism as an expedient, but it is in the nature of the movement to become committed to its devices and to *be* whatever it has become expedient to *use*. In the West, the Communist movement cannot escape its identification with Soviet nationalism. In the Far East, it is equally identified with Chinese nationalism. If any major division is to occur in the movement, it will be the product of the rival nationalisms of the two dominant Communist powers.

5 RUSSIA AND THE NATIONAL MINORITIES

Nationalism in the USSR is uniquely complicated by the ethnic makeup which the country inherited from the tsarist past. The population of the USSR, as of the Russian Empire before the revolution, is only about half "Great Russian" (speakers of the standard Russian language); the rest consists of more than a hundred large and small national minorities. The minorities for the most part live in distinct areas, usually on the borders of the country, and nearly all have been brought under Russian rule by conquest or annexation since the sixteenth century. The tsarist regime had a traditional method for handling the minority problem which its conquests created: Russification. Anyone willing to join the Russian nation by accepting its language and Russian Orthodox Christianity was assimilated; people adhering to the minority culture were discriminated against and subjected intermittently to violent attempts at Russification and repression of the native civilization. Such practices were particularly severe in the nineteenth century, when national consciousness was

growing throughout the world, and the result in
Russian intellectual and revolutionary circles, as
well as among the minorities themselves, was an
intense revulsion against "Great-Russian chauvin-
ism."

Initial Bolshevik views on the nationality problem were ambivalent. The revolutionary tradition
demanded justice for the nationalities, and members of some nationalities—Jews, Poles, Georgians,
especially—contributed disproportionate weight to
the revolutionary movement. On the other hand,
Marxism regarded nationalism as bourgeois and
self-determination as an illusion that distracted
the attention of the workers from the class struggle. Lenin introduced yet another consideration—
promises of self-determination as a purely tactical
concession to win the support of the minorities.

After the revolution Lenin's principle of self-
determination came into head-on conflict with
the Communists' interest in a strong and intact
state. In only one case was self-determination
voluntarily and unconditionally granted—Finland,
whose independence was recognized by the Bolshevik government in December 1917. At the time
the Bolsheviks had high hopes that pro-Soviet
forces would prevail in Finland, but in the Finnish
civil war of 1917–18 the "Whites," with German
aid, defeated the "Reds," and the Finnish government became firmly anti-Communist. All the other
minorities that won temporary or prolonged independence did so only after they were severed
from Russia by enemy occupation during or after
World War I. Poland and the Baltic states declared their independence and were able to preserve it. The Ukraine, Belorussia, and the Trans-
caucasian republics of Georgia, Armenia, and
Azerbaijan were all created by anti-Communists,

but were forcibly delivered into the hands of native
Communist regimes by Russian Communist intervention between 1918 and 1921. In this manner
five new and nominally independent Soviet republics were established, legally linked to Russia
only by treaties, but all under the firm control of
the centralized Russian Communist Party (of
which the Communist organizations in the minority republics were only branches). Legality was
brought more closely into line with reality in 1922,
when the Union of Soviet Socialist Republics was
set up to embrace Russia and the five other union
republics.

The present organization of the USSR reflects
the early Communist adaptation to circumstances
and the effort to reconcile ideals and power. The
forms of national autonomy are scrupulously observed in a complex federal system, but real power
is completely centralized in the hands of the Communist Party of the Soviet Union. Members of national minorities who have merely emphasized
local traditions and consciousness, let alone taken
the theoretical right of self-determination seriously, have been prosecuted for "bourgeois nationalism." On the other hand, the minorities are
recognized as linguistic and cultural entities, with
officially equal rights, and the administrative units
of the union have been carefully drawn to conform to, and even accentuate, the territorial distribution of the various nationalities. Apart from
the major nationalities which form the basis of
the Union republics, lesser groups are recognized
on various administrative levels, ranging from the
autonomous republic down through the "autonomous region" to the "national area," the latter
scarcely more than a glorified Indian Reservation.

By 1939 the number of union republics had in-

creased to eleven, as five new republics were
carved out of the territory of the Russian Republic
in Central Asia: the Uzbek, Turkmen, Tadzhik,
Kazakh, and Kirgiz republics. Additional republics
were added by annexations on the western border
in 1940: the Karelo-Finnish Republic (combining
former Russian territories and the areas taken
from Finland); the three Baltic states of Estonia,
Latvia, and Lithuania; and the province of Bes-
sarabia, taken back from Rumania and set up as
the Moldavian Republic. All five of the new republics were lost to enemy occupation during
World War II but were reconstituted in 1944. In
1956 the Karelian Republic, because of its small
non-Russian population, was reabsorbed by the
Russian Republic as an "autonomous republic."
Fifteen union republics remain. Their theoretical
autonomy has been extended since 1945 to the
point of individual foreign ministries (with separate United Nations representation and votes for
the Ukraine and Belorussia). This is one of the
glaring divergences between Soviet pretensions
and actual practice; needless to say, the minority
republics have no independence in foreign policy
or in any other kind of policy. The controlled
Soviet press publishes in more than a hundred
different languages, but it says the same thing in
every one of them.

Between the mid-1930's and World War II a
major shift occurred in Soviet nationality policy
regarding the relative status of the Great Russians
and the minorities. Essentially the change was
from the circumspect protection of the minority
cultures on a par with the Russians, to a policy of
thinly veiled Russification and the stress on Great-
Russian patriotism as a primary factor of political
loyalty. This was but another aspect of the general

shift toward conservative values which Stalin accomplished in Soviet social and cultural policy. Abandoning the substance of Marxist thought and policy, the Soviet government shifted from class consciousness to national consciousness as the basic psychological source of political unity. This new presumption naturally clashed head-on with the actual Soviet nationality situation. For the Great Russians, patriotism was fine, and they responded well to the rehabilitation of Russian history and Russian nationalism. But just as national consciousness was recognized as a factor of loyalty and unity among the Great Russians, among the minorities it was abruptly judged to be a centrifugal force, undermining their loyalty to the central authority. This no doubt explains why the Communist leaders of the minority republics suffered so severely during the purge of 1936–38. It also accounts for the condemnation of "bourgeois nationalist" tendencies which has constantly been reiterated since that time.

The Soviet solution for the minorities has been to try to create a sense of "Soviet patriotism," a basic loyalty to the "Soviet nation." In substance the national attributes of the Soviet nation are those of the Great-Russian nation. Russian is the common language, taught to all the school children of the minorities as a "second native language." The Great Russians are openly recognized as the leading nationality of the USSR. Stalin toasted the "Russian people" at the end of World War II as "the most outstanding of all the nations that constitute the Soviet Union . . . , the guiding force of the Soviet Union." The historical record of the Russians is the norm against which the history of the minorities must be measured; no conflict of interest, no harm done by Russians

to non-Russians, can be admitted. The absorption
of the non-Russian nationalities into the Russian
Empire became, instead of an imperialist conquest,
a "lesser evil," sparing the peoples concerned from
the tender mercies of Turkish or British imperialism or whatever. Then it was further reinterpreted as a positive benefit, "progressive" in
its social effect. Russification efforts reached their
peak between 1949 and Stalin's death, when Soviet
Russia had returned to the tsarist standard: equal
treatment for anyone who Russifies himself (in
language and doctrine) enough to be considered
loyal; suspicion and discrimination against those
who adhere to native values. For all practical purposes the minorities have no nationality other
than Soviet; they are simply second-class Russians.

The Soviet pattern of theoretical national
autonomy and actual tight central control is
standard for all other Communist regimes which
have extensive minority problems. The major instance is China, where Mongolians, Tibetans, and
other groups number in the millions, though they
are heavily outnumbered by the "Han" Chinese.
China does not profess the federal setup but gives
the minorities administrative recognition within a
unitary state, in districts similar to those of the
Soviet autonomous republics and lesser areas.
Czechoslovakia had an exceedingly acute nationality problem before World War II; it was settled
by expelling the Germans and Hungarians, surren-
dering the Carpatho-Ukraine to the USSR, and
giving the Slovaks theoretical autonomy on a par
with the Czechs. Communist Party control eliminates any possibility of actual political dissension
between Prague and Bratislava.

The Communist policy of forcing minorities to

conform to the dominant nationality is not unusual for a multinational state. National minorities have been suspected and persecuted everywhere in Europe. The points that make Soviet
policy distinctive are first, the magnitude of the
problem, since half the population belongs to minorities; and second, the world-wide propaganda
claims which are made on the basis of the
theoretical Soviet achievements. For the outside
world Soviet Russia proclaims self-righteously and
simultaneously the conservative value of untrammeled national sovereignty, and the liberal values
of nondiscrimination and anticolonialism. In
practice, minorities and nominally independent
satellite nations have little choice but to accommodate themselves to the dictates of the power
centers in Moscow and Peking.

6   COMMUNISM AND SOVIET IMPERIALISM

Among students of Communism who realize
that Marxist revolutionary doctrine does not
really guide the movement, it is popular to fall
back on the explanation of the movement as a tool
of Russian nationalism, and to describe international Communist behavior as a manifestation
of Soviet imperialism. This is paradoxical at
first glance, for international Communism was
launched as an avowedly international anti-imperialist movement, appealing to all victims of
capitalist imperialism whether they fully subscribed to Communist principles or not. Anti-imperialist and anticolonial sentiment became and
remains a major source of pro-Communist feeling,
particularly in the Far East.

Until World War II the Soviet Union was rela-

tively weak and had no occasion to be tempted
into imperialist activity of its own (apart from re-
storing control over some of the national minority areas that were originally taken over by
tsarist imperialism). In terms of political power,
Communism was strictly a one-country affair until the power vacuums created by World War II
opened the way for its expansion. But in the
meantime Soviet values had shifted radically, from
genuine internationalism to a quasi-nationalist
attitude. By 1939 Soviet Russia had become potentially imperialist in two respects: the psychological readiness to use imperialist methods in
the interest of the Soviet state; and the development of Soviet control over the international
Communist movement (at least in the West),
which made it a ready instrument for imperialist
policies when resistance movements and Soviet
military advances in World War II presented the
foreign Communists with opportunities to move
into positions of political power.

   Soviet imperialism in Eastern Europe in both its
direct and indirect forms appears to have
stemmed from three principal motives, none of
them Marxist: security, nationalism, and economic
exploitation. National security—defense first
against a revived Germany and then against the
imagined threats of the Anglo-American bloc—
obsessed Stalin; he was evidently gripped by the
traumatic experience of 1941, convinced that the
next war would again begin with a massive land
invasion of the USSR, and determined that the
Soviet first line of defense should be kept as far
west as possible. A cardinal principle of Stalin's
policy was to rely only on those areas which, directly or indirectly, he controlled. Such an assumption is indicative of the essentially imperialistic

rather than revolutionary character of the Soviet Union's new international outlook in the period of its postrevolutionary reaction. "Friendly governments" in Eastern Europe was the Soviet demand in 1945. Naturally, the Soviet system being as objectionable as it was and Soviet suspicions being as acute as they were, no country could be considered reliably friendly (particularly after the East-West cleavage was clear) unless it had a Communist-controlled government. Not even the pro-Russian but democratic government of Beneš in Czechoslovakia could be tolerated.

Communist governments, in turn, were only a framework for instituting even more direct Muscovite control. Russians were infiltrated into the police systems and military commands of the satellite countries in a technique dramatically exposed both in Yugoslavia in 1948 and in Poland in 1956. Local Communists suspected of resistance to Moscow were ruthlessly purged. Russian social policies and cultural norms were imposed on the satellites. Everyone had to start learning the Russian language. The satellite economies were inextricably geared into the Soviet economic system through unequal trade agreements and interdependent economic plans. Stalin was bent on constructing a permanent Sovietized glacis against the Western foe.

Russia's postwar security mania reflected the upsurge of nationalist feeling. It was nationalist hatred of Germany, and retrospective chagrin over the defeats of 1941, it seems, that dictated the Soviet stand in 1945. Subsequently tension revolved around national power rivalry between the Soviet Union and the United States. Each of the two powers, fundamentally distrusting the other, was determined to get or maintain the position of advantage. The Soviets were prepared to cast political scruple to the winds whenever practical advantage could be reaped by so doing. Practical advantage was neglected only in the cases where nationalistic sentiment transcended the dictates of sober *Realpolitik*.

A striking instance of this occurred when linguistic irredentism made the USSR insist on annexing eastern Poland instead of planning on the eventual Communist rule of the whole country. Most Poles were alienated, despite the compensation of the Oder-Neisse territories taken from Germany—which in turn weakened the Communist cause in Germany. Stalin's priorities were clear: the immediate advantage on the frontier took precedence over the temporally and spatially more distant prospect of Communist control over foreign states. Though Communist rule was successfully established in both aggrieved areas, these territorial changes may yet prove as detrimental to Soviet diplomacy as was the emotion-dictated annexation of Alsace-Lorraine by Germany in 1871. Again, in the Far East, difficulties with both China and Japan were created by Russia's insistence on recovering every scrap of territory and every leasehold that tsarist Russia had lost in 1905 or before. National power and national glory became guiding principles of Soviet international behavior, just as they had become a major inspiration of Soviet internal propaganda and policy.

Soviet Russia's return to old-fashioned imperialist motives and policies did not exclude the economic factor. It is frequently argued by Soviet apologists that Russia's socialized economy rules out the economic motive for imperialism (which is the only one that Marxist theory recognizes as significant). This argument depends on a very limited view of the economics of imperialism, confining the question to the late-nineteenth-century type, in which the quest for markets and investment outlets was an important factor. Admittedly the Soviet economy has no problem of finding investment outlets. It has always suffered from a shortage of investment funds at home, and there is no opportunity for the private profit motive to direct funds abroad. Nevertheless, socialism is no barrier to a country's indulging in the less complicated aspects of economic imperialism—the securing of sources of supplies and the sheer exploitation of subject areas. The latter, indeed, is all the more possible for the Soviet economy precisely because it is socialized—there is no danger that cheap foreign supplies will depress the level of employment at home.

Soviet economic relations with the East European satellite states have been manifestly imperialist in the exploitive sense. Through a variety of devices—joint companies, unequal trade agreements, the purchase of goods by the USSR at artificially low prices, and Soviet acquisition of "German assets" in Eastern Europe (substituting Soviet for German economic imperialism), not to mention reparations—Soviet Russia systematically milked the economies of Eastern Europe until the mid-1950's. The condition of economic servitude which the Russians imposed on Eastern Europe was underscored in the fall of 1956, when the Polish Communists successfully defied Moscow, forced the renegotiation of Polish-Soviet economic relations on a more equitable basis, and in so doing revealed the magnitude of the exploitation which Poland had suffered theretofore. The crises in Poland and Hungary in 1956 alerted the Soviet leaders to the risks of mass hostility in Eastern Europe, and they stopped their economic drain on the region. On the other hand, all the East European states have been still more thoroughly integrated both economically and militarily with the USSR.

In the later 1950's certain significant changes became apparent in the Communist bloc, and outright Soviet domination lessened. The crisis of 1956 had shown the limits to the effective assertion of imperial power, while the growing strength of Communist China put an end to Russia's monopoly of power within the Communist movement. These developments have given the lesser Communist regimes some freedom to bargain and maneuver and to decide their own internal policies. Russia, having succeeded in creating a large multinational alliance of Communist governments, no longer has either the need or the opportunity to indulge in the sheer imperialist domination which typified Stalin's later years. The problem for Russian nationalism now is primarily that of maintaining the leadership of the USSR over the Communist bloc in the face of Chinese aspirations to take the aggressive revolutionary lead. Communism was strictly Russian in its origin, though international in its claims. Now at last it is becoming truly international, though in a direction never anticipated by the forebears of the movement.

6 Communism and the Revolt of the East

Communism has sprung from the unique contemporary situation of a globe at once united and divided as never before, as the non-European parts of the world react to the domination and influence of Western civilization, and seek to relearn and control their own destinies. In the context of East-West relations Communism represents a specific form of the rebellious Eastern reaction to Westernization. The Communist movement acquired this character during the early decades of its development in Russia, when it was transformed from a movement designed to solve the problems of the industrial West, into an attack on the problems of the underdeveloped and nationally humiliated East. Communism in Russia discovered how it could offer the East speedy modernization at the price of dictatorial violence. In the process, all the old humanistic ethics of Western socialism were dispensed with or rendered into harmless catchwords.

This new Eastern character of Communism was implanted by force of Russian control and example upon the entire Communist movement, East

211

and West. To the detriment of the cause in the industrialized West, the Communist movement there has ceased to be relevant to local needs or to local traditions. This is the basic reason for its failure in Western Europe and North America. Even in the Soviet satellite states in Eastern Europe, with living standards higher than in Russia, Communism has come as an alien intrusion and an exploiting occupier, creating more problems than it solved. Only in the underdeveloped areas outside of Europe and North America is the Communist solution relevant. Communism has already proven itself remarkably well adapted to the political and economic problems of China, a meaningful solution there even if not the only alternative. The ultimate paradox is that Marx's heirs have produced a movement fitted to succeed where he saw no hope, and able to succeed on its home ground in the West only as the fifth column of a new invading force from the steppes.

1 REVOLUTION IN WEST AND EAST

"West" and "East" do not—Kipling to the contrary—represent an eternal schism between two entirely disparate worlds, nor is the "East" all of one piece. Nevertheless, there is much validity in this conveniently twofold division of the world. The "West"—i.e., Europe roughly to the Vistula, together with overseas areas of predominantly European settlement—is marked off from the other areas of the globe both by old cultural distinctions and by relatively new economic ones. Western civilization derives its uniqueness from major historical processes operating since the sixteenth century—capitalism, the pluralistic and representative state, science, the ethics of individualism, the spirit of inquiry and exploration. All of these developments contributed to the simultaneous emergence of Europe's technical superiority and to the extension of European power and influence all over the globe. Europe's industrial revolution, three centuries later, followed from some of these same developments, and sharply accentuated the differences between the West and the East. The sequel was the intensification of European world domination through the imperialism of the past century, which brought with it the irresistible impact of Western ways upon the non-European civilizations. Violent reactions were not long in coming.

We have already noted the general conditions which make a revolutionary course of events likely. Misery and oppression alone do not produce revolution, nor does social change per se. Revolution becomes likely when large numbers of people, for whatever reason, acquire the feeling that things could be far better than they actually are or are likely to become under the existing regime. Two situations in particular are apt to create this sense. One of these has been characteristic of certain Western countries in recent decades, while the other is found in the contemporary East.

The typical revolutionary situation in the West is that of a system faltering or retrogressing in its political or economic performance after a period of progress. This is illustrated by the French Revolution. It matters not whether the people are better off than their neighbors (as the French were), if they feel that they are not getting their just deserts. The recent cases are Italian Fascism and German Nazism, where economic and nationalist frustrations produced a wave of disaffection and swept the revolutionaries into power. Had the

United States reached a point of revolutionary crisis in the Depression of 1929–33, the response would no doubt have been similar.

Revolution in the East in modern times differs fundamentally from the Western situation. It is not a purely internal development but the product of outside pressures—specifically, the impact of Western power and example. The hegemony of the West reached its apogee at the end of the nineteenth century, when Europe was the center of world politics, world economics, and world thought. Since 1900, a sweeping reaction to this dominance by the West has set in. The East has been shaken by a rapid succession of revolutionary outbursts, and all of these upheavals have been characterized by violent emotions of anti-Western nationalism. The East is in revolt to win independence from the West and equality with it.

The first wave of the Eastern revolt was centered in the nominally independent empires, notably Turkey and China. The Young Turks of 1908 and Sun Yat-sen's movement of 1911 were both impelled by the nationalistic urge to regenerate their countries and defend their national integrity against the Western powers by overthrowing the old monarchies and revamping their governments on modern Western lines. By the time the nationalists had achieved stable power—in Turkey under Ataturk in 1922 and in China under Chiang Kai-shek in 1927—their movements had become one-party dictatorships, devoted simultaneously to internal Westernization and resistance to external pressures, but cautious about economic development or radical social changes.

Nationalism in countries under colonial rule developed into a major force after World War I, though it nowhere achieved its goal of independ-

ence except in the Middle East (Egypt and Iraq).
The Russian Revolution and the Communist parties
which it inspired contributed to the general ferment, but as late as 1939 European power still appeared as strong as ever. The decisive blow to the
Western position in Asia was dealt by the earliest
Asian power to Westernize—Japan. Emulating the
reactionary aggressive nationalism of the Western fascists, Japan under the control of the militarists in the 1930's undertook a systematic campaign of imperialist expansion at the expense both
of the Western powers and of independent China.
This culminated in the spectacular Japanese successes early in World War II, when the whole of
East and Southeast Asia except the Chinese hin-
terland was incorporated into the Japanese "co-
prosperity sphere." Western authority never recovered from this blow, and the only question after
the war was which kind of nationalist regime
could stand in the place of direct or indirect Western domination. In India the long agitation for
self-rule culminated in the nonrevolutionary
transfer of power by the British to the new states
of India and Pakistan, and the remaining British
and French mandates in the Middle East secured
independence at the same time. The years from
1957 to 1960 have witnessed a like success of independence in Africa. Quickly and relatively easily,
the whole band of countries from the Philippines
to West Africa found themselves free of direct
Western control.

Some Eastern revolutionary movements have
taken the form of nativistic nationalism. Some
have embraced dictatorial rule as a means of
emulating the liberal West. A number of states,
including Indonesia and some of the new West
African republics, have espoused a sort of national

socialism according to which the government is
supposed to accomplish the same sort of social
transformation that it did in Russia. Latin
America, while not experiencing the upset to its
culture which has convulsed Asia and Africa, has
reacted to the challenge of social inequity and economic change with a number of violent anti-imperialist movements, ranging from the quasi-fas-
cism of Peron in Argentina to the native leftism
of Mexico and Peru, and the pro-Communist dictatorship of Castro's Cuba. All of these movements
have in common with Communism the protest
against European and North American domination, political, economic, or cultural. They are all
determined to use the power of a revolutionary government to raise the nation to the European and
North American level of life, and win international respect. Communism is merely one movement of a type, albeit a particularly powerful and
distinctive one.

2 WESTERN IMPACT
AND EASTERN REACTION

The Eastern revolt is anything but a Marxian
proletarian affair, and it defies analysis in Marxian
categories no matter how fervently Eastern revolutionaries may profess the Marxian faith. In its
roots the upheaval of Eastern nationalism is a
manifestation of culture in crisis, with its often
shattering psychological effects on the individuals
concerned.

Thanks to Western domination and the impact
of Western influence everywhere, Easterners (especially the educated and politically conscious
groups among them) are being alienated from
their own traditions by the power and example

of the West. The typical revolutionary today is the alienated Eastern intellectual, rebelling simultaneously against his traditional way of life and against the political and cultural domination of Europe. He wants to emulate the West and at the same time win absolute independence from it.

Acculturation is the technical anthropological term for such a situation where a given culture is subjected to change under the impact of a more powerful foreign way of life. It matters little whether the affected area is a colony or a nominally independent state. Acculturation can occur rapidly or slowly, affecting all of a society or only selected individuals (Asians educated in the West, for example).

Acculturation proceeds in a characteristic sequence, and has effects that are widely typical. The more concrete, practical, and technical aspects of the superior culture are likely to be borrowed first; later come the ideas and social institutions, as well as the social implications of the imported technology. After particular practices and technology have been imported for some time (and, perhaps, after substantial educational influence has been introduced), a mental and institutional crisis is likely. A strong or even violent ambivalence toward the intruding culture can appear. One response is to favor complete adoption of the foreign culture pattern, and the other is to reject it *in toto* and eradicate the influences which have already been felt. Both impulses can appear in the same groups and even in the same individual. People affected by either tendency are inclined to subscribe to some sort of Messianic faith, some doctrine which promises national salvation and triumph, either because the native tradition is held to be morally superior to the foreign culture (for the nativists), or (for the adapters) because the new converts to the foreign way of life are held to be superior and more energetic practitioners of it than the foreigners themselves.

These reactions were vividly illustrated in nineteenth-century Russia, when Russian society had undergone partial acculturation under the influence of Europe, but was still far from conforming to the Western culture pattern. Russian thinkers showed a sharp ambivalence toward Europe as the model to follow or an evil to abhor. Two schools of thought took form among the Russian intellectuals—the "Westerners," who would go over wholly to European standards and seek to follow the European course of development, and the "Slavophiles," who denounced the corrupting effect of European influence and glorified native Russian traditions and the prospect of an independent course of historical development for Russia. As their emotions intensified after the middle of the nineteenth century, the representatives of both groups tended to become Messianic. Slavophiles like Dostoevsky dwelt on the purgative effect which the Russian tradition and the Orthodox faith could have for Europe, while Westerners like Herzen and Bakunin were attracted by the idea of Russia as a revolutionary force that could push Europe farther toward its own destiny.

A similar cleavage occurred over and over again among narrower groups of Russian thinkers and political leaders. In the 1880's the revolutionaries divided into Populists (the later Socialist Revolutionaries) and Marxists, over the question of whether Russia's economic development and revolutionary prospects would take a native course or the European one. The Marxists split in the 1900's between Western-oriented Mensheviks and

Lenin's Bolsheviks, who were much more concerned with adjusting to the specific problems of
revolution in Russia. The Bolsheviks themselves
split after the revolution, between the Western-
oriented Left Opposition and the Russian-oriented
Stalinists, respectively espousing "permanent
revolution" and "socialism in one country." This
doctrinal sifting has given the Communists' initially Western ideology and orientation a redoubled concentration of nativist interpretation
and application. The originally Russian ambivalence toward the West was resolved more and more
in the nativist direction, despite the progress
which Westernization actually made in Russia.

Major responsibility for the disruption of the
cultures of the East lies with the impact of the
Western-dominated world economy. This has been
felt not so much in direct economic exploitation
as in the disruption of traditional economic institutions and ties, and in the force of Western example, even though it might be present only in small
"enclaves" (to use Gunnar Myrdal's expression).
The introduction of Western capital and technique
has invariably raised the economic level of the
native population, but with untoward social consequences. Plantation employment, extractive industries, and imported manufactures everywhere
upset the self-sufficient village society and ruined
native handicrafts. Commercialization and integration into the international economy made
whole populations more vulnerable both to native
exploitation and to the ups and downs of the world
market. Everywhere from Russia to Southeast
Asia and in Latin America as well, the effect of
Western capital or example has been to create a

new proletariat of uprooted peasants, who were
ordinarily left devoid of institutional protection by
their traditionalist governments or colonial rulers.
These people are acquainted with the typically
Western way of life but have little hope of achieving it themselves. Such "transitional" individuals,
as Daniel Lerner styles them in his study of the
modernization of the Middle East, are ready material for any revolutionary movement which is
able to organize and mobilize them.

Westernization's most momentous consequence
has been the acceleration of population growth
in all the underdeveloped countries. This is index
enough of the benefits brought by the West, in
the form of sanitation, drugs and medical care,
and the famine relief afforded by improved transportation. Death rates have been brought down
sharply, but high pre-industrial birth rates have
continued in most of Asia, Africa, and Latin
America. Populations have consequently risen so
fast that average per capita income and living
standards can barely be kept at a minimum level.

Such fundamental problems as population get,
at most, only subsidiary attention from the Eastern revolutionaries, who tend to blame all their
troubles on foreign domination. Where colonial
rule ceases to be an issue, Western capitalism remains the villain. Generally, capitalism is rejected
on principle, because of its association with imperialist domination. This inclines the Eastern
revolutionaries almost without exception to socialism, however they may understand the term.
The Communists consequently find sympathetic
ground for their own ideological fundamentals.

The relationships between dominant West and
subordinate East in the world economy have been

the object of much attention in Communist theory. The attempt to apply Marxism to the analysis of imperialism dates from the decade before World War I, Marx himself having largely ignored the problem. Drawing on his Marxist contemporaries and on the English economist Hobson, Lenin produced a polemic in 1916 entitled "Imperialism, the Highest Stage of Capitalism," which together with some of his miscellaneous comments on the revolution and some commentary by Stalin remains the basis for the Communist view of international relations. The bulk of the argument deals with the drive in modern capitalism to seek new sources of profit by expanding into overseas territories, and the likelihood of war thus created between competing capitalist states. During the 1920's Bukharin, among others, argued that the class struggle had become international, between exploiter "bourgeois" nations and exploited "proletarian" nations, and that Soviet Russia should assume the leadership of the latter. From a very early date the Soviet leaders were aware of the anti-imperialist allies they could find in the backward nations of the East, even though these countries were scarcely ripe for the anticipated proletarian revolution. "The Road to Paris leads through Peking," Lenin is reported to have said in a moment of prophetic insight. In the last year of his leadership he repeatedly stressed that he banked on the revolutionary reservoir of Asia to assure the ultimate world-wide victory of Communism. The anticolonial appeal to all those peoples who seek national independence and racial equality has remained a basic feature of the Communist movement ever since, much as it may have been contravened in practice by Rus-

sian domination of the Soviet minorities and by
Soviet intervention to impose and direct Communist regimes elsewhere.

The effect of acculturation on the individual
member of the backward society can vary a great
deal, but the impact is usually strongest on the
educated or semi-educated classes. Intellectuals,
whose training prompts them to seek logical answers, are the most prone to repudiate traditional
values, beliefs, and loyalties when foreign contacts
and ideas call them into question. As Westernization and public education progress, wider and
wider circles of the population are likely to be
alienated from the traditional social order. A
whole new class of people emerges—individuals
who have acquired some education and aspire to
Western-style intellectual work as a way of escap-
ing lower-class status. They make up what we may
term the "quasi-intelligentsia" or intellectual proletariat, a class peculiar to societies which are
developing under the impact of the West. Such
people are uprooted and ambitious, but they lack
sufficient opportunities for intellectual work, and
they do not usually acquire modern technical
competence. They are condemned to frustration,
and have nowhere to turn except to revolutionary
politics.

The emergence of the quasi-intelligentsia and
its political role is clear in almost every situation
where the Western impact has unsettled other
cultures, beginning in Russia in the second half
of the nineteenth century. Energetic, egomaniac
quasi-intellectuals have been prominent everywhere as organizers of nationalistic and socialistic
revolutionary movements, and they have had no

trouble attracting followers of like mind. Their politics are notably dogmatic, since one of their main needs is the sense of certainty and righteousness that some definite political creed provides. The emergence of the Bolshevik Party in Russia was an expression of the quasi-intelligentsia, and the Leninist type of disciplined party organization seems to have had a pronounced appeal for the quasi-intellectuals elsewhere. The party offers a special mission which sustains the member's sense of particular worth, and its discipline and intolerance offer its mediocre followers a shield against criticism from genuine independent intellectuals who remain outside the ranks of the organization. In its rise to power, the Communist movement permanently institutionalized the force of the quasi-intelligentsia, with the result of an endemic conflict, in every Communist state, between the quasi-intellectual types who run the government and party and have a vested interest in control for its own sake, and the genuine intellectuals and technicians who are required for any real accomplishments but who must suffer under the domination of their politically minded inferiors. Communist concern with ideology and mental rectitude is the direct result of the pretensions and insecurity of the quasi-intelligentsia, as is the tradition that all credit for theoretical originality must be given to the Communist political leaders.

3 COMMUNISM AND EASTERN NATIONALISM

Political emotions demand ideological expressions. This is particularly true of the powerful and complex feelings generated by the Western impact

on the East. Rebellious Easterners, especially the
frustrated quasi-intelligentsia, alienated from
their own tradition by its backwardness and ineffectiveness and from the West by its domination
and exclusiveness, seek a radical new political
commitment, some faith at once anti-Western and
antitraditional. This they find in certain doctrines
emanating from the West itself, above all in nationalism of one form or another.

The appeal of nationalism in the East as in the
West is psychological—an irrational response to
change, frustration, inferiority, and opportunity.
Nationalism admirably fits the needs created by
the Western cultural and political impact on
Eastern societies, in providing a focus for the
sense of grievance, blaming the foreigner for all
the society's growing pains, and creating a channel for the new energies struggling for national
equality. The particular forms and ideologies of
the nationalist effort are largely matters of
chance. Beneath the surface differences of the
various Eastern nationalist movements, ranging
from Communist to pro-American and right-wing,
there are certain basic tendencies which they all
share to one degree or another.

Almost without exception the Asian nationalist
movements have depended on the leadership of
individual strong-men with the self-imposed mission of saving their nations. Chinese Communism,
identified with Mao ever since the early 1930's, is
no exception to the rule set by Sun Yat-sen and
Chiang Kai-shek, Gandhi and Nehru, Sukarno,
Syngman Rhee, Ataturk, Nasser, and Kassim.
Usually their regimes are authoritarian, and more
or less intolerant of opposition, whether or not
they subscribe outwardly to the forms of democracy. Where the nationalist movements have

come to power through revolution or anticolonial war, the government and the leader are identified with the nation, and no meaningful democratic choice is allowed. With the exception of India, the Asian nationalist regimes have not been able to appreciate or to practice the Western standards of individualist democracy. Most of the nationalists are ready to accept dictatorship if they are persuaded of its necessity as the path to national regeneration.

In economics practically all the Eastern nationalists proceed from the assumption that capitalism is bad and socialism (whatever they mean by it) is good. Capitalism is with good reason identified with imperialism and Western domination, and the characteristic demand is to expropriate foreign-owned properties and pursue self-sufficiency with at least some measure of governmental planning. Given this bias, nationalists from Sun Yat-sen on have naturally been attracted by European anticapitalist doctrines and particularly by Marxism. This Marxism, however, is nationalist rather than proletarian. The proletarian class struggle has not figured significantly in the Eastern nationalist movements, not even with the Communists. Native capitalists have fared comparatively well even under Communist rule if they did not suffer the stigma of collaboration with the imperialists or the old regime. The present Indonesian Communist chief, D. N. Aidit, succeeded in jumbling his categories so much as to say, "The Indonesian bourgeois-democratic revolution . . . is something special. . . . It is a part of the world proletarian revolution which firmly opposes imperialism, that is, international capitalism."

Politically and intellectually Asian nationalism

has been quite receptive to Communism, without the objections to Communist method and Communist dogmatism that impede acceptance of the movement in most Western countries. In the East there is no native liberalism to serve as a barrier of principle. For its own part, Communism has come a long way to accept the emotions and objectives of nationalism. As we have seen, the original internationalism of the movement was transformed in Soviet theory and practice into a blatant Soviet nationalism and unabashed imperialism, coupled with the opportunistic courting of non-Communist nationalist movements. So far do Communist and nationalist emotions, tactics, and objectives parallel each other, that in Asia and Latin America it is sometimes difficult to determine whether a man is a pro-Communist nationalist or a pro-nationalist Communist. Communism has come to be simply one variety of Eastern socialistic nationalism, distinguished only by its formal doctrine, party discipline, and loyalty to the USSR. Communist plans for social change have been carefully soft-pedaled or suspended. The Syrian Communist leader Khalid Bakdash, for example, declared in 1944, "We have not demanded, do not demand now, and do not even contemplate socializing national capital and industry." To accommodate traditionalist fears and nationalist emotions, the Communists have sometimes leaned so far over backward that their potential followers cannot tell the difference between them and other nationalists, and fail to develop any exclusive allegiance to the international Communist movement.

The basis of Communism eastward from Russia as a movement of authoritarian national resurgence is underscored by the circumstances in

which most of the Asian Communist parties originated. Whereas the Western (and Japanese) Communist movements came into being through splits
in the existing socialist and labor organizations,
Communism in most of Asia and the colonial
world was born out of nationalist movements. In
the East the class-struggle appeal of Communism
was far outshone by its nationalistic appeal as a
movement against imperialism and Western political or economic domination. Outside of Japan,
none of these regions had much industry or a
strong working class. Typically the Communist
parties were made up, like the Russian revolutionary organizations of the nineteenth century,
of disaffected intellectuals and quasi-intellectual
hangers-on drawn from all strata of society. Genuine working-class leaders have been conspicuous
by their absence. In the Chinese Communist Central Committee elected in 1945, only two of the
forty-four members were known to have proletarian backgrounds.

By and large, the early Asian Communists were
eager agitators, consumed by anti-imperialist
emotion, but almost completely devoid of political
originality. Intellectually they were completely dependent on Moscow's leadership and the Western
ideology of literal Marxism, which they endeavored to apply without any relevance to the facts of
pre-industrial society in the East. This made it
easy for Moscow to maintain doctrinal discipline
among the Eastern Communists, but left the
movement largely cut off from political realities
and cost it all chance of success or major influence
down to World War II—with the outstanding exception of China.

World War II was decisive in the development
of Communism in Asia. Previously the movement

had comprised only a few underground organizations in the colonial areas, and the Chinese Communist peasant army which was barely able to keep itself intact against the harassment of the Nationalist government's forces. Japanese conquest completely upset the established order both in China and in the colonial areas of Southeast Asia, and the Communists found their opportunity. In China the blows suffered by Chiang's government and the opportunity to develop a vast peasant guerrilla movement behind the Japanese lines raised the Communist Party from obscure frontier warlord status to the position of a major contender for power. In Indochina, the Philippines, and Malaya, Communists moved into political prominence for the first time as leaders of the anti-Japanese resistance movement in the countryside. Korea had been ruled by Japan from 1908 to 1945, when Soviet and American occupation forces partitioned the country and saw to the creation of sympathetic regimes in their respective zones. As in Europe, the Communists were never able to come to power or even become serious contenders except in countries where the old government or colonial authority was disrupted or displaced by enemy occupation.

Victory in the Chinese civil war gave the Communists control over the entire Chinese mainland by 1949, and a long and bitter colonial war against the French won them control of the northern part of partitioned Vietnam in 1954. Elsewhere in Southeast Asia, thanks to the achievement of independence, some social reform, and energetic repression, the Communist movement was severely curbed. Indonesia is the exception, where apart from the abortive insurrection of 1948 the party has played a nonrevolutionary role to win influence in the nationalist government of Sukarno, and now enjoys more influence than in almost any other non-Communist country.

In the colonial areas, the success or strength of Communism is directly proportional to the struggle necessary for independence after World War II. India, Pakistan, Burma, and Ceylon, granted independence by the British, have not been seriously threatened by Communism. Likewise the Philippines overcame the Communist challenge bequeathed by the war years. Indochina, which had to fight the French for eight years, ended up partitioned and half Communist. Indonesia, the intermediate case, fought the Dutch for four years and achieved independence under a neutralist nationalist government supported by one of the largest nonruling Communist parties in the world. The Near East, entirely independent by 1945, has suffered radical nationalist turmoil, but no appreciable Communist strength has built up there.

In those parts of Asia not directly upset by World War II, Communism has yet to prove itself a major contender for political power. The Communist Party has built up considerable strength in India, but only after a long history of failure occasioned by slavishly following Marxist doctrine and Soviet foreign policy. Since the early 1950's the Communist Party of India has followed an overtly nonrevolutionary line. It has become the main organized opposition to the ruling Congress Party, and temporarily achieved governmental responsibility in the educated but impoverished Indian state of Kerala. In the Middle East and Africa the role of Communism as dynamic nationalism has so far been pre-empted by native nationalist movements which often oppose both Moscow and the West. In rare instances in Latin America Communists have won influence as col-

laborators in native revolutionary regimes—first
in Guatemala in the early 1950's, and then with
Castro's revolution in Cuba since 1959. Both in the
Middle East and Latin America, Communist influence has depended completely on alliances
with nationalist revolutionary forces, and it remains to be seen whether Communists can maneuver themselves into independent power in such
situations and not be sloughed off as they have in
the past.

The law of Communist success in the East is
simple: Communism wins only as the last alternative, when no other nationalist regime is able
to win independence or maintain the integrity of
the country. Otherwise regimes which are in-
credibly disorganized, shaky, corrupt and aimless
have been able to command the emotional support
of the majority of their subjects and keep power
indefinitely. The Communists have been reduced
more often than not to the policy of alliances—
international coöperation between the nationalist
government and the USSR, and party coöperation
within the country between the nationalists and
the Communists. Such arrangements, following
the pattern set in China in the 1920's, have recurred frequently—in Indonesia, Syria, Iraq, and
Cuba. (Turkey in the 1920's and Egypt in the
1950's were allied with Russia but suppressed
Communism internally.) To the outside world it
usually appears that the country making such an
alliance is going Communist, but (barring subsequent catastrophes like World War II) this
never actually happened prior to the unique na-
tionalist-Communist fusion which is occurring in
Cuba. Ordinarily the nationalists, commanding the
emotional allegiance of the populace, keep the

upper hand, and as soon as friction with the Communists makes the alliance undesirable, they are able to break the power of the Communist Party without difficulty.

The record of Communist successes and failures outside the West indicates serious limits to the appeal which the movement can muster. Communism antagonizes the traditionalists and people who are strongly religious. It is repugnant to the most successfully Westernized elements (and has lost out to Western-type left-wing socialism in the most Westernized Asian country, Japan). With its premium on international discipline and loyalty to the Soviet bloc it runs counter to the complete fulfillment of nationalist emotion. It arouses much opposition because of its discipline and its violent methods of liquidation and collectivization, in so far as people are aware of these features beforehand. Eastern Communism thus hangs in the balance—repugnant to many, but potentially attractive if it becomes the last resort of nationalism. The surest antidote to Communist victory is a successful native nationalist revolutionary movement, which satisfies the same motives that impel a nation toward Communism, and does it without the complications of ideology and international allegiance which often impede the Communist appeal. Communism has become strong in the East only where native nationalism has faltered and proved too weak to satisfy the demand for national achievement.

4 THE PEASANTRY
AND GUERRILLA WARFARE

In addition to the intellectuals (and quasi-intellectuals), the peasantry is one of the decisive classes in the Eastern revolution. Constituting the

overwhelming majority in most Eastern and backward countries, the peasantry defines the basic
problems for the revolution and offers an overwhelming force for anyone who can assume its
leadership. Communism is almost unique among
the Eastern nationalist revolutionary movements
in its readiness and ability to utilize the revolutionary potential of the peasantry. In most Eastern regions where Communism has triumphed or
grown strong it has been as the organized vehicle
of peasant revolt.

Communism's link to the peasantry in the East
is a major paradox, on both historical and contemporary counts. Both the past and the future
of the Communist revolution are anti-peasant:
Marxist theory discounts the peasantry and peasant life as reactionary, and Stalinist-Maoist practice concentrates on disciplining and exploiting
the peasants in the interest of enhanced state
power. Nevertheless, successful Communist revolution both in Russia and in Asia has relied heavily
on the peasantry and its mood of struggle against
a landlord-dominated social system.

Rebelliousness among the peasants of the East
is at least in part the effect of the Western impact
and economic change. While every peasant society
has a history of occasional jacqueries or uprisings,
these were rarely effective until commercialization
began simultaneously to weaken the landlord
classes and open wider horizons to the majority
of peasants. Thus political ferment began to affect
the Russian peasantry in the late nineteenth century, at the same time that population pressure
and the subdivision of the land were actually
lowering peasant living standards. Similarly in
Asia in the present century the bonds of tradition
have been loosened while the pressures of sub-

sistence have intensified. The result in these societies is a vast, if blind and leaderless, potential
for revolution.

One of Lenin's principal innovations in Marxist
theory was to incorporate the stress on the peasantry favored by non-Marxist Russian revolutionaries. Concluding that the volcanic force of
the peasantry would be decisive in any effort to
overthrow the tsarist government, Lenin argued
for an "alliance" in which the proletariat and its
Marxist leaders would take the peasants into their
camp. Both in 1905 and in 1917 Lenin's analysis
was borne out; waves of anarchy in the countryside were a major factor in weakening the monarchy in the first instance, and in undermining
the provisional government in the second.

Once in power in Russia, the Communists revealed a deep ambivalence toward the peasantry.
They proclaimed the transfer of the land to those
who tilled it, and sanctioned the expropriation of
the landlords. On the other hand, circumstances
of economic collapse soon forced them to put pressure on the peasants to assure the urban food
supply, and the result was the notorious history
of War Communism with its committees of the
poor, requisitions, and "extraordinary measures."
The NEP represented a broad strategic retreat to
satisfy the interests of the peasants, whose life
became in that period freer, more individualist,
and more bourgeois than at any time before or
after.

Some Communist leaders, particularly Bukharin, justified the NEP theoretically as the true
approach to Communism. This stand, reflecting
the bias of most nineteenth-century Russian revolutionaries toward the peasant revolution, we
might style "neo-populism." Contrary to Marx, it

held that the socialist revolution around the world depended as much on the peasants as on the industrial workers. The proletariat, Bukharin argued, has to have peasant support both at the moment of revolution and afterward: "The proletariat has *no* choice here; it is *compelled,* in building socialism, to get the peasantry behind it."

The totalitarian politics which Stalin perfected after 1929 permitted an entirely different relationship between Communism and the peasantry. Instead of focusing on the peasants' support and the satisfaction of their interests, the Stalinists imposed the controls on the peasants which would enable them to be used as the economic foundation of the totalitarian state and its industrialization drive. Collectivization is the basis of the Stalinist solution for the peasant problem, to keep the peasants under firm control while the maximum surplus—previously exacted in the form of landlords' rent and taxes—is squeezed out of them in the form of obligatory deliveries and fixed low prices.

Stalin's dragooning of the peasants into the new totalitarian system did not prevent Communists in Asia from successfully utilizing the peasant revolution. Chinese Communism represents the ultimate development of the movement—without any clear plan beforehand—away from Marxism and toward the form of a pseudo-peasant revolution. After the defeat of 1927, the Chinese Communists' reliance on the urban workers and Russian tactical guidance was completely discredited. An alternative appeared by chance when Mao Tse-tung demonstrated the feasibility of using the Communist-type organization to mobilize rural discontent and organize guerrilla armies of peasants to fight the Nationalist government.

Mao's peasant policy was the simple one of concession plus control: an anti-landlord campaign to take advantage of the peasants' thirst for land; substitution of Communist Party rule for that of the rural gentry; and a nationalist appeal to all classes when the anti-Japanese war, beginning in 1937, opened to the Communists the prospect of winning national leadership. The peasantry plus Leninist organization was the key to Mao's success. Mao's approach to the peasants had nothing to do with the theories of Marxism, but was rather a reincarnation of the power base of traditional oriental absolutism. Mao's peasant force was mobilized and disciplined by the party, intellectual or quasi-intellectual in its leadership; the peasants never guided the movement. Success was won through a distinctive new strategy that combined peasant rebelliousness and Communist discipline—guerrilla warfare.

Peasant-based guerrilla warfare has been the path for every Communist victory or near-victory apart from the one in Russia and the artificial revolutions carried out under the pressure of Soviet occupation forces. Special conditions have been required to pursue such guerrilla warfare successfully. Peasants have responded on a large scale to Communist leadership only when a foreign enemy has occupied all or part of their country, and when there is no effective resistance leadership other than the Communists. There have been a number of spectacular Communist defeats where the party did not have a guerrilla base among the peasants. When dictators seized power in Italy in 1922 and in Germany in 1933, Communist strength was easily smashed, and the Communist-infiltrated regime in Guatemala was overthrown in 1954 without any gesture of popular support for it. Even without dictatorial action, successive French governments have been able to deprive the urban-based Communists of their proportionate political influence, and the party has proved powerless to resist. Communists have kept their power intact in adversity only in the presence of foreign rulers or occupiers and only by going out to organize resistance among the tillers of the soil.

The Second World War was the critical event which transformed Communism's potential Eastern appeal into a truly dynamic movement, by affording the Communists in China and Southeast Asia the opportunity for guerrilla warfare where they were at their best advantage. Japanese victories demolished the awe which Western imperialism could previously command, and supplanted Western colonial regimes throughout Southeast Asia, while the Nationalist government of China was crowded into the southwestern mountains. Throughout the Japanese-occupied region Communists seized the opportunity to lead anti-Japanese resistance movements by applying Mao's tactics of organizing peasant guerrilla armies. When Japan collapsed in 1945, all northeast China was honeycombed with Communist guerrilla areas, and the Communists had their solid base for the victorious civil war (partly guerrilla and partly open) against the Nationalists. Elsewhere in Asia significant Communist success came only under the same conditions of leading peasant resistance movements against the Japanese and later against the restored colonial authority or a nationalist regime. Such was the Communist-led civil strife in Indochina, Burma, the Philippines, and Malaya, partly victorious in the first instance and for a long time a difficult problem in the other cases. Indonesia, with a strong non-Communist nationalist movement, never afforded the Communists the opportunity to lead a serious revolutionary movement of their own, and after the abortive insurrection of 1948, they had to play second fiddle to Sukarno's Nationalists. Eastern Europe only confirms the picture: strong Communist-led peasant guerrilla resistance movements against the German and Italian occupation forces in Yugoslavia, Albania, and Greece; victory in the first two instances, but defeat in the third, where Western power backed the restoration of the old regime.

Once victorious, the Communist leaders both in Asia and Eastern Europe saw no alternative but the establishment of the Stalinist system of exploiting the peasants. Under the Communists the peasants had scored gains but never won power; when the Communists had won national power and decided to step up their economic exactions from the peasantry, it was a simple administrative matter to decree the sweeping changes from land reform to coöperatives, and from coöperatives to the severely disciplined system of communes which the Chinese have introduced. Almost overnight, the class which had been the mainstay of the revolution became the chief victim of the revolutionary government. With the Russian experience in mind, of severe losses to animals and crops in the course of collectivization, the new Communist regimes usually moved with caution or moderated their efforts when they met resistance. Now, however, every East European regime except Poland and Yugoslavia has substantially collectivized its peasants. The Chinese began carefully some three years after they took power, with less compulsion and a less completely collective setup. By 1956, however, the collectivization drive had become much more vigorous, and in 1958 it was supplanted by the introduction of the communes, a much more rigorous and collectivist system of rural organization than had ever before been attempted on any large scale, even in Russia. The logic of political and economic success is such that a Communist dictatorship coming to power through peasant revolt in a backward country must sooner or later undertake to make the peasants serfs of the state.

5 THE COMMUNIST REVOLUTION AND ORIENTAL DESPOTISM

As our study of the origins of Communism in Russia has demonstrated, the basic political characteristics of the movement—the party, the dictatorship, the dogmatism, the omnipotence of the state—do not follow from Marxism and are alien to the Western sources of Communist belief. The politics of Communism have been derived from its Eastern setting—specifically from Russia. In turn, the movement is relevant and acceptable throughout that portion of the world where those underlying Eastern political traits prevail—the traditions, assumptions, and methods of "oriental despotism."

While we must not make the mistake of lumping all non-European civilizations together as an undifferentiated "East" and attributing all political evil to it, there are nonetheless certain fundamental historical differences between the politics of the West where Communism has failed and the politics of the regions where it has succeeded. Almost from the dawn of civilization a common pattern of political organization has prevailed over the entire area from Egypt to China—the pattern of the absolute state, with unlimited, despotic power in the hands of an individual ruler who governs through a centralized officialdom and exploits the population in the interest of his own power and glory. This characteristic pattern permits no rival centers of power apart from the state, and very little, if any, local autonomy. The individual has no secure personal or property rights against the state, rarely any independent economic power, and no way of calling the authorities to account except by force—conspiracy and rebellion. There is no "ruling class," strictly speaking. All strata of society must serve the state in their appointed roles, and no one is really free. Dynasties have risen and fallen, empires have expanded and broken apart, but the pattern of centralized despotism has continued unabated for millennia, until the very recent impact of European ways upon the East. The despotic pattern was characteristic for most of the empires of the ancient Near East, India and China until modern times, the Byzantine Empire and its Ottoman successor, and to a considerable degree Russia from the Mongol conquest at least until the eighteenth century. While authorities differ widely in their explanations of "oriental despotism," there is a consensus among many points of view regarding the prevalence of the pattern. Marx treated it as the political superstructure of the "Asiatic mode of production." His disciple K. A. Wittfogel describes it as the product of "hydraulic society," derived initially from the need to maintain irrigation and flood-control systems. Arnold Toynbee recognizes the pattern in the "universal states" which, he asserts, characterize stagnant and decaying civilizations. The Stalinist version of Marxism, on the other hand, fiercely repudiates the notion of a specifically Asian despotic social system, evidently out of sensitivity about the possible applicability of this concept to the rule of the Communists themselves.

The distinctive traits of oriental despotism are readily underscored by comparison with the history of Western Europe, which is almost unique among civilizations in its political decentralization and cultural pluralism. Western government has always been limited, from the very inception of the feudal monarchies, by traditions of law, by individual, local, and corporate privileges, and by the existence of powerful nongovernmental institutions such as the Church. Even the absolute monarchies of the seventeenth and eighteenth centuries, while they did not share their political powers with any representative bodies, were severely limited as to the demands and controls which they could impose on society. First in feudalism, and then with the rise of commercial capitalism, the West experienced a powerful development of individualism, and assimilated the unique assumption that the individual should and could assert himself and his rights against all the powers of the state and society. Such was the social background of the theory and practice of liberal government which spread throughout Europe and the New World, beginning in the mid-seventeenth century and culminating in the mid-nineteenth.

While presumptions of the dignity and rights of the individual became fundamental to the West, they remained almost completely foreign to the rest of the world, where the mere existence of government carried with it the expectation both by rulers and ruled that the government would behave in a despotic fashion. This Eastern trait was no doubt responsible for the colonial successes of the European powers in Asia—they had a much easier time winning the submission of large populations in Asia than in ruling their own brethren in Europe or the Americas.

Westernization, particularly since the nineteenth century, has brought profound crisis for the despotisms of the East. None of them have been able to adjust to the Western challenge and modernize without losing their political grip. They feared and resisted change, but offered no alternative. The Westernization of the educated classes undermined the discipline and self-assurance of these regimes and opened them wide to revolution, if they were not actually overthrown or conquered by military force. India readily succumbed to British rule. The Ottoman Empire, the "sick man of Europe," suffered repeated amputations by its neighbors and subjects as long as it refused the medicine of Westernization. China had virtually bartered away its sovereignty to rival imperialists when the Western-oriented reformers put an end to the monarchy in 1911. Russia, whose adjustment to the West was earlier and less sudden, preserved its political integrity, but the forces of reform and revolution generated by Westernization could not be held back by the old regime. Japan, where the political system was more feudal than despotic, was unique in its ability to assimilate Western influence without a political upheaval.

Westernization has spelled the doom of every despotic regime which tried to resist it. It has not, however, put an end to the political psychology which accompanies and facilitates despotism. When an old despotism collapses, the country is still ready to accept a new one. Revolution in an Eastern despotism undermined by Westernization is not likely to produce a stable liberal regime: both the usual tendencies of revolution and the political heritage of the East point to the opposite. The likeliest eventuality is a new, modernized, and more effective despotism, created by the revolutionary radicals or their successors, even though these people may in the formal sense be attached to some Western ideology derived from liberalism. Marxism was liberal in this East-West perspective, with its humanistic presumptions and its highly negative attitude toward the role of the state either in the past or in the future. But all the cultural background of individualism and liberalism, which lay behind the formulation of such creeds as Marxism in the West, is missing in the East. It is inevitable that the transplanted Marxist belief should acquire a completely different meaning in these alien circumstances. Marxism, embodied in the Communist movement by the Russians, has become the disciplinary inspiration of a modernized system of oriental despotism.

The West, with its liberal background and its economy already developed by capitalism, has little need and less desire for the Easternized despotism which Communism has become. Ever since the foundation of the Communist International a major weakness in the Communist appeal to the West has been the realities of Russian organization and political methods. Communism has made headway in the West only through fraudulent appeals—either the old mask of proletarian revolution or the newer disguise of democratic reform and peace-mongering. In the East, the political reality of Communism has not been so disturbing. Communism's real premises are often taken for granted there, and its appeal lies in the national regeneration that can be accomplished through the methods of revolutionary dictatorship.

The secret of Communist relevance in the East is its role as successor to the old despotic regimes. It is a successor mentally equipped to assimilate everything useful in Western civilization, particularly Western technology and Western industry, but to utilize these Western resources in the service of revived Eastern despotism. This is the synthesis of Western ends and Eastern means which Stalin achieved. The Communist despotism in the East undertakes to copy Western industrialization, but in a totally un-Western way—by state planning and compulsion; and for a radically different purpose—the enhancement of state power and the revival of national vigor.

The industrialization of Communist societies is not likely to engender liberal and individualist tendencies. Industry is not the basis of these tendencies in the West—they go back to pre-industrial feudal and commercial developments—and as a matter of fact individualism has all it can do to survive in the West amidst the problems and pressures of industrialism and mass organizations. Communist industrialization has been undertaken with practically no background of individualism, and both the new industry and the despotic manner of developing it are accentuating centralized bureaucratic controls.

Communism in the East is in a dilemma regarding the two contradictory aspects of its relevance, as nationalist revolt and as modernized despotism. The forces contributing to its victory and the factors involved in its success after coming to power are far from identical. This contradiction is inherent in the Communist movement as it was forged in postrevolutionary Russia and exported abroad. It imposed on a victorious Communist Party the agonizing task of redisciplining all its most enthusiastic supporters, of snatching back from pro-Communist intellectuals and peasants the fruits of the victory they thought they had just won, and of forcing these defrauded elements to bend their efforts none the less to the tasks prescribed by the state. The pattern of despotism requires redoubled despotism for its own effectuation. The party taskmasters' work of curbing the disgruntled and whipping on the faint-hearted is never done.

7 Communism and the Industrial Revolution

The place of industrialization in the Communist appeal is highly paradoxical and widely misunderstood. Communism's relevance to the problems of the East, and its program after taking power in an Eastern country, is represented by its industrialization drive. However, this is not the main appeal of Communism in the East, which hinges largely on anti-imperialism and the naïve belief that once the foreigners are expelled and expropriated, justice and plenty will descend upon the land. Neither does the industrialization function square with the basic premises of Communist theory, which called for the socialist revolution to follow the capitalist industrial revolution and rectify the evils inherent in the latter. The entire socialist tradition, from the early nineteenth century down to the early years of Soviet Communism, viewed the productive forces of the economy as more or less established, and presumed that the task of the revolution was pri-

245

marily to redistribute the benefits of society's existing economic capacity. Once the Communists were well established in power in Russia, they began to realize that the real problems facing their new socialist economic system were quite different. They were compelled to apply socialist methods to the task of creating new productive resources where none existed, and thus to undertake or continue the function of industrialization which Marxist theory had ascribed entirely to capitalism. The upshot was a completely new meaning of socialism—production socialism, where the earlier aims of distributive justice and equality were rudely subordinated to the practical requirements of building, equipping, and operating a modern industrialized economy.

1 THE CHALLENGE OF INDUSTRIALIZATION

The "industrial revolution," so-called, represents a fundamental transformation in the nature of all civilization. For the vast majority of the members of any society it involves a change in their way of living and thinking greater than the transition from the stone age to the early civilizations. It is easy for Westerners to lose sight of the epochal character of the industrial revolution, because they were in the van of the movement and worked it out piecemeal without any outside example. For the civilizations of the East it has been a very different matter. In the past hundred years they have found themselves face to face with the end product of Western economic progress and have had to meet the challenge of quick and thoroughgoing transformation as the price of survival.

The industrial revolution comprises much more than the label suggests. It entails not merely the erection of a machine-equipped factory industry, but the reorganization of life into nationwide economic units and what we might call the "technicization" of life, outside the factory just as much as within it. The self-sufficient rural economy gives way to a complex division of labor and the production of goods and services for vast and remote markets. The traditional routines of a static society yield to the unceasing waves of industrial and technical innovation, where the only thing that does not change is the constancy of change.

Historically the industrial revolution had its seat in Western Europe and above all in England, where its technical, commercial, and psychological underpinnings dated back to the seventeenth century or before. Westerners were unique in their development of what John Nef terms "quantitative precision" in their thinking. No other civilization accorded such prestige to commercial interests, or enjoyed the interchange between the economic and intellectual realms which underlay the birth of modern technology. In the second half of the eighteenth century industrialization and technicization got well under way in England and began to affect North America and the European continent. During the nineteenth century it spread from this center, and by the latter part of the century had reached Russia and Japan. Now no part of the world is untouched by industrialization, though the questions it raises are far from solved in those areas which have most recently faced the problems of modernity. Industrialization, with the problems it entails, constitutes one of the most fundamental and universal historical forces of the

present era. Communism has assumed its present
strength and importance as a direct effect of the
industrialization upheaval.

There are a number of aspects of industrialization which raise critical questions for societies
undergoing the process. Communism has its distinctive answer in each case. A fundamental requirement for industrialization is the accumulation of capital, which in ordinary terms means
the diversion of resources and effort from the satisfaction of immediate consumer wants into the
construction of (or trading for) the plants and
machinery and manifold services that will eventually produce much more bountifully. Communism
has made the solution of this problem of capital
accumulation a major goal, to the extent of fundamentally altering the nature of the movement in
the service of industrialization. Industrialization
entails the development or application of technology, and the training of large numbers of
people in the new skills which the technicized
society requires. For the peasant societies of Eastern Europe and Asia this has involved massive
cultural change; the habits sanctioned for centuries must be uprooted and replaced with completely new attitudes toward work and social
responsibility. In theory the Communists have
ignored this problem of modernizing social attitudes, or have spoken only of overcoming the
habits of "capitalism," but in most of the countries taken over by the Communists, capitalist
modernity had not yet reached the majority of
the population. The Communist answer is totalitarian regimentation and force on the one hand,
and on the other, an intensive effort to develop
mass education, literacy, and technical skills.
Finally, industrialization involves a new massive

system of transportation, communication, and organization: it truly creates the new mass society. Communist totalitarianism undertakes to bring such a system into existence, with the ultimate logic of complete organization.

2 THE SETTING OF EASTERN INDUSTRIALIZATION

The problems of economic development in the East, which underlie the rise and shaping of Communism, cannot be divorced from the overall context of East-West relations and the impact of Western culture on the East. Industrialization in the East must of necessity take place in the circumstances of acculturation. It is one of the major aspects of this acculturation and of the revolutionary reaction which results.

The fact that industrialization in the East is undertaken under Western influence has advantages as well as disadvantages. The Western model is there to copy. The industrial technology and organization which the West had to work out by trial and error over a period of many decades are available in their most modern form at the very beginning of industrialization in an Eastern country. Western capital and entrepreneurial talent are available and even eager to promote Eastern economic development. These Western resources make it possible (though not inevitable) for industrialization to proceed much more rapidly in the East.

Rapid industrialization, however, has consequences which are not always beneficial, particularly under conditions of cultural disparity between the old way of life and European practices. The strains of adjustment can be severe. Develop-

ment is uneven, as modern industrial establish-
ments rise amid conditions of peasant squalor.
For example, in Russia on the eve of World War I
the average industrial enterprise was considerably
larger than in Western Europe, while fifty percent
or more of the population was still illiterate. The
juxtaposition of new and old, progress and backwardness, means that different kinds of problems
and grievances are experienced simultaneously.
A churning social ferment is likely, as impoverished masses find the opportunity to witness modern economic achievements but have no chance to
enjoy their benefits, or as people are trained in
Western ways and then cast loose in an economy
that has no place for them. We find here, in the
circumstances of rapid but partial progress, the
requirements for the classical revolutionary situation: people have awareness of and hope for
a better life, but are balked in the attainment of it.

A revolutionary situation, especially one in
such a sharp form as has been developing throughout the East, is enough to try the endurance of
the most dexterous and far-sighted government.
In most cases, the Eastern regimes of the *status
quo ante* (whether native or colonial) have shown
neither of these qualities. They resist pig-headedly,
only to guarantee that when the forces of revolutionary change have organized themselves sufficiently, the old political order will be demolished
completely.

The basic economic assumption of most Eastern revolutionaries stems from their hostile reaction to Western domination. They are committed to fight imperialism and the capitalism
which they associate with it. They presume that
independence for the national economy will solve

all its problems. Insofar as they grasp the importance of further industrial development they are determined to accomplish it in accordance with the dictates of national socialism—socialistic control by the government, restriction or expropriation of foreign-owned enterprises, and the maximum self-sufficiency. These norms are assumed as matters of moral principle everywhere among Eastern nationalists; the Communists differ only in the intensity and exclusiveness with which they embrace them.

It is easy to see how the assumptions of socialism and autarky follow from the anti-Western revolt. Autarky is the economic side of the independence coin: better no development than that which depends on the imperialists. Socialism too represents independence from imperialism, with which capitalism is identified; socialism means that the nation as such is taking control of its economic destiny. National socialism is the institutional form through which the East is determined to achieve equality with the West.

The bearing of this bias on Communism is immediately evident. Communism, as it took shape in Russia, is by far the most fully developed system of national socialism, ready to meet the aspiration anywhere for independent industrial development. Now fully fashioned in Russia, Communism is ready to be applied—and many Eastern revolutionaries have been predisposed by their own assumptions to look with favor on the Communist alternative. Their socialist bent makes Communism attractive. Their autarkic bent makes Communism necessary. Communism represents the most effective combination of promises and discipline that the Easterners can find to meet their psychological and economic requirements.

The demand for autarkic development makes

for grievous economic problems. It is required of a
shaky economy for largely emotional reasons—the
anti-Westernism and clamor for independence
that stem from acculturation. It makes violent,
dictatorial, even ruthless action virtually inevitable, if a backward nation is to catch up with the
West solely by straining to mount a superhuman
effort. Here is the key to Communist economics—
not "surplus value," not the magic of the plan, but
plain effort, human sweat, which is to be called
forth, if all other means fail, by the oldest induce-
ment of all—the whip.

Under the label of socialism, the East has really
been turning to a managerial bureaucracy as the
system that will administer the building of industry. In this, *nolens-volens,* the East is copying the
trend which has actually taken place under the label of capitalism as the consequence of a developed industrial life—the trend toward the administration of economic activity by a corps of hired
officials working for ever larger and ever more im-
personal corporate entities. "Socialism" in the
Eastern context simply means this pattern carried
to its logical conclusion, with one organization, co-
terminous with the state, embracing the entire
economy. Like prerevolutionary Russian industry
with its higher degree of concentration, the Eastern nations are free to apply some Western forms
more completely than the organic evolution of the
West has permitted, and to an earlier stage of development—the task of building the industry in the
first place. Though Marx may still be the oracle, he
is really irrelevant here. Communism does not
come as the successor to capitalism, but as a substitute for it. It is the totalitarian managerial attack on the problem of rapid economic development.

3 PROBLEMS OF ECONOMIC DEVELOPMENT

The crux of industrial development is the question of capital accumulation. Difficult as it is for backward economies to obtain the requisite investment funds, two of the three possible sources are partly or (by the Communists) wholly ruled out. These are foreign investment capital and private accumulation by native capitalists. There remains, as the chief reliance of the national socialism of the East, accumulation and investment by the state, in the context of a planned economy. By government-directed forced saving, the nation will be compelled to pull itself up by its own bootstraps.

Another difficulty in independent industrialization in the East is that it cannot be successfully carried on at a gradual pace. One obvious reason is the pressure of population increase which Western medicine has unleashed everywhere by cutting death rates. Thanks to current rates of population growth, it is often hard for an Eastern country to stave off actual retrogression in its standard of living. But apart from this, the nature of modern industrial technology is such that a country with no plant at all must make an investment of tremendous scope in a number of large and interdependent enterprises. The steel mill demands coal mines, blast furnaces, railroad transportation, electric power, etc. All of the complementary elements in such an industrial complex must be completed before any will yield a return. Only by giant steps, such as the struggling Eastern economy is not likely to be able to afford without a severe strain, can industrialization of the modern type be economically carried out.

For Eastern countries that have actually gone over to Communist rule, the difficulties of independent development are accentuated by the country's withdrawal from the trading area of the international capitalist economy, and by the insistence on creating heavy industry everywhere. Advantages of specialization, in agriculture or light industry, for example, may be lost because of the determination not to have to depend on the capitalist world for any important commodity. The ethic of industrialization, as we shall see shortly, is such that heavy industry has moral precedence; failure to become independent of other countries in heavy industrial products becomes a stigma of inferiority. Therefore, every Eastern country experiences the compulsion to build itself a heavy industrial plant, regardless of the possibilities for specialization and exchange, and regardless of the inefficiencies of small scale: thus the spectacle of the Bulgarian steel industry. Finally, the demand for autarky raises the problem of indivisibility and complementarity among elements in an industrial complex to a new order of magnitude. The country must provide itself not just with a set of enterprises that are technologically interrelated, but with a much broader set that are economically complementary. The steel plant must be matched with a rolling mill, a machine-tool factory, an automobile plant, highway construction, a petroleum refinery, with enterprises at every stage of the process of translating the work of basic industry into the satisfaction of consumer and governmental wants. The whole chain is necessary before any link of it can bear fruit, as long as the country will not or cannot depend on international trade to furnish the steel, for instance, or consume it and pay for it.

The economic straits which are created by
the determination to industrialize independently
greatly intensify the central problem of capital accumulation, which in any event would be serious
enough. The need for initial accumulation is high,
and all the higher in the more backward country
with less ability to accumulate. The time lapse between the beginning of accumulation and the appearance of obvious benefits to the population is
likely to be considerable. The population is usually
at a bare subsistence level, and is not interested in
yielding up a surplus for investment. In fact, with
Western living standards in view, the masses in the
East are much more demanding of an immediate
improvement in their lot than were their counterparts in the early decades of Western industrialization. Nevertheless, the necessary capital funds,
representing national savings, must somehow
come from the population.

This impasse in the independent industrialization of a backward country has not gone unrecog-
nized in countries facing the problem. It was first
analyzed at length by Communist economists in
Soviet Russia, in the great industrialization controversy of the 1920's. The industrialization controversy was the reflection in economics of the
political struggle that went on during the years
1923–27 between Trotsky's Left Opposition and the
party leadership headed by Stalin and the right-
wing Communists. The Right, bearing the responsibility of government, held to the cautious line on
capital accumulation, while the Left fired critical
barrages of socialist doctrine.

The Left Opposition, whose most prominent
economic spokesman was Evgeni Preobrazhensky,

embraced the ambitious course of rapid accumulation and industrialization governed by state economic plans. They recognized that if industrialization was to be successful, it would have to get under way with a massive effort, which was necessitated both by the Communists' refusal to participate more than marginally in the capitalist international economy and by their determination to become strong enough to avoid dependence on it. Stalin expressed this concern in 1925: "We must build our economy in such a way as to prevent our country from becoming an appendage of the world capitalist system . . . , so that our economy should develop not as a subsidiary enterprise of world capitalism, but as an independent economic unit." Under these conditions of autarky, the necessary capital accumulation could be realized only by squeezing savings out of the Russian population. Russia suffered from rural overpopulation—as do most of the countries of Asia to a much greater degree—in the sense that far more people were living on the land than efficiency required. (Even today, the ratio of farmers to arable land in the USSR is roughly four times that of the United States; in China it approaches twenty times the American ratio.) When a majority of the population consists of subsistence peasants, the problem of domestic capital accumulation reduces to the problem of squeezing food and labor out of the peasantry without a commensurate return to them. Preobrazhensky envisaged the peasant majority in Russia as the "colony" which the industrial sector of the Russian economy would have to exploit in order to lay in a surplus. The masses could expect no return for a considerable period, since the proceeds of this exploitation were to go first to the construction of heavy industry, which was rightly regarded as the foundation of a modern economic system. The equipping of light industry would follow, together with armament manufacture for protection against the "imperialists," and finally a growing stream of consumer goods production would slake the nation's needs with socialist abundance. (We need hardly note that Soviet Russia has not yet fully attained the last stage.)

The main trouble here, as the right wing of the Russian Communists pointed out, was the attitude of the peasant masses during the period when they were being exploited without any immediate recompense. Bukharin and the Right feared that the peasants would turn counterrevolutionary under the pressure of such an imposition, and shake the foundations of the Soviet regime. To forestall such a catastrophe, they argued for and pursued a policy of gradual development, with primary attention to the needs of the population. Rather than exploit the peasants, the Right looked upon a prosperous agriculture as the foundation for the country's economic development. The peasants—who were at this time mostly individual proprietors—would be given technical advice and some equipment, on the assumption that the greatest value with the least investment could be reaped in agriculture. Then, with their income rising, the peasants could afford more consumers' goods; this demand would stimulate consumer goods industry and finance its expansion; the new demand on the part of consumer goods industry would support the expansion of heavy industry. Capital accumulation would come about through state-owned industries making a profit as they supplied an increasingly prosperous population.

This cautious approach to economic development, which the Soviet government actually fol-

lowed during the NEP, was demand-centered
rather than production-centered. In essentials it
conformed to capitalistic economic concepts, even
though Russian industry was state-owned. Only
limited efficacy was ascribed to state action and
state planning. The main virtue in eliminating private capitalists was that the benefits of capital accumulation would presumably accrue to the entire
population.

There is a deep gulf between the economics of
the NEP and the pattern of attack on the problems
of backwardness that the Communists later developed under Stalin's leadership. The gradualist and
demand-centered philosophy which the Communist Right espoused deserves careful attention, for
it is actually a major alternative for people who
wish to avoid the violent totalitarian solution with
which Communism became identified in the 1930's.
The contrast between the two courses of action
can now be observed, for example, in India and
China—the one attempting to use the state to meet
the needs of the population, the other mobilizing
the population to meet the needs of the state.

The prospect for the popularly oriented approach to development is not rosy, as the left-wing
Communist criticism of the right-wing policy
showed. The Left contended on economic grounds
that the capitalistic approach of the Right could
never produce sufficient accumulation to drive Russia ahead on the road to rapid industrialization.
The immediate needs for lump-sum investment,
the Left held, were so great that accumulation
through meeting consumer demand could never be
sufficient, and would even fail to prevent net dis-
investment—the actual deterioration of the country's industrial plant. One alternative was the
course urged by the Left—massive forced saving

and investment carried out by the power of the state. Otherwise, the country would stagnate and find itself forced more and more to surrender the control of its destiny into the hands of small native capitalists and large foreign ones.

Here a political and emotional consideration entered into the calculations of the Left. They were determined to prevent a trend toward capitalism in Russia, even if the needs of the developmental situation which they confronted were such as had been met by capitalism in the West. Implicit in the left-wing critique was the commitment to socialism as an alternative to capitalism. But what kind of socialism?

When taken in conjunction, the two leftist premises—the economic argument for massive development and the emotional presumption of control by the socialist state—pointed to an entirely new political and social system, theretofore only dimly imagined by anyone. The new system would hinge on a state powerful enough to compel economic development regardless of the short-term preferences of the population, and without any reliance on outside sources of capital. It assumed that the state could find resources where none existed before, in the form of additional human effort, to be evoked not by expensive rewards, but by political control and compulsion. It presumed, in short, the totalitarian state, mobilizing the entire population in an industrial army and making everyone strain to the utmost to win the war of modernization.

This implication was not lost upon the disputing Russian Communists. Both Bukharin for the Right and Preobrazhensky for the Left were aware of it and alarmed by it. Fear of totalitarianism apparently was one reason for Bukharin's adamant insistence upon the gradualist program of development. As for Preobrazhensky, he saw no easy way out. Gradualism, he feared, would only lead to untrammeled capitalism and the defeat of the socialist principles of the revolution. On the other hand, the despotic controls implicit in the alternative of rapid state-enforced development he found equally distasteful. The impasse has been described as the "Preobrazhensky dilemma": either capitalism or totalitarianism as alternative forms of industrial development, but none of the equalitarian and libertarian socialism by which the revolutionaries had been inspired up to this time. Preobrazhensky saw only one solution—the same salvation which careful Communist theoreticians in Russia had always had to rely on—aid from a revolutionary West. "The sum total of these contradictions," Preobrazhensky wrote in 1927, "shows how strongly our development toward socialism is confronted with the necessity of ending our socialist isolation, not only for political but also for economic reasons, and of leaning for support in the future on the material resources of other socialist countries." In other words, socialism as theretofore conceived would not work under unrelieved Russian conditions. Marx, it appears, was right after all: the work of capitalism in laying the material foundations for some kind of new equalitarian order could not be avoided. Revolution in Russia, occurring where the prerequisites for the new system were lacking, could not produce the desired result.

The "Preobrazhensky dilemma" did not long go unresolved. A choice was soon made, when Stalin opted for the totalitarian solution (for reasons of short-term political expediency, to be sure, but nevertheless making the commitment final). Given the alternatives of following the West and accepting its domination in the international capitalist economy, or striking out alone whatever the cost, the revolutionary independence-mindedness of the Communists made the latter choice easy to make and easy to enforce on the party. The totalitarian alternative was not an economic necessity but only a possibility; it was political emotion that cast the die.

4 THE FETISH OF INDUSTRIALISM

Industrialization, in areas which are confronted with the ready-made Western example, is not just an economic necessity or a means to the attainment of a better life. Its implications extend deeply into the realm of the political, the emotional, even the moral. Industrialization, for the true Communist (who is an Eastern Communist, wherever he finds himself), is an obsession, a way of life, an ultimate end, to which every human value may have to be sacrificed. Such is the extreme espoused by those who witness another part of the world prospering in the machine age and deriving superiority from it. The Easterner would conquer the machine for his people. The reverse is the result: under Communism as nowhere else, man is the slave of the machine.

The East in revolt is animated by emotional demands to copy the West and defy it simultaneously, to beat the West at its own game. Two contradictory impulses—Westernization and anti-Westernism—are at work here, with conflicting economic implications. Emulation of the West requires industrial development. Independence from the West —autarky, in economic affairs—makes development exceedingly difficult. Rapid industrialization, under self-imposed difficulties, is the Eastern desideratum. This represents a combination of demands that points logically toward only one kind of solution—the totalitarian bootstrap operation that emerged from the Soviet industrialization controversy when Stalin commenced his five-year plans.

This totalitarian solution of Russian Communism is intimately tied to the faith in industrialism. It both utilizes and intensifies the passion to industrialize. Industrialization becomes a moral imperative, far removed from the utilitarian calculations of individual or mass economic advantage which prevail in the West. As Stalin put it, "Industrialization does not consist of any sort of development of industry. The center of industrialization, its basis, consists of the development of heavy industry (fuel, metal, etc.), in the development of what in the last analysis is the production of the means of production, in the development of our own machinery construction. . . . The country of the dictatorship of the proletariat, standing amidst the capitalist encirclement, cannot remain economically independent if it does not produce its own tools and means of production at home." It takes a special effort to comprehend how the Communist *believes in* industry, above all heavy, nonconsumable, industry. Industry is the new deity before which the stern priesthood of the Communist Party compels the masses to bow and sacrifice unendingly.

While Marx applied the notion of a "fetish" to certain aspects of the capitalist mentality, we can detect kindred habits of thought in Soviet socialism under Stalin—practices, standards, or techniques that might lack rational value but which become ends in themselves, idols of the industrializing faith. There was a fetish of heavy industry,

which had to be built at any cost and almost regardless of the utility of its output. The Zeran automobile plant in Warsaw, for example, has never
produced economically, because of insufficient pro-
vision of material and a limited market; the enterprise stands as a symbol of the industrial dream,
but little more. At its very inception the Soviet
First Five-Year Plan was irrationally espoused.
Scientific respect for the facts was abandoned
when the planners were all fired, late in 1928 and
early in 1929, because their plans did not measure
up to the ever-ascending ambitions of Stalin and
his political supporters. A fetish of tempo appeared
—the Stalinist party leaders showed unconcealed
exhilaration every time the planned goals were
raised. The plan was proclaimed completed in four
and a quarter years—a point that reflects ill on the
planning that could not foresee the target possibilities, but speaks volumes for the mentality of
haste, acceleration, and state-commanded effort.
Like the Red Queen, the Soviet government saw no
reason—save sabotage!—why the Russian people
could not run faster and faster.

To a degree rivaling the American proclivity,
bigness and quantity came to be pursued by the Soviets as ends in themselves. A seizure of giganto-
mania impelled Stalin and his government to undertake the biggest dam, the biggest building, the
most lavish subway, etc., without regard to cost or
utility. Output statistics and the fulfillment of the
plan in quantity terms drew all attention away
from considerations of quality, which remains an
endemic weakness in the Soviet economy.

The mentality of industrial haste had unfortu-
nate effects for Soviet agriculture. When Stalin ordered large-scale collectivization of the peasants
in 1929, it was pushed through with a speed and

violence that no one had dreamed of before. Stalin
himself was compelled to call a temporary retreat
in 1930, while making scapegoats of his subordinates who were "dizzy with success." Collectivization was accompanied by intensive mechanization,
necessitated partly by the peasants' slaughter of
their livestock when they were being collectivized,
and partly by the desire to give the government
stronger control over the collective farms. A startling fact about the mechanization of Soviet agriculture is that with rural overpopulation and the
inefficient use of labor in handling machinery, the
net productivity of all people directly or indirectly
engaged in agriculture hardly increased at all.
Mechanization, for all the fervor with which it was
pursued, was not economical. Running as fast as
it did, Russian agriculture only managed to stay
where it was.

A notable change in the economic spirit of the
Soviet regime and its East European satellites followed the demise of Stalin in 1953. As in many
other fields, ranging from foreign policy to intellectual controls, Stalin's departure from the scene
permitted a marked adjustment to reality in the
economic sphere. In 1953 the successor leadership
under Malenkov made dramatic concessions to the
economic preferences of the population, particularly by increasing rewards to farmers and pushing
the production of fabricated consumer goods desired by the salaried officialdom. A certain reaction
set in, in 1955, when Malenkov fell; Dmitri Shepi-
lov, speaking for the party leadership during his
brief period of prominence, maintained that an
equal or greater priority for light (i.e., consumer
goods) industry would "cause great harm to the
entire cause of Communist construction," and
"lead to complete disorientation to our cadres on

basic questions of the party's economic policy."
Since then Khrushchev has observed a certain balance—continuation of the heavy industry priority,
but concerted efforts to raise living standards by
improving agriculture, housing, and wage minima.

The immediate prospect, following the recent
trend, is that the Soviet economy will cater more
and more to the desires of consumers. This reflects
the successful effort to build a heavy industrial
foundation, and the attainment of an economic
level reasonably near the Western. Soviet Russia
has arrived at industrial maturity, and the industrialization fetish has lost its relevance. It has at
last become possible for the Soviet leaders to see
clearly the advantage of winning the population's
loyal support by satisfying its economic needs.

A similar economic relaxation, sometimes even
more striking, has characterized Communist Eastern Europe since 1953. When the moderate Communist Imre Nagy became premier of Hungary in
July 1953, he called frankly for a reduced tempo of
development, with the explanation, "There is no
reason whatever for any excessive industrialization or any efforts to achieve industrial autarky,
especially if the necessary sources of basic materials are wanting." The crisis of 1956 caused the
Russians to suspend their economic exploitation
of the European satellites and to allow further
tempering of developmental plans in order to appease the populace.

The great exception to the rule of Communist
economic moderation is China, which has taken
precisely the opposite course. The Chinese Communist regime moved cautiously after taking over
complete authority on the mainland in 1949, with
modest plans and toleration of private business on
the model of the NEP in Russia. The Chinese First

Five-Year Plan (1953–57) was limited in its objectives, although the peasants were loosely collectivized during this period. In 1957 the Chinese industrial establishment stood, in absolute terms, only about where Russia was before Stalin's five-year plans. Nineteen hundred and fifty-eight was the year of great change in China, with the "Great Leap Forward" proclaimed by Liu Shao-ch'i, and the organization of the peasants into communes. The Communist Party commenced to sacrifice before the fetish of disciplined industrialization more severely than the Russians ever had under Stalin. "Our general line," Liu declared, "is to build socialism by exerting our utmost efforts." The aim, as he phrased it, expresses the essence of Eastern Communism: "We will build our country, in the shortest possible time, into a great socialist country with a modern industry, modern agriculture, and modern science and culture."

Irrational though it is in part, the Communist ethic of production has played an important role in the process of industrialization. Anticonsumptionism has contributed significantly to the extraordinary pace with which a heavy industrial plant—now the world's second largest—has been constructed in Russia. China is on the same path. In the context of the Puritan-like asceticism observed by the Communist regimes, the accumulation of capital has proceeded as an end in itself, with undivided emphasis. The Communist ethic has had much the same function as did the "Protestant ethic" in the industrial revolution in the West, with the premium it put on individual thrift, toil, ambition, self-denial, all of which aided the necessary diversion of funds from consumption expenditure to capital investment.

In both the Western and Soviet cases, the success of industrialization has depended on more then economic factors. A spirit is also required, to sacrifice consumer wants in the interest of future industrial power. Where this spirit is now absent, as it is in much of the East, the road to industrialization is fraught with tribulations. But Communism brings this spirit to the revolutionaries of the East, and gives them both the goal and the determination to attain it by forcing sacrifices on themselves and their compatriots. The intensive industrialization of a non-Western area (which is the characteristic objective of Communism) really means that the whole industrial way of life is forced upon a population. The Communists of an Eastern country confront their own population as missionaries of a new faith and a new system. They must undertake a campaign of conversion—sometimes a long and arduous one, even apart from the task of conquering political power. The work of re-education of a backward peasant nation amounts to no less than a total transformation of its culture if the people are to be prepared for successful participation in an industrial system.

Re-education for industrial life involves not only the work of making the population literate and imparting technical training to an industrial labor force. It means, as the Communists found to their dismay in Russia, the inculcation of an entirely new set of habits and standards—punctuality, accuracy, observation of routine without a lapse of standards, carefulness, cleanliness, maintenance of equipment. None of these considerations means much to a peasant population, but they are all-important in industry. Unfortunately, they cannot be instilled overnight, nor even in one generation, with any thoroughness. Such standards cannot be commanded or compelled—one has to grow up with them. Even in recent years Soviet Russia has suffered from its peasant legacy; while the country's best military and industrial technicians turn out work that is second to none, the mass of workers and soldiers who handle the equipment are sadly inclined to let it deteriorate without proper care.

Industrialization in the East of necessity proceeds under conditions of sharp internal cultural change and conflict. An educated, self-conscious, Westernized but anti-Western elite direct the effort; they find the masses remote, apathetic or disorganized, ignorant; they see an imperative need for political action *against* the masses to mobilize them, drive them, exploit their energies in order to modernize the country. Many Eastern revolutionaries are hostile to their own people—they hate them for being backward, and are prepared to wield the lash in order to drive them ahead, out of their medieval slough. Viewed in these terms, the fury of the collectivization drive in Russia and the wrathful discipline imposed by Soviet labor legislation in the thirties at least become intelligible.

Communism, while accentuating and fulfilling the sense of a campaign against the masses, is not alone responsible for this attitude. It is characteristic of a wide variety of Eastern revolutionaries who have come to the conviction that the masses must be guided or driven and cannot be allowed freely to seek their own destiny. One need only cite Ataturk and Sun Yat-sen in the 1920's, or Nasser and Sukarno at the present time. Sukarno has more and more frankly developed his premises of "guided democracy" and "guided economy." It is but a short step from this frame of mind to the all-out assault on a backward population which the Communist industrialization program represents.

5 EVOLUTION OF
THE PLANNED ECONOMY

The Communist planned economy as it ultimately took shape was never intended to be that way. Its features were evolved, like so much in Soviet political life, as practical measures to deal with unforeseen circumstances or to solve immediate political problems. What eventually became the fundamental objective of the Communist economy—forced-draft industrialization without outside aid—was never foreseen before the Russian Revolution, and only dimly understood for some years afterward.

Certain structural principles of the Communist economy were spelled out in the Bolshevik program, and put into effect soon after the revolution. Corporate capitalism was completely liquidated by the nationalization of industry, and replaced by comprehensive state ownership and control by the time of the Russian Civil War. With the NEP, individual capitalism in farming and trade got a new lease on life, but it was abruptly terminated when Stalin collectivized the peasants and nationalized the NEP-men. The Soviet pattern since the early 1930's—more or less fully copied in other Communist states since World War II—is that of the completely state-owned (barring the coöperative fiction of the collective farms) and state-managed economic system, where private enterprise is ruled out altogether.

At the outset of the Bolshevik Revolution radical innovations in economic organization were attempted. The Bolsheviks and their supporters endorsed the ideal of "workers' control," with managerial responsibility in the hands of workers' representatives, and the observance of complete equalitarianism in wages. Soon after coming to power Lenin recognized that the survival of the Soviet regime required the abandonment of such utopian schemes, and over the anguished cries of his purist colleagues he sanctioned the restoration of industrial discipline and the retention or recruitment of bourgeois managerial "specialists." After the introduction of the NEP a conventional money economy and cost accounting were restored, while managers were invested with authority scarcely different from that of corporate executives in a capitalist economy. Under Stalin in the early 1930's the ideal of equalitarianism was frankly abandoned; wage and salary differentials and incentives were introduced on a scale surpassing capitalism. All revolutionary promises to the contrary, the organization and practices of Soviet industry swung around to a pattern essentially kindred to corporate capitalism, with two major differences: the state was the sole owner of all industry, and the measure of business success was not profit-making but fulfillment of the plan.

Planning is the subject of an extended mythology in the Communist movement. It is typical of the pseudoscientific garb which Communism puts on the elements of its faith. Before the Russian Revolution, Marxist theory dealt very little with the problems, or even the objectives, of postrevolutionary economic planning. All the Bolsheviks had for a guide when they took power was the assumption that when the capitalists were expropriated by the "armed people," everything would become easy to administer. The results were catastrophic, until the Soviet government finally restored order and supplanted its utopian ideals of equality and collective decision-making with an authoritative administrative hierarchy. Even so, for the first six or seven years after the revolution it was all the government could do to get the existing industrial plant back into operation and keep the population fed. The problems of planning new development began to be seriously faced only during the industrialization controversy in the mid-twenties.

For a brief time at this stage of Soviet development there was a serious scientific approach to the problems of economic planning, notably by former Menshevik economists working for the State Planning Commission. The objective now was not a redistribution of the goods of capitalism, but the accumulation of capital and the development of a vastly larger industrial plant. Trotsky gave his whole-hearted endorsement to this effort, but most of the party leaders were cautious to the point of inaction, until Stalin had defeated the Left Opposition and was preparing to dispose of the Right Opposition as well. At this juncture Stalin made the planning issue a political football, and proceeded to attack the professional planners for being too cautious. The upshot—after the planners had been purged—was a five-year plan based not on a rational calculation of resources and problems but on the wishes of the state and the unwillingness of the Stalinists to admit that they had demanded anything unreasonable. The plan was not a schedule to allocate effort, but a target to evoke it. Heavy industry was to be built at all cost, while the populace silently bore the sacrifices exacted from them through the collective farm deliveries and the so-called "turnover tax" (the regressive sales tax that the government still relies upon, with levies on necessities up to fifty percent and more). Any questioning of the priority of heavy industry became and remains to this day a counter-revolutionary thought.

The early Soviet five-year plans were a national

ordeal imposed by the totalitarian state, thanks to which the basic problem of accumulating industrial capital was solved. Between the inception of the plans in 1929 and the German invasion in 1941 the capacity of Soviet heavy industry was expanded roughly fourfold. Steel production, always the critical indicator, was around four and a half million tons in 1928, a figure which barely represented recovery of the pre-World War I level; by 1940, steel production had passed eighteen million tons. Fuel production and electric power capacity showed a comparable increase, while the chemical, automotive, and machine tool industries, starting from very low bases, increased their output from ten to fifty times. On the other hand, consumer goods industry lagged behind; the textile industry, for example, increased only around fifty percent (and this was offset by the decline in rural handicrafts). Housing construction fell far behind the need, as the urban population was doubled by the movement of peasants into the cities to man new industries. When war came, the Soviet government possessed the sinews of a modern war machine, but the population as a whole had suffered a serious depression of living standards and looked back on the period of the NEP as a golden age.

World War II was a time of appalling human and economic sacrifice for the Soviet population, but the effort was sufficient to sustain military production despite the loss of the country's most productive territory to German occupation. The country came out of the war with its industrial base weakened but intact—steel production in 1945 was about eleven million tons—and the ground was ready for the phenomenal industrial expansion which has gone on since that time. By the time of Stalin's death in 1953, Soviet steel production was approaching forty million tons a year, with commensurate progress in other lines of heavy industry, but the pinch was still severely felt in agriculture, consumers' goods, and housing. Only under the successor administrations of Malenkov and Khrushchev has the Soviet regime seen fit to give major attention to the needs and satisfaction of consumers, who have accordingly benefited from an appreciable increase of living standards since that time. Even so, the priority of heavy industry has not ended; another fifty percent of growth has been scored since Stalin's death, and Soviet steel production at sixty million tons a year is well over half the American capacity.

The key to the Soviet industrialization success is the state's relentless allocation of resources to heavy industrial construction, and the absence of restrictions on output which under capitalism are intermittently imposed by profit and loss considerations. However, industrialization has entailed other measures of policy which have been vital to its success—above all, the organization and training of a corps of effective industrial administrators and a disciplined industrial labor force. Since Lenin's time the Soviet regime has been acutely aware of the social requirements of large-scale industry, which have little in common with the revolutionary ideal. A premium was placed on training and incentives, to recruit and prepare the personnel needed for industrial expansion. When these requirements clashed with revolutionary ideals, the latter were forthwith sacrificed. Collective decision-making quickly gave way to the hierarchy of individual authorities, and by the early 1930's the Stalinists had eliminated progressive education and the last vestiges of economic equalitarianism. They presumed that society did not exist for the sake of the individual personality and its development (as the idealists thought), but rather the other way around. Under Stalinism, the individual is expected to exert every effort to contribute to the development of the Communist society, and is rewarded or punished according to this standard.

In all the areas, both European and Asiatic, brought under Communist control after World War II, the same Soviet economic principles have been observed. Heavy industrial development has had unqualified priority, irrational as this might be when applied to each small Eastern European country. Certain Eastern European countries—Bulgaria and Rumania—started from roughly the Russian level of development, and here the cost of progress was high. Others—Hungary and Poland— were at a higher level when Communism came than Russia had been, but the strain of the industrial emphasis was severe here as well, until retrenchments were made between 1953 and 1956. Czechoslovakia and East Germany, on the other hand, were on a higher plane than that of Russia now, and Czechoslovakia made the transition to a Communist economy with comparatively little strain. East Germany suffered unusually until 1953 because it was exploited by the Russians through reparations. Since 1956 diversification and integration of the Eastern European economies has been the rule, and industrial output throughout the region has risen steadily. As far as European Communism is concerned, the problem of how to attain the advanced capitalist level of industrial development has been solved, and full realization of the goal is only a matter of time.

Communist industrialization in Asia—specifically in China—faces a much more difficult situation. When the Communists came to power in

China the country's industry, even in absolute terms, did not amount to much more than that of Russia of the 1890's—i.e., before the considerable capitalistic industrialization of tsarist times. With a vastly larger peasant population living much closer to the margin of subsistence, the Chinese had to commence industrialization from a point far behind the Russian Communists. They proceeded with some caution in the early 1950's, while nationalization was accomplished and agriculture was collectivized. By the end of their First Five-Year Plan in 1957 they had achieved an absolute development of industry somewhat beyond what Russia had in 1913 and again at the end of the NEP. Weaknesses came to light by this time, particularly in transportation and in the agricultural base, and these, coupled with a renewed political fanaticism, prompted the Chinese Communists to undertake a distinctly new kind of economic effort. This was the so-called "Great Leap Forward" proclaimed in 1958—an intensive industrialization drive coupled with the reorganization of the countryside into communes and the dispersion of industry in new small-scale rural enterprises. Making up for what they lack in resources and equipment, the Chinese have relied on organization and effort to transform the country, and the rate of development that has been achieved compares favorably with that of Russia during the early five-year plans. China is well on the way toward creating an independent industrial base for its military power. Whether it will succeed in raising the living standards of its population in the face of an unslackening population increase remains to be seen.

The history of the Communist planned economy shows a steady increase in reliance on the power of the state and the action of authoritative

individuals to effect economic development. Initially the Russian Communists assumed that the
postrevolutionary economy would take care of itself, and throughout the 1920's the predominant
thinking was that economic laws of consumer demand and industrial profit-making, which the
planners would merely study and observe, would
solve the economic problems much as they had under capitalism. Stalin's change of line to forced-
draft industrialization in 1929 was the real revolution in this respect, and the key to the high rate of
industrial progress since then. Chinese Communism has merely carried this shift one step further,
in applying even more rigorous political means to a
considerably more backward economic situation.
The industrial revolution has thus become an entirely deliberate political accomplishment.

6 COMMUNISM AND INDUSTRIAL
MATURITY

While Asian Communism still faces problems
of appalling magnitude which make the full attainment of the objectives of industrialization in
the foreseeable future at best dubious, European
Communism has now broken through to a level
of development quite comparable to the recent
achievements of capitalism. This means that the
severe problems of rapid industrial development
which contributed so much to the evolution of Soviet Communism into its present crystallized form
no longer prevail. In Europe at least, Communism
has outlived the original reasons for its existence,
while industrial maturity has created new problems and new possibilities for the movement.

As the pressures for industrial development
grow less intense, it is easier to see the effect on

Communism of the problems inherent in operating any modern industrial society. Development of industry where none stood before is a temporary challenge, but the industrial society once achieved poses relatively unchanging problems and demands. Insofar as it has adjusted to these conditions, the Communist system can be regarded as a substantially permanent affair.

The first requirement of industrial life, made dramatically clear when the Communists tried to defy it in their early years, is the bureaucratic and hierarchical organization of specialists. Industry and its ancillary services require authority in order to direct large-scale operations quickly and effectively; discipline so that every one on every level fulfills his responsibilities; technical skill appropriate to each level, with a high degree of division of labor, all depending on an extensive system of technical education that can equip people with the myriads of special skills required by industry and technicized life in general. Communism has put a premium on all these requirements of the industrial society, to such an extent that they represent the real substance of the Communist social program. Education is heavily stressed and rewarded, but it is education under strict central supervision and with narrow technical and scientific aims. Training in the liberal arts is virtually nonexistent save for a few specialists in this area; liberal education is replaced by the dismal platitudes which make up the required courses in Marxism-Leninism. Rewards are closely geared to an individual's training, responsibility, and effort, with wide salary differentials, piece rates, and managerial bonuses and prizes, while effort is kept to the maximum by the unceasing pressure to fulfill the plan. Terror is now receding into the background in both the USSR and in Eastern Europe. Rewards, controls, and legally prescribed penalties are much more effective in getting the desired performance in the mature Communist industrial system.

In certain areas of life the Communist stress on bureaucratic hierarchy goes too far. Having made the principle of industrial organization an end in itself, they have imposed it on sectors of the economy which are largely or partly pre-industrial, with uniformly detrimental results. Agriculture is the area which has suffered most from the arbitrary imposition of collective and bureaucratic organization of work. It has yielded the desired tax, but under the collectivized system it has never been accorded the individual initiative and incentive which farming under most circumstances requires for its optimum development. A wide range of secondary economic activities which are by their nature small-scale or unimposing in the national perspective have either been neglected or stunted by the dead hand of the central bureaucracy. In the European Communist regimes such deficiencies have been particularly evident in the fields of retail trade, personal services, entertainment, and luxuries. Until recently such matters have been beneath the dignity of the plan, while the absolute prohibition of private enterprise precludes the satisfaction of any such popular desires by individual initiative.

The completely centralized economy is strong in serving the needs of the state, but weak in meeting the wishes of the population except insofar as individuals must be given incentives to serve the state more effectively. Even from the standpoint of the government's interest, complete centralization has its drawbacks. Local officials, saddled with responsibility but lacking independence, tend to be conservative; they are weak in initiative, and are often obtuse about the needs or potential of the people in their district. To counter the drawbacks of overcentralization, the Soviet regime on Khrushchev's initiative undertook a thoroughgoing reorganization of the economic system in 1957. Most of the central economic ministries were abolished, and their powers turned over to "economic councils," each responsible for the entire operation of economic affairs in their respective territories (corresponding usually to provinces or minority republics). This reform—subsequently copied in Eastern Europe—appears to have been effective, though it entailed new problems when regions failed to coöperate with each other properly. Communist experience, like the history of Russia and the East in general, has conditioned officials at every level to depend on a strong central authority. There are no popular controls, whether political or economic, and very little public spirit, to defend the popular interest in the absence of a firm hand at the center.

In its social structure as in its administrative organization the Communist system has overadjusted to industrialism. There are no pre-industrial social groups or classes left, apart from the peasants; there are no independent businesses or professions. Everyone, literally, has become part of a bureaucratic hierarchy. Public opinion or class interests do not exist in any effective sense. Everyone is an employee of the omnipotent state, as worker, peasant, or member of a category analogous to the salaried middle class of modern capitalism. The Soviet catchall term for the latter group is "employees" (*sluzhashchie*), who range from white-collar workers, through all sorts of technical specialties, to the leading scientific and cultural figures and the top administrative brass. Within this group, numbering some ten million in the USSR (not counting families), there is (as among their American counterparts) intense status consciousness and competition, but much mobility and no sharp class lines. Anyone with ability and energy who gets an education and conforms politically is assured of a successful career in some kind of organization—again like contemporary America.

It is often suggested, as an application of a sort of Marxism-in-reverse, that the growth of the Communist industrial middle class will lead to political changes in the Communist world, and hopefully cause a mellowing of its revolutionary pose and international intransigence. This prediction is based on a number of unfounded assumptions. First of all, as we have noted, there is no particular connection of the industrial salariat with representative government and individual freedom, which are entirely pre-industrial achievements in the West. The education which the Communist technicians get is narrow and dogmatic, and unlikely to make them think any more critically than many an American engineer. Industrial maturity in the Communist sphere has made the power of the party all the stronger. The party's main social roots are in the technical and administrative class (real workers were never a majority in it), but its relation to this class is not representation but control. The higher a man's status in the Communist system, the more closely does he come under the direction of the party, whether as non-member or (more usually) as member. The hopes for a real internal movement of democratization as a result of broadened education and industrial maturity in the Communist system are simply quasi-Marx-

ist illusions indulged in by wishfully thinking
Westerners.

Communism is an instrument of industrialization, or an avenue toward that presumed state of
grace. It is not the only way to reach the industrial
goal, but it is an ever-present and likely alternative in those parts of the world which are trying
to accomplish the industrial revolution with the
achievements of Western Europe and America already in view far above them. The character of
Communism as an approach to industrialization
has become a basic aspect of the movement. At the
same time Communism has been making the adjustments necessary for it to serve as the political
embodiment of accomplished industrialism. Some
of the features of the first role are, to be sure,
needlessly imposed on the second, but this is not
the only instance in history of political arrangements long outliving the circumstances which
called them into being.

Cast in this industrial role, Communism assumed its final form. The core of Communism was
and is the use of discipline to industrialize, together with an industrializing faith which has
served to reinforce this determination. Doctrine,
revolution, Russian circumstances and East-West
problems have all helped create and shape the
Communist movement, but they are no longer of
its essence: its permanent constituents are party,
faith, and industry. Reduced to essentials, Communism is a system of militaristic industrialism.

8 Communism as Totalitarianism

Communism, though a distinct product of particular ideas, individuals, and circumstances, is not unparalleled in our century as a form of government and society. A number of other political movements and regimes have shared some of its most striking—and obnoxious—features, and certain general social trends elsewhere have their analogues in the Communist system. The full understanding of Communism requires us to view it in perspective with other contemporary political movements and developments, and to consider it as a member of a broader political genus, totalitarianism. Our aim here is to determine the extent to which Communism can be explained as one manifestation of this widespread twentieth-century political trend.

1 THE MEANING OF TOTALITARIANISM

Totalitarianism is a familiar phenomenon, all too terrible in its impact on millions of people. The horrors of the recent and present totalitarian movements of Europe and Asia may well make the second quarter of the twentieth century go down in history as one of the most bloody and inhuman eras of all time. The experience of totalitarian evil has been so intense that it is very difficult to inquire into the subject dispassionately. This has all too often obstructed the clear understanding of Communism. Also matters are not helped by the vague meaning of the term "totalitarianism" itself.

Like revolution, totalitarianism is available for study in so few clear-cut instances that meaningful generalization is difficult. It is easy to fall into the circular trap of detailing the idea of totalitarianism largely from Soviet experience, and then explaining the features of the Soviet regime as a manifestation of totalitarianism. Nevertheless, there is evidence enough that the Communist system has much in common with other comparable regimes. The Communist and Fascist-Nazi regimes, and to a certain extent some of the non-European nationalist revolutionary governments, broke deliberately with the liberal democracy which had reached its apogee just before World War I. All these revolutionary movements have emphasized violence, divorce of power from popular control, and extension of the scope of arbitrary and repressive governmental action. Legal violence is the hallmark of the new systems which the present century has spawned.

A ubiquitous feature of the totalitarian regimes is their propaganda, which is both massive and positive. The totalitarians are concerned not merely to suppress oppositional ideas, but to dictate what *shall* be said: unlimited control over thought and culture is the totalitarian standard. Another and equally familiar application of totalitarian power is terror, exercised by a political police, through arbitrary arrest and repression. It is not merely that political opposition is illegal; the subjects of a totalitarian regime cannot win security however much they conform to the law. At times the individual is judged only as a member of a category. Is he a reliable Aryan or worker, or a suspect Jew or kulak?

In political structure as well as behavior the totalitarian systems conform to a type. All have been built around the exclusive rule of a disciplined party—of which Lenin's was the prototype —and most of the time they have stressed the power of an infallible and all but deified individual (the "charismatic" leader, in Max Weber's terminology). All came to power as revolutionary movements, and in every case their policies have represented a curious amalgam of revolutionary and counterrevolutionary influences. All have attacked the status quo; all have been fanatical and humorless.

Finally, there is a political spirit common to all the totalitarianisms—the spirit of "everything for the state." It is one of the obvious ironies of Communism, with its glowing promises of a stateless future, that it proved to be the first and most successful instance of contemporary statism: stateworship, no less. Here is both the inspiration and the justification for the controls over every individual's life and thought which the totalitarians so determinedly have imposed. The state, moreover, in every case has been a national state. Totalitarianism is by nature nationalistic, and belligerently so; it implies war to the death against the decadent democracies.

Many observers with good reason have stressed the distinction between modern totalitarianism and the despotisms or absolute monarchies of earlier times, at least in the history of Europe. One obvious difference is the vastly enhanced potential for totalitarian control which is afforded by modern means of transportation, mass communication, and record-keeping, not to mention armaments. It is physically possible for a government now to aspire to a degree of control over its citizenry which would have been inconceivable a hundred years ago. But paralleling the increased possibility for control are increased aspirations. The modern totalitarian regime lays claim to a far wider competence; the scope of its powers is literally unlimited. The traditional absolute monarchy was content to keep the lid on politically and let established nonpolitical institutions continue undisturbed in everything from religion to economic life as long as they threatened no political trouble. Tsarist Russia, the last European absolute monarchy, came closest (until 1905) to the modern totalitarian pattern, but instead of being a revolutionary attempt to impose new and total controls on society, it was pigheadedly tied to an outmoded social order. To appreciate the contrast, one need only imagine how a totalitarian regime would solve the problem of the Russian revolutionary movement; instead of merely trying to catch the individual revolutionaries, it would have swept away the whole social group of intelligentsia from which they sprang.

Totalitarianism is a distinctly modern phenomenon. At the same time, it is closely associated with revolution—and the present century is manifestly an era of revolutionary upheaval. Totalitarianism is the natural form of postrevolutionary dictatorship under the conditions of social organization and governmental technique which now prevail. World political circumstances have made revolution more likely in our time, and have also made totalitarianism the likely outcome of revolution.

2 MODERN TOTALITARIAN TRENDS

The rash of totalitarian movements in recent decades cannot be understood without taking into account the conditions under which they arose. While we cannot undertake here an exhaustive explanation of all modern totalitarian movements, we can at least point to certain social trends which have contributed to them. These developments, as we shall see, are widespread in Western society, and are by no means confined to the countries which have gone over overtly to totalitarian politics.

The decades since 1914 have seen a recrudescence of violence among and within the nations that has not been equaled since the century of religious wars and persecutions that followed the Protestant Reformation. Violence is the crucible of totalitarianism; in violence were the totalitarian movements conceived, and through violence they came to power. International conflict paved the way, setting the psychological stage for internecine struggle within nations. The critical date was 1914; since the outbreak of that bloody ordeal of attrition now known as the First World War, violence has been the norm.

Since World War I ushered in the era of totalitarianism, we have seen mankind sink to depths of cruelty and degradation which the nineteenth century, luxuriating in its illusions of "progress," had thought forever transcended. The revival of Europe's traditional anti-Semitism, but in a form more vicious than history had ever witnessed, is but one example. Whole nations have flung themselves into orgies of cultivated barbarism and sadistic purgation with calculated defiance of all the standards of civilized behavior that have been built up so laboriously over the centuries. Democracy, justice, tolerance, mercy, legality, political decency in every sense, have been subjected to mortal challenge, just at the point when they had scored an almost universal triumph. Ironically, the first totalitarian upsurge came in Russia, where the newest democracy was still struggling to be born.

Totalitarianism has fed upon a number of deep-seated social developments which in one way or another stem from the permanent revolution in economic life which has been going on in Western society for the last century and a half. Some of the consequences of industrialism, respecting the organization of economic life into very large, complex, and disciplined industrial and administrative units, point obviously in the totalitarian direction. Other effects, in the psychological realm, have been more subtle, but no less profound.

Despite the fact that economic individualism flourished in Western Europe and America during the century of the industrial revolution, the industrial way of life has given sweeping impetus to a trend toward organization at the expense of individualism. This is perfectly evident in relations among the units of economic activity—the tendency toward ever larger capitalistic units, mergers, and cartels. Such are the technological conditions of modern industry (especially its most modern branches) that progress *ipso facto* implies organizational concentration. The centralizing trend may be fought by democratic governments, or helped along to its logical conclusion by socialist acts of nationalization, but its existence can hardly be disputed.

Within individual economic units, and within society as a whole, the trend has been to closer integration of individuals in an ever more complex division of labor, and with more and more reliance on bureaucratic command and subordination. Not only have government and industry followed this pattern everywhere; it has extended even to such traditionally individualistic professional areas as law, medicine, and scientific research. Such tendencies toward the organization of individuals in administrative hierarchies have proceeded rapidly in every reasonably advanced country in the present century, independently of totalitarian political movements. But the reverse influence undoubtedly holds—such developments have facilitated the growth of totalitarian politics, which logically completes the organized hierarchy of society. The assumption that industrialization promotes democracy is totally unwarranted. The relationships which industrialism demands, facilitates, and rewards with success are actually those of authority, subordination, specialization, and overall control —just the sort that characterize society at large when a totalitarian movement takes over politically. Totalitarianism in certain respects is simply the factory writ large.

Complementing this organizational trend in the totalitarian direction are certain psychological effects that stem from industrialization or from its organizational consequences. Old communities, old values, old loyalties are disrupted; work is overspecialized and one-sided; the individual is progressively alienated both from nature and from the natural society of his fellows. Isolated and frustrated, the modern individual becomes ripe for a movement which offers him an organized sanction for an outburst against the constraints of civilization. He is ready for an orgy of class, race, or national hatred.

The sheer scale of life as it has come to be lived in industrial societies makes it almost totalitarian by nature. People by the thousands find themselves engaged together in activities from manufacturing to education, where formerly they figured only in dozens or scores. Obviously the relations which earlier prevailed no longer suffice; organization is necessary, and control, of a minute sort never before thought necessary. Millions take part where only thousands used to be—in armies, in politics, in audiences for the spoken or printed word. The nature of what is said, performed, and printed cannot remain the same on such a vast scale. The phenomenon we are dealing with here is the "revolt of the masses" long ago discerned by Ortega y Gasset. Entering by the millions into all the complicated and refined activities that were worked out in the course of the development of civilization, the masses by their very numbers overwhelm the subtle values embodied in these higher realms. They exacerbate the damage by the fact that they retain their mass attitudes, the thinking and emotions which were appropriate only to their former condition as the mute multitude.

The mass man, according to this reasoning, is a natural totalitarian. The mass man, in Ortega's phrase, makes no demands on himself; he appreciates nothing, and has no critical power, while at the same time his influence has become decisive, through the sheer weight of the numbers in which he has invaded the upper regions of society. The mass man is a fertile subject for demagogy, and the might which he now represents offers the demagogue a ready road to the acquisition of power—totalitarian power. Totalitarianism, in this perspective, is the rebellion of the upsurging mass

man against civilized society, which he resents
both because it formerly dominated him and because it still holds up to him standards of accomplishment to which he cannot or will not
measure up.

Here is one of the roots of twentieth-century
violence. It is the violence of the mass man vent-
ing his frustrations in whatever direction he feels
them. Such consequences of the social and political
dominance of the masses and the mass mentality
are traceable in turn to industrialism. Industrialism has produced the foundation for totalitarianism, both directly by creating the technological
and organizational conditions for totalitarian rule,
and indirectly by encouraging a social psychology
—the revolt of the masses—which is favorable to
the emergence of a totalitarian movement.

With the social hegemony of the mass man
and the evolution of communications technology
in the present century, a new set of institutions
has acquired decisive political significance—the
media of mass communication. Much larger audiences can be reached, with ever greater impact (as
the field has been developed in succession by mass
journalism, radio, and television), and the mass-
minded audiences are far more amenable than
their predecessors to suggestion and control. These
audiences, in turn, are the decisive force in society
and politics: what they think is what the nation
thinks, for all practical purposes. Thus the channels of mass communication have become the
keys to a nation's mind and to its action as well,
entirely apart from any deliberate political effort
to establish such control.

Accompanying this accretion in the influence
which the mass media wield is the concentration
and simplification of the content of the media, a
development which is also encouraged by the

technological nature of the media. Everyone is tuned in to the nation-wide broadcast; scores of millions can hear and heed one voice. But fewer and fewer people contribute to the content of the media; and those who do, do so less and less as independent individuals, but rather as members of organizations. Opportunity to speak, perform, and print does not expand with the audience; dissemination of the word is so much wider that fewer voices can reach—and control—the greater audience. In turn, those fewer voices are dependent on the media of communication which give them their audience, and consequently they must heed the wishes of the still fewer individuals who control the media.

Still another significant development is a change in the content of what is communicated over the mass media. It ceases to be straightforward interpersonal communication of information and ideas in a context of presumed rationality. More and more, communication is used to further a purpose not explicitly stated in the matter that is communicated; communication becomes advertising, promotion, propaganda, whether under private or governmental aegis. Such promotion of ulterior objectives, moreover, proceeds in a new context where the basic assumption is the irrationality of the audience. The audience is to be manipulated, through the use of verbal symbols and the emotional responses which these can evoke. Those who control and utilize the channels of communication are, in the phrase which Stalin eagerly borrowed from Maxim Gorky, the "engineers of men's minds." Under Communism, and elsewhere as well, society is close to the dictatorship of the symbol-manipulators.

The social trends of a totalitarian nature may facilitate the establishment of totalitarian government, and they are always put to use by the political totalitarians after they come to power. Such use naturally accentuates the original totalitarian trends. Nevertheless, these trends of social totalitarianism are not identical with political totalitarianism. The political totalitarians—the revolutionaries who establish a totalitarian government —may stand quite apart from the trends of social totalitarianism, if they hail from countries where this aspect of modernity has not taken hold, or they may even react violently against such trends. Their motives depend on their circumstances, which are basically different in East and West.

3 EASTERN AND WESTERN TOTALITARIANISM

While the main features of totalitarianism are standard everywhere, the circumstances giving rise to totalitarian dictatorships are quite different in different parts of the world. We shall distinguish two basic types of totalitarianism—one characteristic of Western Europe, generically known as Fascism, and the other essentially a phenomenon of the East. Eastern totalitarianism is synonymous with Communism. Many of the Eastern nationalist movements have created dictatorial regimes, but none has approached the intensity of real totalitarianism. The Japanese military regime of the 1930's and '40's, arising under circumstances which were economically like those of Western Europe but culturally different, should probably be considered an intermediate case between Eastern nationalism and Western Fascism.

To understand Communism as the totalitarianism of the East, we must first clarify the nature of the recent Fascist totalitarian regimes in the West. While the makeup of the Fascist movements was complex, they had one striking theme—the political and psychological alienation of large numbers of people from the developments that were transpiring around them. Fascism embraced elements from every social level: the "Lumpenproletariat"—the dregs of society, the unemployed, the "ragged proletariat" that this German expression sums up; together with much of the lower middle class—the petty bourgeoisie caught between the millstones of big labor and big business; and together with these the biggest industrialists and property owners, as well as traditionalists of all descriptions. Fascism is a catchall, promising all things to all men, but it has a common denominator. All its supporters are among the alienated—i.e., the "proletariat," if we take it in its broad sense to mean all those elements of a population who are alienated from the existing order of things—who find that the course which society is taking is leaving them behind or destroying the position which they have hitherto enjoyed.

Western totalitarianism is a movement of the people who are alienated because they are opposed to, or sloughed off by, the prevailing social totalitarian trends. It is moreover a movement of the alienated which repudiates the great prophet of the alienated, Karl Marx. But when the alienated take power, paradoxically, they immediately accelerate the centralizing and totalitarian trends to which they were apparently opposed, and translate the social trend overtly into the political sphere.

Communism in the East is likewise a revolt of the alienated, but in the East alienation has occurred among different groups and for different

reasons. As we have already seen, the alienated
people first in Russia and subsequently in Asia
were those who were aroused by the beginnings of
Westernization into an attitude toward the West
which was one of simultaneous admiration and
resentment. Toward their own ruling groups they
grew violently antagonistic, as these rulers failed
either to resist the West or to model themselves
successfully upon it. As the theoretical inspiration
for these Eastern revolutionaries nothing was so
well-adapted as Western doctrines of criticism
and protest, in the acceptance of which the Eastern revolutionaries could simultaneously endorse
Western standards of achievement and repudiate
existing Western governments and influence. Eastern totalitarianism—i.e., Communism—is a movement primarily of the alienated educated class
who, in the name of a Western prophet of revolution, aspire through the seizure of power and
totalitarian rule both to Westernize their countries and to win a position of independent power
from which they can defy and even humble the
West.

Meanwhile, where Communism had a foothold
in the West, it was losing its revolutionary élan.
After the mid-1930's, the Communist movements
of the West had for all practical purposes become
reformist rather than revolutionary in regard to
the internal affairs of their respective states.
Where it has survived as a significant force—
mainly in France and Italy—Communism is a
movement not of the alienated fringes but of the
organized working class (together with numerous
intellectuals). The Western Communist parties
are not so much a revolutionary repudiation of
the social order as they are a pressure group
within the existing society, without the total repu-

diation of the whole trend of society and its ethic which characterizes both Western Fascism and Russian and Asian Communism. Only with their reformist and nationalist pose dating from the Popular Front have the Communists been able to hold any significant strength in the West. Western Communists are going the way of the Social-Democratic Marxists before them. They would have sooner, were it not for the doctrinal restraints exercised by Muscovite control—which remains a decisive force in shaping the international attitudes of the Western Communists.

Even where Communists are in power in East-Central Europe, the weakening of Russian control permits the Western reformist tendency to assert itself, as the events in Poland after the crisis of 1956 clearly showed. Communism in the West is totalitarian only in the measure that the Russian model of Eastern Communism is enforced upon it, and it seriously threatens to impose totalitarian rule only insofar as it is backed up by the national might of Soviet Russia. Only thanks to constant Russian pressure was Communist totalitarianism implanted in Eastern Europe, where direct Russian police and military control together with periodic purging of the local Communist leadership was required to maintain the desired degree of totalitarian rule on the Russian model. Yugoslav Communism is still authoritarian, under the personal dictatorship of Tito, but the structure of totalitarian control both in economics and in intellectual life was largely dismantled after the break with the Soviet bloc in 1948. Elsewhere in Eastern Europe, the relaxation of Russian control attendant upon de-Stalinization in 1956 was sufficient to permit an acute crisis, as anti-Russian and anti-totalitarian forces raised their heads in Poland

and Hungary, and in Poland scored some slight successes.

In one respect, Eastern totalitarianism—both Communist and non-Communist—is more consistent than the Fascist version. Eastern totalitarianism is typically a movement of intellectuals who are alienated both from their own national traditions and from those of the West. They are rebelling against national backwardness and subservience, against colonial rule or native regimes which seem to be tools of Western "imperialism." They have been characteristically inclined toward totalitarian means of attaining their objective. Communism, even where it is not yet in power, is a movement in accord with the general trends of social totalitarianism that characterize the modern world, rather than a defiant outburst like Fascism, trying to reject these trends though actually accentuating them. Accordingly, it is possible for Eastern totalitarianism to be much more rational than Western totalitarianism, which is psychologically less in accord with the totalitarian social trend of the present era and hence relies more heavily on virulent and aggressive nationalism and its offshoot in the barbarities of racism. Communism in the East is a deliberate revolutionary application of totalitarianism, both social and political, in an effort to modernize a non-European society. Even so, the political side of Communism still bears the character of the alienated non-European intelligentsia: they wish to use the totalitarian social trend, but they are not part of it. The Communist party men are, no more than their Fascist counterparts, to be identified with the technically competent managerial class.

The contrast between Communism and Fas-

cism with respect to their causes and in relation
to the trend of social totalitarianism is sharp indeed. Fascism is a disease of modern Western
society in crisis. The more modern the society, the
worse the attack of the disease, as the German
case testifies. The Fascists react against the modern trend, but when they come to power they take
command over it, accommodate themselves to it,
and exaggerate it. Communism is a malady of
antiquated (and usually non-Western) society in
crisis—a crisis of modernization and Westernization. The more disruptive the condition of change,
the more likely the revolutionary and totalitarian
outcome. The more stressful the conditions such a
movement confronts, the more likely is it to take a
Communist form. The Eastern Communists are reacting against Westernization, but not just backward; they are determined to take the process of
Westernization in their own hands, apply Western
forms of social totalitarianism to accelerate its
completion, and thus win equality and independence vis-à-vis the West. In Russia and particularly in China, the flux of revolution has allowed
the realization of the most extreme totalitarian
trends in modern society.

Both Western and Eastern totalitarianism are
intimately connected with nationalism. Totalitarianism demands that society be welded into an
integral whole, and given the prevailing division
of the modern world into national states, the nation is the social unit within which the totalitarian goal is usually pursued. The two tendencies
stimulate each other: nationalist emotion, especially when frustrated, contributes to the forces of

political totalitarianism, and the totalitarian regime encourages nationalism in order to make itself more acceptable. Outright international conflict, especially when it results in defeat, is a powerful factor contributing to totalitarianism, and totalitarian regimes, inherently committed to revising the relations which prevail between their respective countries and the rest of the world, inevitably accentuate international tension. The logical end point is total control internally and a total struggle with outside forces.

Here, however, we must consider an important difference in the nationalisms of Eastern and Western totalitarianism. Nationalism has been a much more central and critical aspect of the Fascist regimes than of the Communist. Nationalism was the doctrinal core of the Fascist movements, and was much more intensely felt by them. It supplied the emotional cement that united the alienated but otherwise disparate groups which made up the Fascist following. Shocks to sensitive nationalism were the specific reason for Fascism's success in Germany and Italy.

Eastern nationalism is far less a phenomenon of psychopathology than the madness of the Western totalitarians, which culminated in the insane butchery perpetrated by the Nazis under the banner of "Aryan" racial supremacy. Eastern nationalism is more rational, more concrete, and more justifiable, even though the consequences have been upsetting to the West. Eastern nationalism, including that of the Communists, is the nationalism of people who have experienced what has been from their national point of view the long indignity of alien—i.e., Western—superiority, sometimes politically and always culturally and economically.

The Eastern nationalist espouses totalitarianism for the perfectly rational purpose of quickly taking advantage of the achievements of European civilization in order to end direct or indirect domination by the West and to put his country on a level of independent equality with the West.

The Eastern totalitarian, apart from the political methods which he adopts, has a much more positive attitude toward both the rationalist and democratic elements of the European tradition than does the Western totalitarian, who is reacting irrationally against such ideas. The Easterner is not opposed to Western ideals and achievement—quite the contrary: he complains only that the West does not live up to them, especially in its dealings with the rest of the world. It is no accident that Marxism, as a Western doctrine of social and political criticism, presuming both rationalist and democratic values, has become the official inspiration for the major totalitarian movement of the East.

As far as its literal doctrine is concerned, Communism is much closer to the Western rationalist and democratic tradition, and to the present liberal exponents of the latter, than it is to Fascism. Here, of course, is a major source of confusion: Communism's doctrinal cloak has made the movement reasonably respectable in the eyes of many people who would instantly reject the unabashed politics of totalitarianism. In reality, the dictatorial governmental structure and the manipulation of doctrine for political purposes are basic features of both kinds of totalitarianism. Nevertheless, doctrine has governed attitudes, negative as well as positive. The wide gulf between their doctrinal sources and their way of thinking

has set the Fascists and Communists against each
other most of the time despite the similarity of
their political systems and methods.

4 THE TOTALITARIAN
DICTATORSHIP

Totalitarianism in power is the product of specific political movements and specific political
situations; it is the work of people who want total
power, strive for it, and when the time is ripe,
seize it. Revolution naturally leads to dictatorship,
if the upheaval is sufficiently pronounced. Revolutionary dictatorship under twentieth-century conditions (of industrialism, political technique, and
mass communication, together with the social
change represented by the emergence of the mass
man) is *ipso facto* totalitarian dictatorship. To put
this differently, revolutionary outbreaks in our
century offer the chance of success to totalitarian
movements, which have independently been generated by twentieth-century social strains. The
totalitarians have qualities of organization and
ruthlessness which, under the circumstances of
revolutionary tumult, make them invincible. Overt
totalitarianism appears only in revolutionary
situations, however, because only then can the
totalitarian movements seize their advantage and
impose themselves on an inherently unwilling
population.

Totalitarianism is not based on the political
domination of society by one ruling class. On the
contrary, the naturally dominant stratum—in
modern society, the managers and experts who direct all the institutions of social totalitarianism—
is strictly subordinated to the political totalitarians who come from the ranks of the alienated.

Once in power, the political totalitarians take over the channels of communication and command, and become the agitators and propagandists, spies and censors. This function, the party people exercising it, and their dominant political position, are almost identical in Western and Eastern totalitarianism. The function, of course, is also present in the Western countries where the totalitarian trends are not overt and political—it is the function of the promoters, advertisers and public relations men, and opinion mobilizers, the symbol manipulators, and the investigators and snoopers of all sorts.

Both Fascist and Communist regimes experience serious tension between the ruling group of political totalitarians and the natural ruling class of managers and technicians. The party men defensively assert a capricious authority which is naturally resented by the technical people. As a result, the totalitarian party experiences recurring trouble in getting the desired performance from its industrial administrators, its armies, the churches, cultural and scientific specialists, everyone who has a particular technical or organizational speciality.

The tension between the politicans and the specialists has been particularly evident in the Communist world since the death of Stalin. Malenkov seems to have catered to the managerial group when he was in power from 1953 to 1955, while Khrushchev's victories over Malenkov in 1955 and over the whole group led by Malenkov, Molotov, and Kaganovich in 1957 had overtones of the politicians' supremacy over the specialists. During the crisis of 1956 there were signal attempts, universally supported by intellectual circles, to throw off the stifling ideological controls imposed by the

party officials—notably in Eastern Europe and in
China. The ferment of 1956 even affected the USSR,
but there the principle of party supremacy had
been so long established that it was comparatively
easy to maintain discipline among the elite. Still,
the tension remains. The Stalinist totalitarians—
the party hacks—fear the challenge of the technically competent people in every field, and are
prepared to fight to retain their status. Here, perhaps, is material for a resurgence of the totalitarian spirit in the Communist world.

The nub of the totalitarian system—the institution through which the "totalitarian class" of
alienated rebels establishes and maintains its
sway—is the party. The totalitarian party is a
phenomenon entirely different from the political
parties of Western parliamentary systems. In the
preparatory stages it amounts to the union of the
alienated, giving organizational expression to their
determination to seize power and reconstruct the
social order on the lines of a past or future utopia.
To know the characteristic form of the totalitarian party we need only recall our discussion of
Lenin's doctrine of the party organization. Lenin's
Bolshevik Party was the first clearly formed totalitarian movement, with its determination to push
for revolutionary change as an end in itself, its
principles of discipline and doctrinal unanimity,
and the implied proposition, realized during the
revolution, that no other political organization
nor any other political voice was to be tolerated.
The Bolshevik Party became the model for the
Fascists and non-European nationalists, however
much they disagreed with the Bolsheviks in doctrinal terms. Not only the Communists, but the

Nazis, the Italian Fascists, the Rumanian Iron
Guard, the Spanish Falange, the Argentine Pero-
nistas, the Chinese Kuomintang, the Turkish Republican People's Party under Ataturk, the "Imperial Rule Assistance Association" in prewar
Japan, potentially Nasser's National Union in
Egypt, Nkrumah's Convention People's Party in
Ghana, Toure's Democratic Party in Guinea, have
been Leninist movements to one degree or another.
This is true both in organizational structure (combining features of an army and a religious order)
and in the function of total control to which the
party aspires.

The party plays a decisive role in the establishment and operation of every totalitarian regime.
One of the most economical definitions of totalitarianism is simply rule by a single party (of the
Leninist type) which excludes all rivals and sets
up unlimited controls over the population, whatever the ideology and presumed objectives of the
movement may be. The victory of the totalitarian
party means that the alienated individuals who
make up its most active element are no longer
alienated—they now rule *over* the social system
which either because of its organizational trend or
because of its backwardness, had previously thrust
them *aside*. The party and its success permit the
alienated to transcend their alienation and to act
out their hopes, fears, and frustrations as they
violently impose their will upon the population.

The party as an institution is responsible for
some of the major distinctions between modern
totalitarianism and old-fashioned despotism. The
old despotism rests on top of society and sup-
presses its opponents, but it has no way to reach
down to the masses to organize, control, and mobilize them. This the totalitarian party does do—it

integrates the whole population into the regime, leaves no proletariat alienated, allows no room for opposition even to exist.

Rule by a totalitarian party is always accompanied by a political police and all the machinery of repression and terror. In part this follows logically from one-party rule: if opposition is not to be tolerated, it has to be suppressed. If the mass communications in the hands of the totalitarian regime are to be one hundred percent effective, the private circulation of opposing views must be prevented. But the motivation of political terror under totalitarianism appears to go much deeper than these mechanical considerations of sustaining the monopoly of political power and public discussion. The totalitarians behave violently because they *like* violence. No doubt one of the main reasons for people's devoting themselves to the cause of a totalitarian revolutionary movement is to win the opportunity for violently asserting themselves against the people or institutions which they feel have balked them. Suppression of opposition thoughts is likewise impelled by more than considerations of maintaining power; the totalitarians are psychologically too vulnerable to tolerate criticism. Finally, totalitarianism requires a scapegoat, an internal but alien group which is outlawed and made the target for artificial mass hatred and unlimited repression. The nature of the proscribed group can vary widely—kulaks, Communists, agents of imperialism, wreckers, Jews, Zionists, nudists, Freudians, Jehovah's Witnesses, corrupters of the national morality however defined. Nevertheless, the significance of the proscription and the treatment of the condemned group are basically the same in every case. The totalitarian regime must maintain a constant state of internal war. If the enemy does not exist, he must be invented.

Together with the party there is one other political feature which all totalitarian regimes have in common. They have all been dominated by individual dictators. In every case, one man was the creator and director of the movement, organizer of the party, and dictator of the country after the party took power. All non-Communist totalitarian movements have lived and died with a single leader. Only in the Soviet case have there been interludes of group dictatorship—the two episodes of collective leadership following the deaths of the individual dictators Lenin and Stalin.

The influence of the individual leader can be enormous in creating and shaping a totalitarian regime. If the leader of a revolutionary movement is circumspect, he may be able to forestall political totalitarianism altogether. Jawaharlal Nehru is a case in point. Where a movement does become totalitarian its traits are inseparable from the character of the leader, as the roles of Lenin and Stalin in shaping Communism indicate.

Usually the totalitarian dictator answers to Max Weber's description of the "charismatic" leader, who has the mysterious power to attract enthusiastic popular support, to lift people out of their accustomed routines, and to rearrange the institutions of society. The Communist historian Pokrovsky wrote of Lenin, "There was above all, his enormous capacity to see to the root of things, a capacity which finally awakened in me a sort of superstitious feeling. . . . I ceased to dispute and submitted to Lenin even if logic told me that one should act otherwise." If, like Stalin, the leader does not have a magnetic personality by nature, "charisma" can be created artifically through the devices of propaganda like the "build-up" of politicians which the mass media can accomplish even in democratic states. Without determined individual leadership of a charismatic nature the forces of totalitarianism would remain formless, and fail to win power.

While leadership and conspiracy are essential to a successful totalitarian revolution, they are not sufficient to explain the success of totalitarianism in particular countries. We have already surveyed the complexities of revolution. A society must be seriously disturbed before a major revolutionary outbreak can materialize. Conspirators aplenty are available under such circumstances; the country is ready to follow any of them; and it is a matter of chance as much as anything else that a particular revolutionary leader succeeds. On the other hand victory of a particular leader with certain ideas can shape the future decisively. Such were Lenin's victory in Russia in October 1917, and Stalin's in the mid-1920's.

We have already analyzed the totalitarian pressures of the situation in which Stalin found himself. The Soviet government was a postrevolutionary, quasi-dictatorial regime, and by that very fact subject to the totalitarian trend common to all modern revolutionary governments. The Communist Party was totalitarian in its organizational principles, and was in the difficult position of an extreme revolutionary group clinging to power after its time had past. Above all, the problems of Russian backwardness and the tasks of industrial development gave a practical appeal to the totalitarian alternative.

The evidence of Stalin's opinions and actions—

his dislike for anyone with marked ability, originality, or prestige, and his progressively heightened mania for self-justification and self-glorifi-
cation—is strongly suggestive of the Western
totalitarian rebel, the alienated individual who re-
acts against the world of organized experts with a
counterorganization that puts itself at the head
of the totalitarian trend. A typical totalitarian
party man, Stalin was thus a natural rallying point
for those like him in the organization, who had no
particular competence except the ability and
willingness to wield power and take command
over the experts.

Stalin's personal success and his historical accomplishments are opposite sides of the same
coin. He became dictator because he identified
himself with the totalitarian trend in all its aspects. Becoming dictator, he guided Russia's destiny toward totalitarianism in the extreme. Stalin
the man was the catalytic agent that determined
the permanent shape which all the situational
forces would give to the Communist movement in
Russia and abroad.

Communism can be brought into clear focus as
an example of political totalitarianism. The totalitarian regimes are the products of revolutionary
movements, succeeding as a result of different
circumstances, but all imposing their rule through
similar twentieth-century devices of political organization and technique. Communism, like its
Fascist and nationalist counterparts, is a movement of inspired leadership and disciplined following, organized in the party; violence and terror are
practiced habitually. Total control within the national unit, and successful defiance or domination
of foreign forces, are standard objectives. Finally,
the totalitarian regimes have in common an at-

tachment to their respective doctrines, the inculcation of which demands the subjection of the nation to rigorous and pervasive thought controls. To
this, the mental aspect of totalitarianism, we now
turn.

5 THOUGHT CONTROL

A definite, official, and exclusive doctrine is
characteristic of practically all of the totalitarian
movements. Enforced unanimity in all channels of
public communication is a *sine qua non* of totalitarianism. This unanimity is not just the negative
product of censorship and control. Typically, the
totalitarian regime does not confine itself to re-
straining ideas which it does not like, but actively
creates and imposes the positive content of everything that it wants the nation to think.

The totalitarian doctrine may rest on an elaborate and originally sophisticated philosophical
system, as Communism uses the ideas of Hegel and
Marx, or it may be an illogical mélange of myths
and hatreds such as the Nazis subscribed to. Whatever its form, and whether it is coherent or not,
the doctrine is obligatory for every citizen under
the totalitarian regime. The imposition of doctrine
is the mental counterpart of totalitarian political
rule. No activity having even the slightest doctrinal implications can escape from the control
which the totalitarian orthodoxy demands.

In the emotional intensity which it evokes
among its believers, and in the fervor with which
it is enforced, the totalitarian doctrine is closely
analogous to religious faith, especially as faith was
felt in centuries past, when it was a matter of
salvation or damnation and toleration was un-

thinkable. The appearance of a militant and exclusive faith, under modern conditions, can hardly avoid implications of political totalitarianism. In the Communist case, the influences worked both ways; there has been a powerful interaction between Communism as militant doctrine and Communism as a totalitarian political movement.

We have observed that totalitarian leaders and governments exhibit a passion for self-justification. They absolutely cannot tolerate the slightest criticism. They are totally lacking in a sense of humor—that treasure among the political graces. The totalitarian cannot laugh at himself. Perhaps this is why he becomes a totalitarian.

The premise that all criticism, opposition, and political jokes must be suppressed is of course not new. Among the earliest achievements of civilization were the establishment of *lèse-majesté* and blasphemy as capital offenses. In this respect the behavior of the totalitarians is only a relapse harking back to the standards of earlier despots. The difference in modern totalitarianism is just here, in the fact that it is a *relapse*. Ancient despotism, and even regimes as recent as seventeenth-century absolute monarchy, could rely on tradition for the positive doctrines which would uphold the authority of the state. They were therefore able to confine their active interference to the repression of attacks on the tradition. Negative controls were enough. Modern totalitarianism is trying to *create* a tradition to uphold its authority, and moreover must do this under circumstances where the educated circles of the population have become used to making up their own minds. The whole modern tradition of independent and critical thought has to be uprooted, and a new doctrine which justifies the regime has to be implanted positively.

Faced with these formidable difficulties, the totalitarians have usually reacted by setting their doctrinal sights even higher. It is not enough, apparently, to assert that the government and the leader *do not* make mistakes; the leader is declared to be infallible—he *cannot* make mistakes. Hence, merely to question whether such and such an action is mistaken constitutes an assault upon the proclaimed sanctity of the leader, a mortal offense against the faith.

The leader's claim that he can never be wrong (possibly sugared, as it was by Stalin, with assurances that he was not being "dogmatic") has serious consequences. It is because of this, and this alone, that the totalitarians are compelled to resort to the rewriting of history and the suppression of the past wherever it embarrasses the present policies or pretensions of the dictator. The claim also leads to embarrassing difficulties with the totalitarian doctrine itself when, as may often happen, it gets in the way of what the leader wants to do. The upshot is that the doctrine, like everything else, is subjected to the will of the leader. Doctrine is treated with reinterpretation. Doctrine, like history, is made to say what the leader wants it to say, to mean what he says it means, and nothing more.

The pressures to rewrite history and reinterpret doctrine were particularly strong in Soviet Russia because of the ups and downs of the revolutionary wave which the ruling Communist Party was nervously riding. Holding power, the Communist Party ran into exceptional difficulties in justifying itself in terms of its own original revolutionary doctrine. The situation was particularly acute under Stalin after 1929, with the country under a postrevolutionary dictatorship and entering the postrevolutionary conservative shift (the Soviet "Restoration"). A revolutionary doctrine had to be restated so as to rationalize and justify a counter-revolutionary regime. The consequent stresses were enormous—and it is probably not just coincidence that the Great Purge occurred at precisely this point.

Here we see how the pressures for thought control, most extreme in the Soviet case, were compounded. The totalitarians want to suppress criticism and opposition; they have to root out habits of free thought and substitute a rigid orthodoxy; they insist on total justification of themselves through their doctrine, and claim infallibility. This requires historical and doctrinal manipulation that makes them all the more liable to criticism. They are all the while trying to bridge ever-widening gaps between doctrine and reality. Every step adds its weight to the need for thought control, and the very measures of control themselves require further justification and further control. There is no logical stopping point short of total indoctrination: the party, with one will, shall be the nation's only mind.

The year 1929, when Stalin assumed unchallenged power over Soviet political life, marks the decisive turning point in the development of totalitarianism in Russia. Organized opposition and public exchange of political opinion (confined to Communist Party ranks since about 1920) had come to an end. The great efforts at government-directed social change—collectivization of the peasants and intensive industrialization—were being launched. Finally, the authority of the party to control every sphere of life and thought was being boldly asserted.

Prior to 1929, the Communist Party leaders had not followed up the implications of their political position to claim total power over all fields of thought. Their position was rather on the order of the old autocracies; they were content with negative action against overtly antigovernmental political talk. Both Lenin and Trotsky expressed a certain self-restraint when it came to party incursions into such areas as the arts. Party-line history, while violently opinionated, was not widely subjected to gross factual distortion until Stalin began to bend the record to his own advantage during his struggle with the Trotskyist Opposition.

The totalitarianism which Stalin put into practice after 1929 demanded an unlimited extension of party controls over thought. There was no logical escape from this, nor would the personality of the dictator permit any. Justification of the regime required total control. Total control in turn required further justification, which locked the monolith into position. Stalin gave his endorsement to those Communist theoreticians who asserted that none but "proletarian" ideas could have validity—while "proletarian" was defined as being imbued with "party spirit" and serving the political objectives of the party. From this time on, everything that was said or done was subjected to overriding standards of political judgment. Anything that failed to conform to the party's standards of propriety and usefulness—anything from economics to aesthetics to education—was condemned as "bourgeois" and hence counterrevolutionary. In every important field of thought the machinery and doctrine of party control were perfected. Then these controls were put to work, from 1934 on, to condemn most of what the revolution had stood for, and to cultivate, in the name of the revolution, the traditionalist thought and policy which the government, as a postrevolutionary dictatorship, liked or thought expedient.

Thought control does have its limits, though they stem not from any sense of proper restraint on the part of the totalitarian regimes. The limits are of a practical nature, which even under conditions of instantaneous mass communication prevent the complete realization of the ideal of total control. A regime which has worked its way through the ups and downs of revolution is inclined to make doctrine its servant rather than its master. When doctrine begins to interfere with tangible accomplishments in any field, ranging anywhere from foreign policy to the control of juvenile delinquency, controls will be relaxed or the doctrine will be reinterpreted to conform to whatever policy is found most opportune. Notable recent adjustments of this nature in Russia were the rejection in 1950 of the Marxian linguistic theory expounded by N. Y. Marr, and the dethronement of the anti-Mendelian geneticist Lysenko after Stalin's death.

A much broader limitation on thought control is sheer boredom, admittedly a pervasive problem in Russia and Eastern Europe and a serious obstacle to the hopes of the Communist regimes to implant positive belief. Indeed, the entire system of belief, as Soviet experience has shown, is likely to lose its vitality and dry up into a set of ritualistic formulae, which everyone knows he must

314 Communism as Totalitarianism

mouth, but which not many take seriously. The effect of control is likely to be the absence of any ideas at all. This still leaves the totalitarian regime vulnerable. The stifling effect of control creates an underlying hunger for ideas and foreign contacts, which is ready to assert itself as a profoundly subversive influence at any time when the system of control may be relaxed. This effect could be observed in Russia and even more in Eastern Europe following the effort of the Soviet regime to cleanse itself of the taint of Stalinism in 1956. Short of permanent mass hypnosis, which no one has yet developed, there seems to be no way for totalitarian regimes to surmount the problem of controlling the human mind.

9 Communism as a Faith

We have at length established the main
forces which have contributed to the shaping of
Communism, and have analyzed the basic political
and social forms which distinguish the Communist
system. We have not, however, fully accounted for
the spirit, the emotions, and the loyalties that have
sustained and fed the Communist movement. The
completion of our analysis requires the application
of one final perspective, in which we shall assess
Communism as a unique movement of nonreligious
religion.

Communism is often defined as a "secular religion." As an organized system of belief with a
definite group consciousness and missionary spirit,
Communism displays obvious social and psychological parallels with the familiar supernatural
faiths, though the deep philosophical differences
must not be lost sight of. The relationship of Communism to religion can best be explained by con-
ceiving of a broader category of "faith movements," which includes as subtypes the strictly
religious movements on the one hand and the
militant nonreligious faith represented by Communism on the other.

315

1 THE PATTERN OF FAITH MOVEMENTS

Comparative treatment of faith movements encounters the same difficulty as the analysis of the great revolutions and totalitarianism—there are too few cases from which to generalize reliably. It is impossible to decide with any certainty what the essential features of the general phenomenon are, as against the individual variations. Furthermore, as with political upheavals, it is necessary to distinguish between the major organized faith movements, and those forms of religious life which do not involve a systematic effort to expand, win converts, and impose a doctrine wherever possible. Christianity and Islam are the most obvious examples of universalistic expansionist religious movements, and it is to them, and to Christianity above all, that we shall make primary reference in discussing Communism as a faith. Other religions of roughly comparable nature are Zoroastrianism and Buddhism. Primitive animism, its polytheistic refinement in the Graeco-Roman religion, and communal faiths such as Hinduism and Judaism do not fall within the type under consideration here; they are systems of religious practice, but not "movements." Confucianism, while never a movement in the mass sense, does parallel Communism as a more or less secular political ideology.

The common denominator of the various faith movements is the fact that they do "move," and have a distinctive drive and self-consciousness. They arise in an established society, as the result of the deliberate effort of an individual or group to expound and propagate new teachings. Initially, they defy tradition. Essential to the new faiths is the element of protest, which may be moral or political, or more often both in combination. Oppressed classes or nationalities, as well as guilt-stricken members of the dominant group, are among the people who turn to the new faith as a vehicle to express their rejection of the old order. The faiths, in their origins, are closely related to revolution: a new religion is revolutionary, and the modern revolutions have had strong religious overtones. Both are rooted in a moralistic protest against the injustice and immorality of the *ancien régime*.

It is the conviction that the old regime is evil or degenerate (whatever influences may lead to this conviction), rather than specific doctrinal propositions and theories, that gives the religious or political enthusiasts their great energy. Indeed, the question whether such a protest movement takes the form of religious deviation or political revolution seems to be largely a matter of the epoch in which it occurs. Prior to modern times, the religious form was the usual one, whereas in the last two centuries particularly, it has been the political form. The English Puritan Revolution of the seventeenth century was a transitional case, simultaneously a religious schism and a political upheaval.

The more recent instances of total revolution, though they have not been linked to religious faith in the specific sense, have invariably involved both organizational and doctrinal attacks on the existing system of belief. The French revolutionaries were bent on the creation of a national church, and from there the extremists went on to contrive their cult of the goddess of reason. The Russian Revolution was militantly anti-Christian in its active phases. The Chinese Communist revolution has undertaken to demolish the Confucian tradi-

tion of thousands of years' standing. In every case
the new revolutionary ethic demands the repudiation of the old morality and the old belief, as false,
corrupt, reactionary. Political revolution and religious schism are the two sides of the same coin.
Both are likely to cut across national boundaries,
and in an epoch of upheaval in politics and faith
such as the present, they leave little chance for
unruffled peace in the world.

While faith movements may begin as strictly
moral rebellions, almost invariably they become
organized and acquire a political aspect. The separation of church and state is only a rather shaky
accomplishment of the modern West; much more
normal, in the experience of human history, has
been the effort to combine or coördinate religion
and government and use each for maintaining the
authority of the other. If only to put an end to
persecution, faith movements have been driven to
seize political power. The devices of persecution
are then readily turned against their former employers. Nothing succeeds like success, which
brings opportunists in droves clambering onto the
bandwagon. The movement which begins as an
idealist revolt soon becomes primarily attractive as
a system for acquiring, exercising, or propitiating
the powers of government. The persecuted sect of
yesterday is today's state religion.

The dynamic faith movements are universalistic. They proclaim the truth for all men, and
hope to carry their word everywhere. Their missionary fervor is unbounded. They move readily
through an existing political entity, as did Christianity through the Roman Empire during the first
three centuries A.D. When they assume governmental power they may strike aggressively to expand the limits of their spiritual and temporal em-

pires concurrently. Peripheral peoples and those lacking strongly developed faiths of their own are readily incorporated into the world of the new expanding faith, which confronts them with a power both political and intellectual that they are unable to resist. This can be seen readily in the expansion of any of the major faiths. It is well illustrated both by the spread of Christianity into northern and eastern Europe in the Middle Ages, and by the expansion of Communism westward and eastward from Soviet Russia. Except for serious geographical obstacles, the only thing that seems able to stop the expansion of a militant faith is another faith.

Political success, welcome as it may be, has untoward consequences for the faith. With the natural desire to hold the positions it has conquered, the movement acquires the responsibilities, in whole or in part, of governing and organizing the life of society. In spite of itself the movement is profoundly transformed, as a band of hunted rebels becomes a ruling bureaucracy. As a social institution the successful movement comes to resemble the old order more than the protesting sect from which it sprang. The course of development is closely analogous to that observed in the process of revolution; in either case, political revolution or religious upheaval, success rapidly causes the new movement to lose its original apocalyptic fervor and utopian idealism, and a conservative trend sets in.

This inevitable conflict between theory and practice has a profound impact on the movement. To borrow Karl Mannheim's formula, a "utopia" is transformed into an "ideology"—the ideas which inspire a rebellion are converted into a system for rationalizing and defending the new status quo.

Meanwhile the trend toward conservatism and reconciliation with the world as it has been prompts new dissident sects to speak out in the original spirit of the faith. It becomes necessary for those in authority to spike such embarrassing use of the doctrine. An official interpretation of the belief is laid down and enjoined upon all believers. Doctrine is converted into dogma, whose acceptance is enforced with all the compelling power available to the state church and the church-state. As the psychoanalyst Theodore Reik puts it, "Dogma arises as a reactive phenomenon, reacting against heresy . . .; it is born of the defensive battle against doubt."

After the new faith has become stabilized in power, doctrine ceases, by and large, to be an active inspiration for the powers-that-be in their day-to-day activity. The function of doctrine becomes less that of guidance and more that of justification of things as they are or as the authorities wish to make them. To make doctrine serve this purpose a pattern of manipulative techniques is developed, to which we can apply the generic term "scholasticism." In this frame of mind, thought is not empirical but authority-bound. Justification for present action or custom is sought by culling and reinterpreting the scriptural canon for the appropriate literal sanction, while the spirit of the prophets of the faith may be evaded altogether. Lenin once protested, apropos of this, the tendency to convert dead revolutionaries into "harmless icons," to assuage the masses and at the same time to dull the revolutionary sense. He hardly expected the same to happen to himself.

In the long view, the alternation of reforming fervor and bureaucratic self-justification seems to be an inherent and inescapable feature of human

history. Max Weber's conception of the polar at-
tractions of "charisma" and "bureaucracy"—the
disruption produced by emotion-stimulating leadership, and the complacent stability of routine—
aptly illuminates the process. Puritan fervor and
moral earnestness cannot be sustained indefinitely;
the contrary human impulses will intrude themselves into any movement, however exalted its
original professions. By the same token, no matter
how far the doctrine of the faith may be com-
promised in practice, the moral elements in the
system retain their power to inspire new protests
in the name of the original spirit of the movement.
Every faith, once established, seems destined for
an endless tug-of-war between the compromisers
and the reformers, the realists and the utopians.

2 COMMUNISM AS A FAITH MOVEMENT

Like the other faith movements to which it is
related, Communism began as a movement of the
oppressed or disaffected. These rebels rejected the
existing order with great moral indignation, embraced the teachings of certain prophets (Marx
and Engels), and commenced to organize and
proselytize with the aim of putting their ideals into
practice. Once achieving power, the movement
made its compromises with social reality, and
placed its reliance on authority and dogma to keep
its believers in line.

As was the case with Christianity, Islam, and
Buddhism, the center of gravity of the Marxist
movement shifted from its original locale to a
partially alien culture—from Western Europe to
Russia. Russia did not conform to the literal speci-
fication of prior industrial development which

Marxist doctrine laid down for its own success.
This, however, was no obstacle to embracing
Marxism as a faith, but one of the reasons for it.
For all its effort to be scientific, Marxism failed to
comprehend its own nature and its appeal as a
faith. It did not succeed for the reasons given in
the Marxist doctrine, i.e., as the political response
of the proletarians of the most industrialized
countries, but for reasons of faith, in those parts
of the world where conditions made the faith
attractive.

The development of an idea, a set of teachings,
a political philosophy, or the pronouncements of
a prophet, into a faith movement, cannot be explained on the basis of the original doctrine alone.
The conditions for the development of a new faith
—just as for a revolution—must be sought in the
society in which the faith develops. The particular
prophet with his doctrine is only the catalytic
agent, setting off the reaction when the required
ingredients are present—i.e., when the traditional
way of life is challenged and cannot answer, when
it ceases to make sense. In the modern era, such
breakdown of traditional patterns is most commonly to be found in the areas where Western
European influences come suddenly into contact
with an established civilization and throw it into
a chaos of flux and change. As we have already
noted at length, the impact of Westernization and
modernization on the East is the basic factor making the ground ready for the Communist faith.

The fideistic character of Marxism as the Communists profess it is the result of a gradual development, connected with the shift of locale eastward. The Marxist movement in Russia became
much more of a faith than it had ever been in
Western Europe, where it was shedding its fideistic

character altogether by the time of the Russian Revolution. Eastern conditions impelled people to Marxism for reasons of faith and caused the propositions of Marxism to be recast on more fideistic lines. The only material consequence of this adoption of a logically inapplicable doctrine was to accentuate the difficulty of protecting the faith against free-thinking critics after the Communists came to power. The defense of the Marxist faith in Russia implied additional need for censorship and thought control. The faith is even more irrational and psychologically demanding in the scene of its more recent success, Communist China.

A remarkable, if irreverent, parallel can be drawn between the respective developmental steps of Christianity and Communism: each has its early prophets, its doctrinally revered founder, its successful revolutionary leaders, its notorious heretics, and finally its established bureaucratic rulers. Thus:

The Hebrew prophets	The Utopian Socialists
Jesus	Marx
St. Paul	Lenin (doctrinally)
Constantine	Lenin (powerwise)
Arius	Trotsky
Papacy	Stalin and his successors

We may note the deviators—Jews and Social Democrats—who shared the teachings of the prophets but refused to go along in the development of the new faith. To carry the analogy even further, Titoism in its relationship to the Communist movement is remarkably like the Protestant Reformation, a national rebellion against the universal authority, based on an alleged appeal to the original spirit of the movement. Perhaps there is something of a Counter Reformation in the post-Stalin reforms in Soviet Russia. The analogy fails, of course, when the time span is considered; the development of Communism (and of Islam) was greatly accelerated by comparison with the centuries which Christianity required to go through the process.

Communism in power displays all the traits of a state religion. The old rebels become the new oppressors, doctrine becomes orthodoxy, and heresy is hunted down with all the inquisitorial resources at the disposal of the state machinery. The natural missionary fervor of the faith is supplemented, wherever possible, by the aggressive expansion of the state which embodies the faith. As in early Islam, especially, the Communist drives for imperial expansion and propagation of the faith become inextricably combined. Where one such expanding faith encounters another system of equal vitality, the result is a state of religious war. The clash of Communism and the West resembles the hostility between Islam and Christianity, intermittently bitter but in the end indecisive.

The analogy between Communism and religion goes further than the simple pattern of a protest movement gaining power and imposing its new orthodoxy. The manner and system of Communist belief, as distinct from the specific tenets of the faith, are characteristically those of a universalistic religion. Fervor, dogmatism, fanaticism, dedication, atonement, martyrdom can all be observed in the Communist movement. The Communist Party, like a church, provides the institutional context for feeling and expressing common belief. Belief supplies a sense of group identity, and defines the group toward which loyalty is affirmed. Belief at the same time provides and defines the enemy—the unbelievers, "reactionaries" and "counterrevolutionaries," meaning, in the Communist jargon, those who reject the beliefs and professions of the movement.

So far does the character of the Communist's allegiance to the movement correspond to religious commitment that we can even observe the intensely emotional phenomenon of religious conversion when individuals are persuaded to embrace the Communist faith. "Brainwashing" is the vivid term the Chinese have given us to describe this process, which is naturally distasteful for the adversaries of the faith to contemplate. Force, pressure, and ulterior inducements are commonly present in Communist proselytizing as they were in the expansive phases of the major universalistic religions. Where Communism is in power, the compulsory aspect of the process is clearly uppermost; nonetheless we must not underestimate the appeal of Communism to the person who needs a new faith.

As with other faiths, the emotional appeal of Communism as a faith does not depend primarily on the specific items of belief which may be professed at any given time. The attraction of the movement is above all that of a dynamic force with which the individual can identify himself and whose fortunes he can make his own: it is the appeal of the movement as a going concern. Consequently, the movement is able to hold the loyalty of most of its following through the most drastic changes of form and of doctrine, which in the Communist case have come with bewildering ra-

pidity. It is significant that the defections caused
by changes in the party line have occurred largely
among the leadership and some of the intellectual
hangers-on—people who have joined for more
conscious and more specifically doctrinal reasons
—while the mass membership, especially in countries where the party is strong, has been kept remarkably well in line. To the really committed individual, the movement supplies the purposes and
values around which he orients himself and which
he cannot dispense with. For the true believer,
excommunication is a fate worse than death. That
this is literally true is shown in the 1938 show-trial
plea of Nikolai Bukharin, the Right-Communist
leader whom Stalin had removed from power in
1929: "When you ask yourself: 'If you must die,
what are you dying for?'—an absolutely black
vacuity suddenly rises before you with startling
vividness. There was nothing to die for, if one
wanted to die unrepented. And, on the contrary,
everything positive that glistens in the Soviet
Union acquires new dimensions in a man's mind.
This in the end disarmed me completely and led
me to bend my knees before the party and the
country. And when you ask yourself: 'Very well,
suppose you do not die; suppose by some miracle
you remain alive, again what for? Isolated from
everybody, an enemy of the people, in an inhuman
position, completely isolated from everything that
constitutes the essence of life. . . .' And at once
the same reply arises. . . . The result is the complete internal moral victory of the USSR over its
kneeling opponents. . . ."

The religious character of Communism does
not end with the psychology of the movement and

its appeal. The very foundations of Marxian doctrine have a religious coloration, which cannot be accounted for other than as the incorporation of basic assumptions and modes of thought bequeathed by the whole Judeo-Christian tradition. Here we find the roots of that crucial aspect of the Marxian theory of history which, rather than following logically from the rest, seems to be imported from outside—the apocalyptic hope that the next revolutionary upheaval will put an end to all the agonizing travails of human history and usher in the bliss of the classless society. Marx's theory of history is only St. Augustine's in modern dress, as the following parallel suggests:

Garden of Eden	Primitive communism
The Fall	Onset of class societies and class struggle
The Earthly City	Class society (feudalism, capitalism)
The Day of Judgment	The proletarian revolution
The City of God	Communism

Some writers have gone even further to suggest that Marx's faith in the proletariat expressed the idea of the "chosen people," on the model of the Jews, though this is perhaps far-fetched. The essential point is that the Marxian theory of history, and through it the Communist movement, involve certain eschatological assumptions—a mythology about beginnings and endings—which are 1) derived from Christianity, and 2) indispensable ingredients in the emotional appeal of the movement. Communism as a faith is Christianity brought down to earth. It is easy to suspect, though proof is lacking, that these religious habits of Communism were reinforced in Russia by the deep heritage of the Russian Orthodox Church, whose emotional impact is no doubt still not entirely lost upon the Russian Communists, much as they may profess their formal atheism. The Communist pattern of reasoning, despite their assertions to the contrary, is metaphysical in both the strict and derogatory senses. Communism does lack any reference to the supernatural, strictly speaking, but the "Dialectic" represents almost as much of a cosmic will as the vaguely metaphorical theism of liberal Protestantism, not to mention the ethereal abstractionism of some schools of Hindu and Buddhist thought.

Like any systematic religion, Communism has an elaborate theology. The mode of thinking which prevails in the movement is religious: it involves unquestionable truths, the proper profession of faith, the observance of liturgical rigor in the formulae of belief and ritual. Under Stalin, Marxist-Leninist doctrine was codified into a set body of principles, with official explanations of all questions. Thought proceeded from fixed categories; then hairs would be split in applying these arbitrary concepts to reality. The way to understanding man and society was primarily restricted to the study of the holy books, the works of Marx and Lenin (and later Stalin's own). A full-blown Communist Scholasticism was the result.

Communist categories of thought are Platonic or "realist" (in the medieval sense)—the idea or abstract concept is accorded a degree of reality above that of the specific, tangible instance or event. Thus, "History," "Revolution," "Proletariat," "Socialism," are more real and more important in the Communist mind than are specific events, revolutions, workers, or socialist policies. When the general rule and the specific instance do not jibe, the specific instance is dismissed as defective or transitional; the prior idea is never questioned. Two examples may show how this mentality operates in various spheres. In 1921, when opposition to Lenin's leadership was widespread among the Communist workers in Russia, the party leaders asserted that criticism of the "party of the proletariat" merely proved that the worker-critics were really unproletarian. In 1934, when Stalin wished to repudiate the socialist policy of equalitarianism, his technique was to assert that equalitarianism was not socialist, and was unworthy of a Marxist. In every case, the term "proletarian" or "socialist" is adhered to rigidly, while the content is freely manipulated, and general ideas of revolutionary virtue are of little avail when it comes to the fate of the particular individual who gets in the way of the machine.

There is one further respect in which Communism partakes of the essential character of a religious movement—in the moral realm. All the major religions involve codes of conduct and norms of social life which initially represent a protest against what is considered the corruption and depravity of the previous social order. Religions, like revolutions, have an essential puritanical element. Observance of the new code is much more than a matter of rational conviction about the merits of the particular norms in question—it stems from, and supports, the passionate sense of righteousness. The sense of righteousness, attached to a particular organization or social entity, is the emotional foundation of the phenomenon of faith movements which we are here analyzing.

Communism, despite what seem to be incon-
sistencies in the political methods which it permits, is actually an extremely moral—or moralistic
—movement. Moral protest is deeply imbedded in
Marxism. The source of Marxist revolutionary
fervor is moral indignation over the condition of
the worker under capitalism—shackled in "wage-
slavery," dehumanized by the machine. Capitalism
is rejected on grounds more moral than economic
—it is evil because it rests on "the exploitation of
man by man." The phrase is still current among
Communists, the pinnacle of their moral sense.
The profit motive and the mores of a commercial
society are condemned on the grounds that they
asphyxiate the human spirit—both of the rulers
and the ruled. Morally speaking, Marxism and
Communism are zealously antimaterialist. More
evil has probably accrued to Communism through
its excess of moralism than through any deficiency
on this score. Many of the greatest crimes of
history, after all, have been committed in the name
of some great principle of faith. Too much zeal for
a particular moral objective begets the unmatched
cruelty of the fanatic, who disregards the mundane
decencies of workaday humaneness in favor of
some lofty principle which he will enforce at the
expense of every other human value.

When the new faith succeeds and begins to take
root, it must undergo a serious crisis of transformation in the moral sphere as well as in the doctrinal. The system of morality must be converted
from an expression of protest into a buttress for
the newly established social order—it must be
changed from a radical ethic to a conservative
one. Communism accomplished this alteration in
two ways—in part through reinterpretation of the
ethic, and in part through the actual substitution

of conservative norms for earlier radical aspirations. Such latter-day moralism concentrates puritanically on peccadilloes like sex, jazz, and loafing, while the real crimes of social injustice receive pious sanction. This was one of the most striking aspects of the conservative phase in Stalin's Russia. Once the teeth of revolutionary doctrine had been pulled or filed down, the moral tenets of the faith could be employed to good effect in rationalizing the new order in both domestic and foreign propaganda.

3 THE PARTY AND THE FAITH

In the institutional respect, as in the psychological, Communism's distinctive nature places it clearly in the religious category. The Communist Party is a sect, with beliefs, mission, priesthood, and hierarchy. It is a church, in the very obvious sense that it is the institutionalization of belief. It is the organization which bears and propagates the faith. In power, it assumes the exclusive right to teach belief. Within the party one belief—the official version of Marxism-Leninism—has a doctrinal monopoly: one church, one faith.

In actual structure and compass the Communist Party is midway between a church and a priesthood. As originally conceived by Lenin, it was much closer to the latter—he preferred to keep the organization small, tightly disciplined, and totally dedicated to the revolutionary cause. The conquest of power in Russia introduced profound changes in the nature of the party. It became a mass organization, numbering over half a million by 1921, as ambitious individuals of every sort flocked into the party's ranks. This growth, coupled with the postrevolutionary disorganization of the country, imposed mammoth organizational tasks upon the party. To meet this need, Lenin's earlier organizational precepts were elaborated upon, producing a new institution within the party, the "apparatus" of professional party organization men. This, of course, was the basis of Stalin's ascent to personal dictatorship.

The party "apparatus" under Stalin took the place of Lenin's narrow party in filling the Leninist requirement for a hard core of dedicated and disciplined individuals. This group is more strictly like a priesthood. The analogy is closer in Chinese Communism, however, where the "cadres" of party organization men are subjected to a special indoctrination so strenuous as almost to efface individual belief and personality altogether. (The Chinese subject their own men to the psychological breakdown techniques that the Russians reserve for prisoners whom they want to confess.) Simple party membership, on the other hand, has progressively lost distinctive meaning, and in Russia is now merely the usual concomitant of social status in the bureaucratic pyramid (extending to about three percent of the population in the USSR at present). Certain auxiliary organs bring the party's leadership and doctrinal guidance to bear on much wider circles of the population. These are the "transmission belts"—trade unions, local government, educational institutions, etc.—used to carry the holy word to the rank-and-file citizen. The party's own recruiting base, the Communist Youth Organization (Komsomol), is itself very broad, with a membership larger than that of the party, and including roughly a third to half of the population in the eligible age group. Through its auxiliary organizations the party encompasses everyone in the Communist society, and is no less universal than an old-fashioned state church. No one is free to disbelieve in the party or its mission.

For the faithful, the party organization is inseparable from the faith. The party is the vehicle of truth, and nothing can be correct outside the party or against the party. Trotsky tried to defend himself in 1924 by declaring, "None of us wishes or is able to be right against his party. The party in the last analysis is always right, because the party is the sole historical instrument given to the proletariat for the solution of its basic problems."

The origin of this close bond between the organization and the belief is to be found in Lenin's idea of the role of ideology in the revolutionary struggle. "Without a revolutionary theory there can be no revolutionary movement," Lenin wrote in 1902. "To belittle the socialist ideology *in any way, to turn away from it in the slightest degree* means to strengthen bourgeois ideology." By implication this betrayed a lack of faith in Marxian determinism, a fear that the proletarian revolution would not take care of itself. Such a fear was appropriate enough under the circumstances, since the "vanguard of the proletariat" was not led by proletarians but by disaffected intellectuals, and was advancing without the benefit of the extensive economic development that was supposed to precede the establishment of socialism. Lenin was quite right in arguing that a "proletarian" revolution in Russia depended on a pure and narrow doctrine and the maintenance of tight discipline among the believers. Only if doctrine welded them together as a dedicated sect could the Bolsheviks successfully impose their will upon the stream of history.

The justification, formulated then and adhered to since, of the demand for close conformity to the party line is drawn from Marxism, and represents yet another contribution of the parent philosophy to the Communist faith. The argument derives from the Marxian proposition that political and social theories are deeply influenced by the social and economic structure and reflect their authors' positions in relation to the class struggle. Corresponding to the proletarian movement there can be only one proletarian creed, an exclusive proletarian truth. The party knows the interests of the proletariat best, better than any individual proletarian; therefore what the party says has to be right. With this, Marx's attempt at a sophisticated sociology of ideas becomes a crude defense of dogmatism. Correct proletarian ideology is what the leader says it is, and every nonconforming notion is liable to be expunged as a "bourgeois" intrusion. An effort to explain thought has been converted into a reason for controlling thought.

The arrogant assertion of exclusive truth has gone further. All nonproletarian thought stands condemned because it represents lost causes and hence cannot look objective reality in the face. Only "proletarian" thought is considered to be in tune with the inevitable trend of events, and hence objectively valid. Under Stalin, in the early 1930's, this reasoning was pushed even further: anything which momentarily aided the historical progress of the so-called party of the proletariat (and this meant, in effect, Stalin's policies), was held to be objectively true and commendable. Anything which obstructed the proletarian cause (as Stalin interpreted it) was a work of the devil. Thus originated the doctrine of *partiinost* or "party spirit," the guiding principle in Soviet thought control ever since.

Stalinist Communism is distinguished by the

complete correspondence of belief and organization. Party and doctrine mutually reinforce each other in a system of unprecedented mental rigor. The monopolistic controls of the party enforce the exclusive faith. The faith justifies and buttresses the controls of the party. There is no room for relaxation without threatening the very fundamentals of the system. None of the reforms granted by Khrushchev has allowed any real relaxation in the doctrinal authority of the party. On the contrary, the official press in every Communist country has not ceased to echo the themes of cultural and doctrinal discipline—"guidance by the party," "Communist education," "ideological battle against the influence of bourgeois culture," etc.

The shifts of line as the Communist leaders adapt their dogma to changing realities create chronic difficulties in maintaining the unquestioning belief which they insist upon within the movement. In the long run, however, the changes of line and the disciplinary action which they necessitate actually make belief firmer, at least among the hard core of Communist old-timers. The changing line has forced Communists either to quit the movement or to surrender their own minds and their own judgments altogether. At one time or another every conceivable alternative of policy has been under condemnation by Moscow. Contrary to the official pretense, there has been no straight center path which the properly inspired Communist could follow on his own. It is literally impossible for anyone to have remained in a Communist party for any length of time without being forced on some occasion to repudiate his own beliefs and feelings in favor of the new line commanded by the party. After this has happened once or twice the party has an unshakable hold

over the member, who must permanently justify
the correctness of the party in his own mind, or
face up to the stupid and erroneous self-abnega-
tion he committed when he followed the earlier
zigzags. To defend the ego which he has committed to the party, the Communist becomes
fanatically loyal. This is undoubtedly one of the
chief mechanisms in the maintenance of discipline
in the international Communist movement.

Sometimes the grip of orthodoxy is actually
strengthened by defeats and persecution. This
clearly happened among the Bolsheviks between
the Revolution of 1905 and World War I, and
also during the Civil War. It is also possible that
Stalin contributed to Muscovite discipline in the
international Communist movement by the defeats and embarrassments which his tactics occasioned. Such setbacks often drove the independent-minded out of the movement in disgust
and reduced the rest of the party membership to
a demoralized and embittered herd who would
follow the movement no matter where in order to
justify to themselves their own commitment to it.

The relation which the party bears toward
Communist doctrine goes far to explain the role
which the party has assumed in Communist society. Like an exclusive church, the party organization has the responsibility for upholding faith
and morals for the entire population. The party
has had to develop an elaborate machinery for
inculcating and enforcing correct belief. Everything that is printed, everything that is taught,
everything that is said in public, must not only
conform to the party line but also be positively
aimed, in the last analysis, to further the power
and policies of the party and its leadership. The
party has taken upon itself the task of laying

down standards for literally every field of human thought and endeavor. There is no area of thought or behavior that has any claim in principle to be exempt from these controls. Everything that is said or done is supposed to be under the control of the party and to advance the political interests of the party. Communism means the primacy of politics—it has become a secular theocracy.

The Communist subjection of all thought and action to narrowly political standards and objectives stems from the thinking of the Russian radical intellectuals of the third quarter of the nineteenth century. Trying to express their rebelliousness in a fashion that would pass the censors, individuals like Chernyshevsky and Pisarev made literary and artistic criticism the vehicle of a revolutionary credo, and began judging the arts as political weapons. The Bolsheviks, following in this tradition, took it as self-evident that every human activity had political significance and that everything should be judged primarily in terms of its impact on the political struggle.

Complementing this politicalization of all aspects of life is the desperate and deadly seriousness which Communism has injected into human affairs. There is no room for humor, no room for frivolity—these are presumably qualities which may disarm the "proletarian" cause in the face of the capitalist threat. The Bolshevik Party resembles the old religious orders of fighting monks—political ascetics, in this case, who put aside all regard for their personal safety and fortunes, in order that the cause may prosper. Until a decade after the revolution the ascetic ideal was embodied in the "party maximum" that prevented any party member from drawing more

than a worker's wage. The party still demands
that everyone devote himself to the serious business of contributing to the Communist cause. This
schoolmasterish state of mind appears to have
survived with scarcely diminished strength the
decline of ideological fervor and the crisis of the
repudiation of Stalin. On the surface of Communist
society, at least, an astringent puritanism still
prevails.

4 THE COMMUNIST APPEAL

The central role of the party organization in
the Communist movement makes it easy to over-
look some of the less mechanical aspects of the
movement and to regard it as a dehumanized
monstrosity. To many anti-Communists the Communist movement seems like the work of individuals as far removed from ordinary humanity
as men from Mars, who appear from nowhere to
do the work of the devil when circumstances
permit. We must remind ourselves of the obvious
fact that Communists are human beings who for
various combinations of motives, some of the
worst and some of the best, have been attracted
into the Communist movement and persuaded to
devote their utmost efforts to its success. In certain places at critical times Communism is able
to win the allegiance of some of the most talented,
energetic, and persevering individuals, who then
give the Communist revolutionary movement superior qualities of organization, discipline, dedication, and action—as well as a fanatical ruthlessness that can be called into play at any time.

The Communist movement exercises at least
four distinct kinds of attraction. The most obvious,
and the one naturally stressed by the Communists

themselves, because of its conformity with the postulates of historical materialism, is the promise of alleviating economic discontent. The conviction that Communist leadership best serves their material interests and gives them the most to hope for is far and away the most influential factor in holding the allegiance of the working class in France and Italy, as it was for a large segment of the German workers before Hitler, and indeed for a majority of the Russian proletariat at the time of the revolution.

From the religious aspect of the movement, two major forms of the Communist appeal stem— the psychological and the moral. The moral appeal has been of outstanding importance in attracting nonproletarian adherents to the movement— notably the Russian founders of the Bolshevik Party. These people are impelled on primarily ethical grounds to repudiate the societies in which they live, above all because of the injustices of exploitation and class privilege. They embrace the revolutionary goal as an end in itself, an Armageddon, an essential and inevitable purgation of the sins of class society. The historical materialism of Marxism provided an admirable rationalization for this attitude, by assuring the revolutionaries that their cause was absolutely right and irresistible. But doctrine did not create the motive force. The moral element in Communism dramatizes the affinity of the movement both with other revolutionary movements and with religious movements of the traditional supernatural form. The moral element is the key link, the common denominator between religion and revolution.

While intelligible in itself as a motive based on rational conviction, the moral factor in Communism is closely related to what we may term the psychological or irrational attraction of the movement. Intense moral repudiation of the existing order usually stems from an individual's effort to establish identity with a larger group. The individual, particularly as exemplified by many European proletarians and by intellectuals around the world, loses the sense of a community of values with the society in which he lives, and finds himself fundamentally alienated. Movements of political radicalism offer an escape from such alienation by constructing an ideal image of society or idealizing some segment of society and living for the day of total change.

The Communist movement provides a special haven for the alienated. It is a cause to identify with, a group to belong to, and can offer an embittered and rootless individual an opportunity to remake his personality around the movement. The powerful influence of this type of attraction has been made abundantly familiar by case after case of ex-Communist confession, especially among Americans. The social bond of the party has often caused disillusioned members to prolong their membership in the face of repeated insults to their self-respect dealt them by the party disciplinarians and the zigzagging party line. In many cases, psychological ties to the movement are so strong that breaking them can be the crisis of a lifetime.

The political effect of this irrational group-solidarity kind of appeal has sometimes been exaggerated. In the first place, while it certainly helps keep members active in the party, it is far less important in bringing them in to begin with. It is the moral disaffection from the existing social order, more than anything else, that makes a person ready for Communism. Moscow reaps the advantage simply by default—there are usually no serious radical alternatives, and the conservatives' incessant identification of radicalism and Communism makes the decision for the radically inclined individual a simple one. He goes to the most widely advertised vehicle of radical protest.

Radically alienated and uprooted individuals have played a disproportionate role in the Communist movement, as indeed they have in the establishment and propagation of any new faith. The history of Communism is replete with people from Lenin on—not to mention Marx—who, like missionaries, have devoted themselves to the movement. They are driving egoists, rarely enjoying normal family life or employment, always on the move to organize, agitate, and impose themselves on their followers, ascetic in their habits and paranoid in their attitudes. They sacrifice themselves in the service of their fanaticism, and then must sustain their dogmatic belief to justify the sacrifices that they have made. They represent the antithesis of the settled bourgeois life, but they also contrast starkly with the Communist officialdom which develops after the party has consolidated its power or even where the party is in opposition but successful and bureaucratized (as in France and Italy). Psychologically speaking, nothing spoils a revolutionary like success, and this is why we can never expect a successful revolutionary movement to sustain its original spirit.

The psychological appeal of Communism depends most of all on the degree of individual and group alienation in a given society. Such circumstances have prevailed most intensely, in the present century, in the societies of the East, and it follows that the psychological appeal of Communism is particularly strong and distinctive there. Communism is ready to enter the scene as a new religion wherever the old religion is particularly moribund—notably in the Far East, among the anticlericals of Latin Europe, and among the intelligentsia in some parts of the Moslem world. Viewed in a broader perspective, this is not surprising. Most major religious overturns have occurred in situations of acculturation and alienation, where outside influences undermine the old faith, or where the ossification of a society's old beliefs invites new ideas from without.

A fourth element in the Communist appeal, in addition to the economic, psychological, and moral, is the strictly intellectual attraction of Marxist-Leninist doctrine. Communism has a coherent body of belief, a systematic philosophy that covers everything, relates everything to everything else, and purports to explain everything. At the same time, the character of Communism as an intellectual authority leaves no room whatsoever for doubt. Communism is one way to fill the intellectual gap in a society that is tired of its skepticism. Here again, Marxian philosophy plays an important role. Marxism is a towering landmark in systematic speculative thought, and for all its biases and inaccuracies remains the most internally coherent and yet comprehensive system of social thought ever produced. It is a monument to the age of the scientific and evolutionary mentality—a sort of Summa Theologica of the nineteenth century.

Like any religion, Communism takes as its starting point the prevailing assumptions of the age. In the Communist case, these center around science, which is invoked as the last word to sanctify the propositions of Communism, just as the supernatural premises and mysticism of the past necessarily had to be incorporated in the old strictly religious movements. Thus the philosophical difference between the traditional religions and Communism is more apparent than real. What they do with their philosophical premises is basically the same—they create a binding faith and elaborate a doctrine in order to sustain the authority of whatever original postulates the movement is committed to. The Communist believes in Science, but in an unscientific way; Communism makes mystical deities out of Marx's efforts to grasp the truth about human history. Given such a context, any serious attempt within the Communist movement to create a genuine social science is anathema, just as Galileo's discoveries were to the Catholic Church.

Despite these dogmatic limitations, Communism is markedly superior as a modern intellectual system to many of its ideological competitors—anachronistic laissez-faire liberalism or reactionary nationalism in Europe, or the confused revolutionary nationalism whose several variants have been sweeping the East. In places as widely separated as Guatemala, Syria, and Malaya, Communism has distinguished itself by a coherent, pseudoscientific, ardently revolutionary appeal to otherwise confused and floundering intellectuals and quasi-intellectuals. Such people in these areas find Communism the most effective and intellectually articulate faith available.

In the Communist faith there is much that partakes of the religious mentality of earlier days. Communism surpasses most of the conventional religions of the present day in the intensity of its emotional fervor. The party member characteristically exhibits complete devotion to the movement. He has faith in the infallibility of the party, its leaders, and its line. He exhibits what Marx might have called a fetishism of the party. Questioning of the party's revealed truth evokes furious wrath—not because the dissent is wrong, but because it is evil. The true believer makes such a condemnatory judgment because he cannot stand to hear that his faith may be based on an arbitrary and unfounded choice.

The circumstances of joining and leaving the movement are particularly revealing about the religious character of Communism. Typically, accession to the movement is accompanied by a conversion experience; the new recruit "sees the light" and the whole world suddenly looks different when it is viewed through the lenses of faith. When a member breaks with the movement, his former associates regard it as an act of unspeakable treachery—it is apostasy. This intense feeling about adherence to the movement certainly contributes to the psychological difficulty which individuals experience when they try to leave it, and accordingly buttresses the discipline which the leaders of the movement are able to exercise.

The evidence of religious devotion, dedication, and dogmatism within the Communist movement, in Russia and abroad, is overwhelming. It extends even to cases of masochistic guilt-atonement, when a self-effacing privileged individual turns against the society that has given him unfair advantage over his fellows, and joins the Communist underground. The movement has no shortage of martyrs, and makes the most of them. It has even succeeded in making martyrs of some of its members who were victims of the excesses of the movement itself—the Stalinist officials who were liquidated by their boss in 1938, and posthumously depurged in 1956. The atonement complex no doubt has contributed to the facility with which the movement both in Russia and abroad has been built up on disciplinarian lines: guilt-ridden intellectuals, feeling still more guilty because they are nonproletarians in a proletarian movement, allow themselves to submit to the allegedly proletarian virtue of Leninist discipline. Loyalty to the movement supports the doctrine by excluding all doubt and all real criticism as the work of the counter-revolutionary devils. As long as genuine religious emotion is strong in the movement, even the most devasting doctrinal attacks upon it are unlikely to enjoy appreciable success. A decade of doctrinally well-founded Trotskyist polemics in the International served only to solidify the ranks of Moscow's loyal legions.

5 RELIGIOUS WAR

A major political function of fideistic belief, which Communism has in common with most major religions, is to define a struggle and an enemy. A state of religious war, active or latent, is the international or intergroup consequence of any militant faith. In the expansionist religions, the crusading spirit is inseparable from religious fervor, while religious emotion can hardly be kept at a high pitch without the challenge of the infidel, the heathen, or the heretic.

There are roughly three general forms of group strife engendered by religion: friction as a militant faith spreads through a society where there is no comparable rival; a direct clash where two rival faiths collide; and the violence occasioned by a split in a faith movement and the efforts of each

offshoot to dominate the whole. We will consider
the impact of Communism from the point of view
of each of these three types of conflict.

Where no strong prior faith is involved, the
progress of a religious movement is not likely to be
marked by open warfare, though civil unrest and
persecution (of and by the new faith) naturally
accompany the social upheaval which the emergence of a new faith reflects and intensifies. We
can compare Communism in Western Europe and
America with the position of Christianity in the
Roman Empire in the first three centuries A.D. and
with Buddhism during its rise in the Far East—
all of them were looked upon with varying degrees
of enthusiasm, skepticism, or antipathy; sometimes persecuted (with varying degrees of effectiveness), sometimes tolerated; combated less on
grounds of faith than as a challenge to public
order and national security.

More properly speaking, religious war is the
conflict that occurs between competing faith
movements in the territories where they impinge
on one another and where they struggle for domination. The long history of warfare between the
Muslim world and Christendom is the most obvious
example of such a contest. The struggle is intermittently bitter, and a state of firm "peace" is
rarely reached. While fighting may not be continuous, the state of belligerent hostility on both
sides is relatively constant, and the best form that
relations can take in a situation like this is the
informal truce.

Here we have a remarkable likeness to the relationship between Communism where it is in
power (particularly Soviet Russia) and the non-
Communist world. Strong suspicion and a con-

viction of eternal enmity have marked both sides
ever since the Bolshevik Revolution. The cleavage
of the non-Communist world into Fascist and
anti-Fascist blocs and the alliances of the Second
World War temporarily glossed over the hostility
between the bearers of the Communist faith and
the adherents of the established order in the West,
but with the defeat of the Axis powers and the
greatly enhanced power of the Soviet Union after
1945, the conflict was bound to erupt again more
bitter than ever. Perhaps the most remarkable
aspect of the struggle was the fact that despite
the outbreak of fighting between adherents of the
two systems in many parts of the globe, general
war was avoided during the most acute phase of
hostility from 1948 to Stalin's death in 1953.

For portions of Western society the clash between the competing Communist and anti-Communist allegiances has a specifically religious
character. This is particularly true for the Catholic
Church, and as regards nations as a whole, for
the United States more than for Western Europe.
Religious antipathy is a major element in American anti-Communist emotion, and perhaps out-
weighs all other considerations taken together.
This may well explain why alarm over the Communist threat has reached much greater proportions in the United States than in any Western
European country, despite the exposed geographic
position of the latter.

There is another perspective of religious war
in which Communism can be viewed. By analogy
with the Reformation of the sixteenth century,
Communism can be considered the product of a
schism within Western civilization, where rival
groups have drawn antithetical conclusions from

their common cultural heritage, and have partitioned the Western world into zones where their respective faiths prevail.

An extended parallel can be drawn between the Reformation cleavage and the twentieth-century antagonism of the "bourgeois" and Communist powers. In both cases the initial rebellion (Luther's and Lenin's) provoked an equally vigorous counteraction—the Catholic Counter Reformation of the later sixteenth century, and in the recent case, the emergence of Fascism. From the point of view both of fifteenth-century humanism and of nineteenth-century liberalism, the revolutionary and counterrevolutionary movements are equally bad. Mutual counteraction causes violence, intolerance, and persecution to increase on both sides. The rupture of a civilization's unity of faith is the signal for invigorated faith and fanaticism on both sides of the schism.

The only escape from such a state of affairs seems to lie through mutual exhaustion in a stalemate, the subsiding of religious fervor, and the recognition that the religious issues dividing the respective camps have become either meaningless or politically unimportant. It is not unreasonable to expect a development of Communism and anti-Communism analogous to the seventeenth-century subordination of religion to politics and the religious toleration and indifference of the eighteenth century. Indeed, there have already been signs of such a tendency, beginning with the political mating of the two fanatic antagonists in 1939, and reappearing with the post-Stalin Soviet foreign policy of alliances with non-Communist but anti-Western nationalist movements.

We have already noted another application of

the Reformation analogy, to the Titoist revolt of Yugoslavia. As in sixteenth-century Christianity, a conflict over the conduct and power of Communism's Soviet center led to an international split in the movement and the formulation of significant doctrinal changes in the camp of the schismatics. Tito and his supporters took the stand that they were the true Marxist-Leninists, and that Stalin's Russia was marred by "bureaucratic degeneration." In 1955–56, Khrushchev tried to end the schism by appeasing the Titoist "Protestants" both in Yugoslavia and in the Eastern European satellites. His maneuver was a resounding failure. Communist schismatics remain in power in Yugoslavia, mutter behind the scenes in Poland, and had to be put down by a bloody "Counter-Reformation" in Hungary. Finally, a schism on the scale of the Rome-Constantinople split in Christianity is now opening up in the Communist world, with the growing evidence of political and doctrinal discord between Moscow and Peking.

6 THE TRANSFORMATION OF THE MOVEMENT AND THE FUNCTION OF DOCTRINE

The importance of doctrine to a faith movement does not lie in its literal terms. Its essential role, as the Communist experience shows very clearly, is to justify power, sustain group consciousness, and express the group's commitment to the faith. The followers of the faith embrace the doctrine not because it passes a particular test of metaphysical or historical truth, but because it conveys a sense of the exclusive possession of truth. The Communist is sure that he is right and that all his adversaries are wrong, even if the party line has just been reversed yesterday and will change again tomorrow—though it must be noted that some of the most extreme zigzags, notably the German-Soviet pact of 1939 and the posthumous dethronement of Stalin, have been hard for many comrades to take. Specific doctrines may come and go, but—barring the exceptional shock—the faith and the sense of orthodoxy remain.

In the early stages of a faith movement, doctrinal evolution is almost unconscious. It can be observed in the syncretism whereby most of the major religions have in the early stages of their growth incorporated all sorts of doctrinal elements from the peoples and areas which they absorbed into their orbits. Just as Islam, sweeping though the Byzantine Near East, came to resemble Christianity more than its own Arabian origins, just as Far Eastern Buddhism became more Chinese than Indian, Bolshevism became much more a Russian than a Western doctrine, in spite of the professed continuity of belief.

The leaders of a faith movement, once in power and confronted with major (in the Communist case, total) responsibility for organized social life, demand a different service from their doctrine. Where the original doctrine continues to play its inspirational role it threatens to become an embarrassment, as in the case of the Communist oppositionists who challenged, in the name of proletarian orthodoxy, both the correctness and the justification of what the Soviet leadership was doing. Such application of doctrine the leadership of the movement could not or would not tolerate. The further the process of reinterpreta-

tion went, the more violently heresy was condemned. The more the change in the doctrine, the
more obligatory belief was politically enforced and
the more dogmatic the whole system became.
Ideologists who did not conform to the requirements of scholasticism and Stalin-worship were
liquidated in a series of purges between 1930 and
1938, until the men were found who would give
Stalin the kind of totally contrived justification
he demanded.

The primary function of doctrine in the Soviet
Union and probably in most other Communist
states is self-justification for the leader or leaders.
The Communist regime depends heavily on the
doctrine for this service, and the leaders cannot
dispense with the faith even in their own minds.
The faith is upheld determinedly, even at the cost
of the crippling burden of thought control which
the minute enforcement of a totally unreal orthodoxy entails. The propaganda function of doctrine
is probably not as important for internal purposes
as is commonly supposed. While most of the Soviet
population accept the premises they are fed in
the official propaganda, not many become actively
enthused about it. In the East European satellites
a large proportion of the citizenry are still altogether anti-Communist in private. In Communism
gone conservative, the purpose of the endless
political indoctrination to which the people at the
more responsible levels are subjected is largely a
negative one—to keep people's political thinking
smothered under the official line, to stifle the development of a frame of mind that could support
independent criticism, and in general to keep people bored with politics and passively content with
the status quo. Indications are that the Soviet

regime has succeeded in achieving a general, if
passive, acceptance of its principles of rule, except
among a quiet minority of the intelligentsia.

Abroad, the propaganda function of doctrine
is considerably more important. The allegiance of
foreign Communists has depended in large measure on the maintenance of the terminological illusion that Soviet Russia is the beacon of their
hopes. While reinterpretation can be enjoined
upon the movement abroad, it is a much harder
process than it is within a state where the facilities
of totalitarian government are available, and
therefore abrupt changes of line always cause the
defection of some foreign sympathizers. A latent
tension remains in the discrepancy between Soviet
reality and the idealized image which inspires the
Communists abroad (or most of them, if the leaders are really cynical careerists).

In the relationship between the Communist
states and the outside world, doctrine has been
of central importance. The militaristic pattern
and spirit of Communist organization require for
their effective functioning a sense of conflict—
there has to be an enemy somewhere. As it becomes more difficult or less expedient to find
enemies at home, they must be sought abroad.
Communist doctrine serves the essential purpose
here of providing and defining the enemy—
capitalistic imperialism, at present.

Doctrine, finally, is an important element in the
system of totalitarian control. The organizational
essence of Communism here meshes with its character as a faith movement—discipline and belief
mutually reinforce one another, and each is required to maintain the rigid strength of the other.
Ideological standards of conformity are indispensable in establishing and upholding the authority

of the party in intellectual and cultural life in particular, and this is why such an intense effort has been made over the years to subject practically every field to the stifling and often ridiculous dictates of party doctrine.

The Communist faith suffers, as have all others, from the fact that the intensity and purity of belief cannot be kept at the highest pitch indefinitely. In the measure that the movement succeeds, wins power, eliminates competitors, and becomes bureaucratized, its motive fluid of genuine religious emotion and moral fervor ebbs away. The zeal of the true believer is supplanted by the personal ambition of the careerist and the jurisdictional jealousies of the bureaucrat. In Russia, the puritanism characteristic of any religious-revolutionary movement has steadily declined, though its imprint on the surface of things is still obvious. The doctrine, as far as Russian Communists are concerned, has changed from a "utopia" to an "ideology." The problem is no longer to eliminate opponents of the doctrine; instead, those who threaten to take the doctrine too seriously have to be restrained. The most articulate critics who privately challenge the official faith are those who style themselves "neo-Leninists."

The decay in Communist zeal was undoubtedly hastened by Stalin's dictatorship and the hypertrophy of control which came with it. Khrushchev's rule, with its relaxation of the Stalinist terror and its gestures of proletarian spirit, has possibly achieved a moderate revival of genuine Communist feeling, of course in its latter-day form with strong nationalist and industrialist content. Even with the worst of the dictatorship past, however, it is doubtful whether Communism can recover much intellectual and emotional vitality in Russia. It is a faith which does not appear to have great prospects for enduring as an inspiring force over the centuries, as have some of its rivals. Where an easing of the heavy hand of Muscovite control can allow some upsurge of vitality in the movement, it is likely to become so deviant that it escapes from the bounds of the present Communist faith altogether. In the long run, political-religious zeal and the organizational essentials of Communism do not appear to be compatible.

A tendency to accept things as they are is apparent even in the foreign Communist parties which are not in power, and the extreme twists to which the Soviets have subjected their ideals have not produced as much tension between the Mother Church and its branches as might be expected. The foreign parties have become less and less revolutionary, more and more "revisionist" (though that nasty word is naturally not accepted). Western Communists now get their sense of righteousness from a comfortable bourgeois morality, not from any really rebellious and independent moral standpoint.

There is one major exception to this trend of relaxation, and it is likely to be the main source of discord in the movement in the near future. This is Communist China, which represents the fruition of an independent revolutionary process that is still in a much earlier phase than Communism in Russia. The Chinese are still zealous and fanatic; their revolutionary emotion has climbed to a new peak, like that of the Stalinists after 1929. Revolutionary hatreds are still a driving force in China, in both internal and foreign policy. All this is now very embarrassing to the Russians,

who look with equal disfavor on the Chinese commune experiment and the Chinese readiness to
use force in international disputes.

The depletion of the emotional wellsprings of
faith has not and will not bring an end to the
Communist problem. Religious war and international conflict have had people at each other's
throats over sufficiently long periods to show that
recovery of the new faith from the first flush of
crusading zeal is no guarantee of peace. Indeed,
the post-zeal situation, when utopia has become
ideology, and when the revolutionary regime is
striving to maintain its doctrinal identity even
though it has ceased to care about the specific
content of doctrine, can be even more dangerous.
International and religious conflict are essential
to keep the population mobilized around the regime and its empty slogans. To cite a recent example, the Suez crisis of 1956 was successfully
manipulated to create an upsurge of genuine self-
righteous Soviet patriotism, which conveniently
shielded the Soviet regime from some of the moral
impact of the Hungarian repression.

There is nevertheless ground for optimism in
the decline of emotional fervor in the Communist
system. Leaders have or will come to the helm who
are accessible to rational argument and who will
more readily see when pragmatic interests cut
across the dictates of doctrine. The masses, be-
lieving only nominally, are already prepared to
accept new points of view, if only communication
from the outside can be achieved. We may hope
that the time will come—Poland is near it already
—when no one in the Communist system will really
care whether the literal doctrine is enforced or
not, and then the censorial rigors of theocracy can
give way. When this happens, we can finally ex-

pect the Communist leaders to act according to
the normal considerations of national interest and
international stability.

7 ENDURING COMMUNIST BELIEFS

In its basic doctrinal and organizational forms
the Communist movement has been fully evolved
and stabilized for two decades or more, except in
the Far East. Discounting the pretensions of the
party line, it is possible to state with fair com-
prehensiveness the actual substance of lasting
Communist belief. We have already encountered
most of the aspects of this belief in our previous
analysis, and it only remains for us here to sum
up the thinking of those persons in the Communist movement who are still fervent believers.

The institution of the Communist Party, as a
latter-day theocratic church, is still fundamental
in Communist thinking. True Communists can
conceive of no political order, no social activity,
apart from the guidance and control of the Communist Party. Communists assume that organization plus party control is enough to accomplish
any objective whatsoever. The party is monolithic,
exclusive, and infallible. There can be no dissent
outside it or inside it. Criticism must be confined
to the details of policy execution, and is particularly directed against individuals who attempt to
preserve their own intellectual integrity. There is
a complete taboo on public criticism of the top
leadership, and any fundamental disagreement
over policy is condemned as heresy—either "revisionism" on the right or "sectarianism" on the
left.

To be sure, the party's operations are graced
with elaborate democratic trappings, but the latter

are devoid of significance except at the very top
and the very bottom of the Soviet institutional
structure, where the central authority organizes
the rank and file as a check on the lower officialdom. Even under the collective leadership following the death of Stalin, there was no public exchange of conflicting opinions. In the public
pronouncements of the party's nominally sovereign Central Committee, not to speak of the party
congress, unanimity prevails absolutely. The leaders' very position in command of the state seems
to strike most Soviet citizens as evidence of both
their right and their ability to exercise the power
which they wield. This assumption, that governmental power is its own justification and no business of the man in the street, is not confined to
Russia; it appears widely in the non-Western parts
of the world and is, in fact, one of the major
obstacles to the progress of democratic government in many areas.

In economic life the Communist state reigns
supreme. Communism is totally committed to the
socialist pattern of governmental ownership of
the means of production, and in the USSR any
attempt at private trade or production actually
runs afoul the law as "speculation." A strong
moral condemnation of "the exploitation of man
by man" continues to be echoed with real conviction, though exploitation by the state has to be
borne in silence. Economic policy is guided by
what amounts to the moral priority of heavy industry, and the drive to catch up with the capitalist West in industrial development is relent-
lessly pushed by the Communist governments.
With the notable exception of Yugoslavia, the
Communist states are also committed to centralized state control and planning. State-run

industry has become so axiomatic that even anti-Communist émigrés and disaffected students almost unanimously defend it. Industrialism and its requirements have shaped Communist behavior to such an extent that the old socialistic protest about the dehumanizing and alienating effect of industrial life becomes a penetrating criticism of Communism itself. Needless to say, no such protests are allowed to be articulated in a Communist society, and the heritage of Marxism becomes a sort of ideological vaccination to shield industrialism from humanistic objections. In no other system is man as much a slave to the machine.

Culture, like economic life, in the Communist view is equally a subject for party control, though the actual effect of such discipline and organization is far more detrimental in intellectual life. Communism, like any dogmatic faith, accords the individual thinker no right to his own mind. He must always be subject to the authority of the party, which may correct his "errors" and guide his work toward the social purposes defined by the party.

The real Communist philosophy of society is the antithesis of individualist liberalism. Like the conservatism which animated most of the European opponents of the French Revolution, it presumes an essentially military mode of life, with ranks, discipline, and commands. The individual finds his justification only as a part subordinated to the whole. Private power and independent individual action in the political and economic realms are completely excluded. The same applies to the intellectual and cultural realm insofar as the Communists can enforce their controls. These are the enduring premises of a mature totalitarian system.

Communist leaders make much of what they call "Communist morality." This has several aspects, which in part sustain the totalitarian features of the system, but which are not altogether foreign to familiar "bourgeois" or Christian morality. Communist morality means in the first place a Victorian code of personal conduct—honesty, cleanliness, punctuality, and abstention from sexual irregularities. The Komsomol, which is charged with much of the enforcement in this moral realm, sometimes strikes the observer as a politicalized jamboree of overage boy scouts. Like most revolutions Communism is puritanical, and its puritanism was only partly relaxed in Stalin's counterrevolution. Moscow's night life still leaves a good deal to be desired from the standpoint of the average Western patron of evening entertainment. But apart from the inhibition of frivolity, there is a positive side to Communist morality, with its effort to inculcate a sense of social duty and solidarity. The state's interest here is obvious, but there is undoubtedly psychological strength in this emphasis. No one can feel left out—even if he wants to—and this may offset some of the tendency, evident in the West, for modern urban industrial life to isolate and atomize the individual.

The individual in Soviet society is the duty-bound executor of the state's commands. He is held strictly accountable for his shortcomings, while successful performance brings substantial individual rewards. Marxist assumptions to the contrary, social circumstances are not admitted as excuses for individual failings, as Stalin made clear when he put an end to the doctrine of "objective conditions." The psychology of the unconscious is also rejected. This is understandable: no ruling power can allow the blame to be placed on circumstances or forces for which the system

is responsible or for which the individual cannot
be held accountable. There is a natural tie between political conservatism and the philosophy
of individual moral responsibility, as there is between political radicalism and the notion that the
system, not the people, is to blame for what goes
wrong. The Communists have repudiated economic
and social determinism; now it is "survivals of
capitalism in people's consciousness," like the
temptations of Satan in ages past, to which con-
traventions of the moral code are attributed. The
Soviet citizen is free, presumably, to choose between good and evil, and if he chooses what the
regime regards as evil he is punished accordingly.

Metaphysically, Communism sticks firmly to
the letter of dialectical materialism. Religion,
while tolerated if it doesn't involve international
alignments, is impeded by lack of personnel and
buildings, and is subject to continuous disparage-
ment in the schools and the press. The Communist
atheists protest too much; one wonders how free
they are from religious questions and doubts.
Natural science, on the other hand, is a deity
worshiped more ardently in the Communist orbit
than anywhere else in the world. Education has a
high priority, with a primarily scientific and
technological content. In form, Communist theo-
rizing is strong on philosophical abstractions, but
the overwhelmingly practical and technical emphasis in the Communist educational system
shows what they are really interested in.

Most of the real fervor in Communism concerns the relation of the Communist movement
to the rest of the world, and specifically its challenge to capitalism and to the alliance of democratic powers led by the United States. The
emotions in this competition have long since

transcended the old terms of the world proletarian revolution; they are now primarily a matter of nationalism or supernationalism, in which the two super-powers mobilize their allies and preach their respective ideologies while maneuvering to maximize advantage and minimize risk in the present atomic stalemate. War has become an avoidable horror to all but the fanatic Chinese, and the Russian Communists content themselves with the ambition of producing more butter and consumer goods and thus presumably defeating capitalism by winning a sort of productivity race. Internal discipline is meanwhile sustained by appealing to the Marxist myth of the capitalist menace, implacably hostile yet doomed to disintegrate. Marxism becomes an ideology of totalitarian Babbittry.

The picture which we can infer as to the real values prevalent in Soviet society is remote indeed from the spirit of revolution. It is a measure of how far the processes of historical evolution have run their course in a scant four decades. The Communist system is predicated on the integration of every individual, of all action and all thought, into a single-minded whole, with a common purpose which it is obligatory for all to serve. The purpose is neither Marxist nor utilitarian except in a certain subsidiary way—it is the power and grandeur of the machine-age nation. "Militaristic industrialism" is the simplest term in which the real essence of Communist belief can be encompassed. To this must be added the matter of belief itself, for whatever else may change, the supreme value for Communism, as for any religious movement, is to keep the faith.

Conclusion:
Communism
and the Future

It is not only natural but vital in studying pressing political problems to look to the future and to try to anticipate the outcome of the
situation one is analyzing. This is not a matter of
passive prediction, which could not accurately be
done in any event, and which moreover involves
a fatalism that is not warranted by the nature of
the historical process. Nothing in human affairs
is inevitable except death, and this is only an
individual fate. As Machiavelli expressed it, "I believe, if we are to keep our free will, that it may
be true that fortune controls half of our actions
indeed but allows us the direction of the other
half, or almost half." The future of human society
will be the product of human decision and action,
though the decision may be warped by ignorance
or prejudice and the action limited by circumstances. The accuracy of decision and the effectiveness of action depend on intelligent understanding of the forces and conditions which
operate in the present. Only by dealing carefully
and far-sightedly with the realities of our time
can the leaders of the non-Communist world plan
362

action to make the future yield the success and
security we hope for.

Discussion of the future of Communism is
often confused by the Communists' own Marxian
philosophy of historical inevitability, according to
which they claim they are bound to win everywhere. Many anti-Communist observers virtually
concede to Communism the inevitability of history,
and frenetically search for means to stem this
onrushing flow of events, or else they mistake the
Communist philosophy to mean a moral commitment to make Marx's prediction come true at any
cost, and gird themselves for battle. Our analysis
has shown, however, that Marx's scheme of history is neither inevitable nor even relevant. Success has come to the Communists for reasons that
they themselves do not really understand. Even
the aspirations of the Communists are not im-
mutable; Communism is—or has been—significantly malleable. The molding of the movement by
events and circumstances has proved this.

The problem for Western policy-makers is also
their opportunity: to influence and restrain Communism by using the various powers at their command—political, economic, ideological, military—
to shape and manipulate in a way favorable to
the West the environment in which Communism
operates. Naturally the West is far from omnipotent in taking such action; Western leaders no
less than the Communists must realize the limits
to their powers and the difficult circumstances
with which they must deal. However, in this contest of statesmanship the Western world has one
immense potential advantage to draw upon—the
manifold intellectual resources of a free society
that permits free thought. The Communists are
shackled by dogma—we are not. We can see them

and the situation in which they operate with infinitely more clarity and realism then they can see us, or themselves, or any other forces in the world.

We have oserved in a number of contexts that Communism—in Soviet Russia and Eastern Europe —is in the later stages of a very profound transformation. We can readily summarize the present trends of social change in the Communist orbit apart from China and draw some inferences about the future of that part of the movement which looks to Russia as its head.

Communism, as a totalitarian onslaught upon the problems of modernization and industrialization, is now erasing the justification for its own existence, as far as the Soviet orbit is concerned. It has built a vast industrial plant, including the East European economies which are integrated into the Russian, and has accomplished the cultural revolution of mass education and technical training. It has created an elaborate hierarchical organization of society, and has nurtured a technocratic upper class of administrators, engineers, and communicators who operate the system. Productivity has reached the level where military strength can be maintained while the population is allowed a steady and appreciable rise in living standards. The reasons for totalitarian political and economic pressures on the population are disappearing, and to a considerable extent those pressures have been eased.

Communism's material success and relaxation have permitted a gradual but profound change in the spirit of the movement in Russia and points west. Communism has provided Communists with status, careers, and comforts, and latterly even reasonable security against arbitrary arrest. The revolution is over. Partly to meet its requirements of economic progress, and partly as a result of that progress, Communism has created a new bourgeoisie, statist rather than individualist, but otherwise much akin socially and psychologically to the salaried middle class in the West. With rare exception, these people are not personally fanatic; belief is a matter of conformity and comfortable self-righteousness, if the individual is not actually one of the numerous secret dissenters. The Communist movement demands unquestioning loyalty to its authority, but apart from this, belief plays no guiding role. It serves only the functions of self-justification and control characteristic of a complacent long-established church.

In the realm of ideas, all the distinctive features of the Stalinist mentality are still evident— assertion and enforcement of an official body of doctrine, the pose of unanimity about all important issues and decisions, and the basic principles of thought control. The latter have been measurably eased in application, if only because the practical damage due to excessively rigorous intellectual and cultural regulation became evident. Nevertheless, it is still explicitly asserted that the overriding considerations for any intellectual activity are political—the goals and standards of the party and the success of its efforts. Such pronouncements demonstrate that the statist bias which Stalin gave the Communist movement— the presumption that human life draws its value and meaning not from the development of individuals but from the purposes and achievements of the national group, as determined by its leaders —remains in full force. Where any freedom for the individual is allowed under Communism it is not a matter of principle but of limited expedient. Totalitarian government, a rigid state religion, and the devotion to industrial and military power continue to be the basic features of Communist practice. Were its essential Stalinist features to go, the movement as we know it would cease to exist.

Since Khrushchev's ascendancy in Russia in 1955 there have been efforts to combat the desiccation of Communist belief and win renewed authority for the party. As we noted in the chapter on revolution, Khrushchev made gestures of a return to earlier and more proletarian policies. The Soviet regime took on a pro-worker cast which it had not had since the 1930's, with steps to equalize wages and pensions somewhat, and emphasis on party control over the technocratic middle class. In 1959 Khrushchev returned to old Marxist propaganda themes with the announcement of the beginning of "the period of all-out building of a communist society," which he described as "the most just and perfect society where the best moral traits of free men will be fully disclosed." The road to this utopia, however, was only more of what the Soviet citizenry was already getting—strict state and party controls, the continued emphasis on heavy industry, and no diminution of salary differentials: "Equalization would mean not a transition to communism but the discrediting of communism."

Present Soviet circumstances are so different from the economy of spontaneous abundance envisaged by Marx that Khrushchev's talk of the "transition to communism" can only be regarded as the farcical juggling of labels, to get for the present regime the emotional benefit of old so-

cialist ideals. "Naturally," says Khrushchev, "in
a communist society there will be planned and
organized distribution of work according to various branches of production, and social regulation
of working time," while "certain public functions
will remain, analogous to present state functions."
The "withering away of the state" is thus redefined to mean nothing but the transfer of functions from central to local agencies or from the
government to the organs of the Communist
Party, while the blissful prosperity of complete
communism will supposedly be attained when the
Soviet Union passes the state of Vermont in the
per capita production of milk and butter. The
"dictatorship of the proletariat" is officially terminated by the 1961 party program, but it yields only
to "the state as an organization embracing the entire people," while the role of the party as "the
leading and guiding force of Soviet society," with
all its unity, discipline, and ideological rigor, is re-
affirmed in full force with no terminal date whatsoever. The substance of these current Communist
professions only adds proof to our conclusion that
Soviet socialism is merely a dictatorial alternative
to capitalism as a system for creating material
wealth. This is still socialism, but it is not in any
meaningful sense specifically Marxist; the Communists have kept no more of Marx's ideas than
those which he shared with a multitude of other
socialist thinkers of his time.

We now find in Russia a permanent state of
tension between the modern hierarchical industrial
society which Communism has created, and the
Communist instruments of control which were responsible for creating that society. The Communist
Party has exclusive power, and there is no immediate possibility of an evolution in the democratic di-

rection. The real question is the future of the relation between the party and the technocracy. Will
the party accommodate to the technocracy sufficiently to permit unhampered economic progress
and rising living standards? Is the party apparatus
becoming just another branch of the administrative hierarchy? Or will the party feel compelled to
find artificial grounds for continuing its function,
put new stress on ideological controls and conformity, and enter into a renewed cold war with
its own society? The latter eventuality would mean
that the Communist totalitarian politicians had
succeeded in shifting from an Eastern to a Western
pattern as they transformed their own social base
from the backward Eastern to the modern industrial type—a final "Westernization" of Communist
totalitarianism. In any case, the pressures and the
resources sustaining totalitarianism are sufficient
to keep Communist Party rule firmly entrenched.

Recent political developments both in the Soviet Union and the East European Soviet orbit have
reflected the dilemma of adjustment versus control which confronts the Communist rulers. Khrushchev, when all is said and done, has succeeded
remarkably well in reforming the regime and renouncing the most oppressive features of Stalinism without altering the foundation of totalitarian
rule. He did risk serious trouble when his attack on
Stalin in 1956 raised excessive hopes for liberalism
among the Soviet intelligentsia, but he was able to
restore discipline, purge the disgruntled Stalinist
die-hards, and reap the benefits of a reformer's
popularity. In the East European satellites Khrushchev was much less fortunate—gestures of reform and relaxation were taken as the signal to
throw off Soviet influence altogether, and the result was the necessity for the infamous and bloody

intervention in Hungary. Moscow emerged from the crisis of 1956 with the realization that it had to be much more circumspect in its relations with other Communist states, allow them some latitude in their internal policies, and abjure the pose of outright domination. Communist loyalties around the world had been sorely tested by the events of 1956, but the movement weathered the storm with its strength and discipline largely intact, thanks in part to the inability of Communism's opponents to take advantage of their opportunity.

One branch of the Communist movement emerged from the crisis of 1956 not only with its strength unimpaired but with a reassertion of the most uncompromising attitudes of Stalinism. Communist China momentarily responded to the crisis by relaxing, with the policy of tolerating critical opinions and letting "a hundred flowers bloom," in 1956 and early 1957. This interlude was rudely ended in mid-1957 by a "rectification campaign," the condemnation of "rightists" throughout the administrative structure, and the suppression of critical ideas as "poisonous weeds." Mao Tse-tung was more than ever the object of his own "cult of personality," and he began to assume the status of an independent Marxist oracle on a par with Lenin and Stalin. In the economic realm, the Chinese Communist government launched schemes of reorganization and development—the communes and the "Great Leap Forward"—that exceeded in their rigor and ambition the Stalin revolution in Russia in the early 1930's. Politically, doctrinally, and economically, the events in China since 1957 have corresponded closely to the transformation of Russia from 1928 on, and the prospect is for an intensification of all the attributes of Stalinism in China. This extends to foreign policy as well, as the

Chinese Communists remain gripped by the blind passions of anti-imperialism and anti-American-ism.

Communism in China may in fact be evolving into a distinctly different form of totalitarian society. China faces generations of crisis and agonizing effort before she can achieve the Soviet level of industrial maturity—if the population problem does not cause some kind of explosion before then. Chinese Communism is not bourgeoisified; it is still fanatic, and its fanaticism has been stepped up since 1957. Totalitarian controls in China, as represented in "brainwashing" and the communes, for instance, are considerably more severe than they ever were in Russia. The Chinese and Russian revolutions are out of phase; the Chinese are still whipped up by domestic and international attitudes which the Russian Communists are relieved to have outgrown. The Chinese are undoubtedly chagrined about the insufficiency of Russian aid either for their internal development or for the realization of their aims of conquering Formosa and expelling American influence from Asia. The Russians may well be apprehensive themselves over the possibility of China's upsetting the peace and over China's potential threat to Russian influence not only in Asia but in the whole Communist movement. Tension between the two partners was notably revealed in the summer and fall of 1960, when tactical differences and the issue of ultimate authority in the Communist movement brought from the Russians and Chinese thinly veiled charges of "dogmatism" and "revisionism" respectively. This was accompanied by a notable diminution of trade and personal and press exchanges between the two states. There is every reason to expect this cleavage between the young and mature

Communist revolutions to become more accentuated as time goes on.

Since the Second World War, Communism, as an expanding revolutionary faith movement, has caused the polarization of international relations into two great hostile camps—Russia and her satellites plus Communist China on the one hand, and the alliance of Western democracies led by the United States on the other. There are neutrals, particularly among the Asian and African nationalists, and national-Communist Yugoslavia, but so far the neutrals have lacked the power to resolve or change the basic Russo-American cleavage of world power.

Paradoxically, the international expansion of Communism in 1945–49 came at a time when true ideological fervor had largely withered away as the real motive or guide of Soviet foreign policy. Doctrine had been reduced to an instrument or justification of Soviet power moves, in a pattern of bold enhancement of national power. The conflict between the United States and Russia lacks real issues of either the material or ideological sort; like European power rivalries from the seventeenth to the nineteenth century, the conflict persists of its own momentum, simply because the two big powers and an atmosphere of suspicion between them exist. This great-power conflict becomes progressively less a matter of faith and principle, and increasingly a matter of the pursuit of strategic advantage.

Technological changes in the art of war have given the two superpowers one fundamental strategic interest which they share in common. This is to avoid obliteration by an exchange of thermonuclear bombs. Distrust persists; the commitment to the forms of Marxist ideology from which the Soviet leaders cannot extricate themselves creates a presumption of mutual hostility both on their part and in the Western camp; but both sides recognize that a nuclear war would be a mutual disaster no matter who won. Each side maneuvers for its advantage or security and is ever on the alert against pressure from the other, but the fact of coexistence is not really disputed.

"Peaceful coexistence" such as the Russians now espouse is not peace in the traditional American sense, which meant the absence of any international tensions or threats. However, it is clearly not war; it is, in fact, not far removed from the familiar form of competitive international relations so long practiced in Europe. Both America and Russia have had to revise their theoretical predilections—isolationism and world revolution, respectively—to take account of present realities. The Russians, for their part, have performed remarkable ideological gyrations to try to demonstrate that the policy of peaceful coexistence flows logically from the pronouncements of their founding father Lenin. This is but the most recent of their maneuvers to preserve the sanctity of doctrine by denuding it of its meaning.

The dynamic and unpredictable factor in the international arena, as in the internal development of the Communist bloc, is Communist China. The disparity of phase and direction between the Russian and Chinese revolutions has led to growing differences between the two Communist giants over the strategy and tactics of dealing with the West. Russia seeks conferences and agreements; China insists on the need to use or threaten force both to check the Western alliance and to advance the cause of Communism in new areas. In China revolutionary fervor has merged with inflamed nationalism, and in their passion for incorporating Formosa and ending the career of Chiang Kai-shek the Chinese Communists can see nothing internationally save the prospects of violent conflict.

In contrast to Soviet domination in Eastern Europe, the main bonds between Moscow and Communist China have been the less tangible ones of a common ideology and a mutual need for support against the Western alliance. Ideology, however, has long since ceased to be a primary guiding force in Communist affairs. Ideology is only an instrument to justify what the Communists feel are their practical interests, and if practical interests point toward a cleavage between Russia and China, the ideological bond can easily turn into a forum for mutual accusations of heresy. The more purely strategic considerations govern Communist policy-making, the more likely an open Russian-Chinese cleavage becomes.

The nature of the present world conflict and international alignments is changing, just as international affairs shifted from the religious basis to the power basis in the seventeenth century. This trend does not mean the end of conflict, but it does mean that the danger of imminent mutual annihilation is lessening. For the Western powers, concerned both to keep the peace and to maintain the security of their national institutions, values, and lives, the problem is to keep Communism in check while avoiding war, until the whole ideological cleavage between Communist and non-Communist subsides. Much can be accomplished by a Western ideological counteroffensive to expose the claims of the Communist faith and to distinguish it from genuine radicalism and nationalism. If we can live through the next half century, the leaders of every power in the world may at last be able to see their mutual advantage in creating a real international organization that will finally deliver mankind from the shadow of the mushroom cloud.

In the longest perspective, the ideological contest of Communism versus democracy is not our most serious problem. The Russians can live with themselves and we can live with them, but the nations of Asia and of tropical Africa and America are in the midst of an economic and demographic crisis that may well destroy the world we know. Communist China already represents one of the dangerous forces stemming from this Eastern crisis. Whether the West can go on living with Communism will very likely depend on the outcome of events in the underdeveloped and uncommitted countries. If Communism—particularly on the Chinese pattern—should make sudden new gains in these regions, the future is dark indeed. From 1949 to the present the Communists have not progressed much: the stage has been filled with a procession of triumphant nationalist movements. To sustain these often ill-prepared regimes or other non-Communist alternatives, in the face of the social crisis confronting the underdeveloped areas, will require on the part of the West a prolonged effort of statesmanship of the highest order.

Communism professes to be the successor system to capitalism. In reality, it is an alternative, but an alternative based in large measure on certain features of modern capitalism that are made the basis of the entire social organization under Communism. These Western elements which Communism incorporates and elaborates include not only the industrial economy, but the bureaucratic managerial system of industrial organization (in contrast to the workers' control which was the original Russian revolutionary ideal), the administrative hierarchy in all areas of life, and mass communications. Soviet society is the corporation writ large, with the ethic of the Organization Man, plus the spirit of a faith and the discipline of an army. Communism is an adaptation to the challenges and problems of industrialism that is more advanced than the complex accretion of disparate habits and institutions characteristic of the pluralist societies of the West, and yet at the same time, with its despotic controls and its history of terror, it is by comparison barbaric.

We can see in each camp, though more clearly among the Communist, trends of social totalitarianism that hint at no reasonable prospect of reversal. Each camp draws a sense of purpose and a justification for its totalitarian tendencies from the existence of conflict between the two camps, with both the totalitarianism and sense of conflict much more sharply pronounced in the Communist camp. We must not forget, however, that the West itself has already been afflicted once with virulent totalitarianism in its midst. There are totalitarian attitudes on both sides which are served by international conflict. We must recognize this before we can detach the conflict from the psychological needs that feed it, meet the needs otherwise, and try to resolve the conflict. The real danger is that reason will fail on both sides, and that we will head toward George Orwell's nightmare of monolithic superstates blindly and bloodily struggling with each other without end.

Bibliographical
Note

The literature on Communism is of vast proportions, although it is not always qualitatively adequate on every aspect of the movement. I shall attempt here no comprehensive survey of the material; I only present a guide to some of the most significant literature in English representing the various perspectives developed in this book, and indicate those writings which I have found particularly helpful in my work of synthesis.

Marxist doctrine is well summarized in R. N. Carew Hunt, *The Theory and Practice of Communism* (New York, Macmillan, 1951), while its internal limitations are effectively criticized by Max Eastman in *Marxism: Is it Science?* (New York, Norton, 1940), by John Plamenatz in *German Marxism and Russian Communism* (London and New York, Longmans, 1954), and by Alfred G. Meyer in *Marxism: The Unity of Theory and Practice* (Cambridge, Harvard University Press, 1954). The most significant political writings of Marx and Engels are conveniently available in Lewis Feuer, ed., *Marx and Engels: Basic Writings on Politics and Philosophy* (New York, Doubleday-Anchor, 1959). Among Marx's most important works, from the standpoint of understanding Communist theory, are the *German Ideology* (1845–46), *The Communist Manifesto* (1948), the introduction to *The Critique of Political Economy* (1859), and *The Civil War in France* (1871). Marx's theory of history is dissected in Karl Federn's *The Materialist Conception of History: A Critical Analysis* (London, Macmillan, 1939). Herbert Butterfield in *History and Human Relations* (London, Collins, 1951) discusses some of the positive contributions of Marxist thought. My article, "Fate and Will in the Marxian Philosophy of History," *Journal of the History of Ideas,* Oct. 1960, treats the problem of inevitability in Marxism. Karl Mannheim in *Ideology and Utopia* (New York, International Library of Psychology, Philosophy and Scientific Method, 1936) expands on Marx's key concept of "ideology." The best Communist statement of Marxian theory is Nikolai Bukharin's *Historical Materialism: A System of Sociology* (New York, International Publishers, 1925). James Burnham's *Managerial Revolution* (New York, John Day, 1941) is a provocative effort by an ex-Trotskyist to bring Marxism up to date as a general theory of corporate concentration and totalitarianism.

The Russian background of Communism is dealt with in a number of works on the revolutionary movement, of which the most solid is perhaps Franco Venturi's *Roots of Revolution* (New York, Knopf, 1960); see also my article, "Lenin and the Russian Revolutionary Tradition," *Harvard Slavic Studies,* IV, 1957. Nicholas Berdiaev in *The Origin of Russian Communism* (London, Bles, 1937), and Edward Crankshaw in *Russia and the Russians* (New York, Viking, 1948) offer insightful, if debatable, suggestions on the relation of Communism to the Russian national character. John Maynard in *Russia in Flux* (New York, Macmillan, 1948) deals with the interaction of Russian life and the revolutionaries, before, during, and after the revolution. The coming of Marxism to Russia has been ably treated with a psychological emphasis by Leopold Haimson in *The Russian Marxists and the Origins of Bolshevism* (Cambridge, Harvard University Press, 1955). Lenin has been the subject of several good studies, including David Shub's *Lenin* (New York, Doubleday, 1948), Bertram Wolfe's *Three Who Made a Revolution*—i.e., Lenin, Trotsky, and Stalin—(New York, Dial Press, 1948), and Alfred Meyer's *Leninism* (Cambridge, Harvard University Press, 1957). Lenin speaks for himself quite candidly, and may be consulted in the two-volume English edition of his *Selected Works* (Moscow, Foreign Languages Publishing House, 1950–52). His fundamental statement of doctrine, method, and intent is the lengthy pamphlet,

378   Bibliographical Note

"What Is To Be Done?" of 1902. Trotsky's distinctive
prerevolutionary views are represented in his *Our Revolution* (New York, Holt, 1918).

The study of the Russian Revolution in relation to
other revolutions must begin with Crane Brinton's
Anatomy of Revolution (revised edition, New York,
Prentice-Hall, 1952), but George S. Pettee's *The Process
of Revolution* (New York, Harper, 1938) is a thoughtful
book in the same vein. See also Isaac Deutscher, "Great
Dilemmas, for Stalin and His Heir," *The New York
Times Magazine*, Mar. 13, 1949, and Paul Federn, *Zur
Psychologie der Revolution: Die vaterlose Gesellschaft*
(Leipzig and Vienna, Anzengruber, 1919). William
Henry Chamberlin's *The Russian Revolution* (2 vols.,
New York, Macmillan, 1935) is basic for a connected
account of the events of 1917–21, while E. H. Carr's
volumes on the revolutionary period in his still un-
finished *History of Soviet Russia* (New York, Macmillan, 1951–   ) offer a series of penetrating topical
studies. No comprehensive Soviet work on the revolution has yet appeared (save G. N. Golikov's "Sketch of
the History of the Great October Socialist Revolution," Moscow, State Press for Political Literature,
1959). The nearest thing to an official account is Trotsky's literary monument, *The History of the Russian
Revolution* (3 vols., New York, Simon and Schuster,
1932). N. N. Sukhanov's *The Russian Revolution, 1917*
(abridged translation, London and New York, Oxford
University Press, 1955) is the most famous eye-witness
account.

General, comprehensive histories of Soviet Russia
are not numerous. The most fully adequate is Georg
von Rauch, *History of Soviet Russia* (New York, Praeger, 1957). Other works with a special emphasis but
broad coverage of Soviet history are Isaac Deutscher,
Stalin: A Political Biography (New York, Oxford University Press, 1949) and Leonard Schapiro, *The Communist Party of the Soviet Union* (New York, Random
House, 1960). For the official Soviet view, see V. N.
Ponomaryov et al., *History of the Communist Party of
the Soviet Union* (Moscow, Foreign Languages Publishing House, 1960). For a collection of excerpts
of the most important Communist policy statements
representing all tendencies in the movement from

Lenin to the present, see my *Documentary History of Communism* (New York, Random House, 1960).

The structure of Communist rule in Russia is explained in detail in Merle Fainsod, *How Russia is Ruled* (Cambridge, Harvard University Press, 1953). The history of the Communist factions and the early evolution of the Soviet regime are treated in my *Conscience of the Revolution: Communist Opposition in Soviet Russia* (Cambridge, Harvard University Press, 1960). On the purge era see Zbigniew Brzezinski, *The Permanent Purge* (Cambridge, Harvard University Press, 1956), and Bertram Wolfe, *Khrushchev and Stalin's Ghost* (New York, Praeger, 1956), which includes the text of Khrushchev's secret speech attacking Stalin in 1956.

The changes in Soviet domestic policies under Stalin are dealt with in Nicholas Timasheff, *The Great Retreat* (New York, Dutton, 1946), Trotsky's *The Revolution Betrayed* (New York, Doubleday, 1937), and Klaus Mehnert, *Stalin vs. Marx* (London, Allen and Unwin, 1952); see also my article, "Soviet Thought in the 1930's," *Indiana Slavic Studies,* I, 1956. Stalin's major policy statements are available in various editions of his selected writings and speeches entitled *Leninism* or *Problems of Leninism* (Moscow, Foreign Languages Publishing House). This does not include his important article, "Concerning Marxism in Linguistics," which is available in pamphlet form (New York, International Publishers, 1951). For comments on Stalin's use of theory see G. L. Arnold, "Stalinism," *Political Quarterly,* No. 4, 1950; George Lichtheim, "Soviet Marxism: from Theory to Ideology," *Soviet Survey,* Jan.–Mar. 1959; and my article, "The State and Revolution: A Case Study in the Genesis and Transformation of Communist Ideology," *American Slavic and East European Review,* Feb. 1953. The best general treatise on Soviet doctrine is Gustav Wetter, *Dialectical Materialism* (New York, Praeger, 1959).

The history of the Soviet economy is covered thoroughly, though from a Marxist standpoint, by Maurice Dobb in *Soviet Economic Development since 1917* (New York, International Publishers, 1948). A good critical and analytical survey is Harry Schwartz, *Russia's Soviet Economy* (New York, Prentice-Hall, 1950). Past and present problems of the planned economy are analyzed in Alexander Erlich, *The Soviet Industrialization Controversy* (Cambridge, Harvard University Press, 1960) ; in Abram Bergson, ed., *Soviet Economic Growth: Conditions and Perspectives* (Evanston, Ill., Row, Peterson, 1953) ; and in Oleg Hoeffding, "Substance and Shadow in the Soviet Seven-Year Plan," *Foreign Affairs,* April 1959. Problems of the technocracy are treated in Joseph Berliner, *Factory and Manager in the USSR* (Cambridge, Harvard University Press, 1957) and in Solomon Schwarz, *Labor in Soviet Russia* (New York, Praeger, 1952). On the Soviet class structure and the everyday life of various groups in the population, see Alex Inkeles, "Social Stratification and Mobility in the Soviet Union: 1940–1950," *American Sociological Review,* Aug. 1950; Robert A. Feldmesser, "The Persistence of Status Advantages in Soviet Russia," *American Journal of Sociology,* July 1953; David Dallin, *The Real Soviet Russia* (New Haven, Yale University Press, 1947) ; and W. W. Kulski, *The Soviet Regime* (Syracuse, Syracuse University Press, 1954 and 1959). Raymond A. Bauer, Alex Inkeles, and Clyde Kluckhohn, *How the Soviet System Works* (Cambridge, Harvard University Press, 1956), reports the findings of the Harvard Project on the Soviet Social System, which conducted extensive interviews of Soviet displaced persons. Two very revealing articles on deviant attitudes among Soviet students are Tim Callaghan, "Studying the Students," *Soviet Survey,* July–Sept. 1960, and David Burg (pseud.), "Observations on Soviet University Students," *Daedalus,* Summer 1960. For a general survey of Soviet education see George S. Counts, *The Challenge of Soviet Education* (New York, McGraw-Hill, 1957). The best history of religion in the USSR is John Shelton Curtis, *The Russian Church and the Soviet State: 1917–1950* (Boston, Little, Brown, 1953). There is no comprehensive study of Soviet intellectual life, but George S. Counts and Nucia Lodge, *The Country of the Blind: The Soviet System of Mind Control* (Boston, Houghton Mifflin, 1949), is a penetrating account of the enforcement of the party line in cultural matters between 1946 and 1949.

The problem of nationalism and the non-Russian minorities of the USSR is covered in Richard Pipes,

The Formation of the Soviet Union (Cambridge, Harvard University Press, 1954), and Frederick Barghoorn, *Soviet Russian Nationalism* (New York, Oxford University Press, 1956), as well as in some of the general political studies cited above.

A variety of scholarly opinion on various aspects of recent events in the Soviet Union and the rest of the Communist bloc is available in the journals dealing especially or frequently with current Communist affairs. Among the most useful are *Soviet Survey* (London), *Problems of Communism* (Washington, US Information Agency), *World Politics* (Princeton), and *Current History* (Philadelphia). See also *The Annals of the American Academy of Political and Social Science,* May 1949 and Jan. 1956 issues entirely devoted to the USSR. Current information from Soviet sources is regularly translated in the *Current Digest of the Soviet Press* (New York). The prospective evolution of the Soviet dictatorship is assessed optimistically by Isaac Deutscher in a number of articles (see his *Russia in Transition and Other Essays,* New York, Coward-McCann, 1957) and rather more conservatively by Barrington Moore in *Terror and Progress: USSR* (Cambridge, Harvard University Press, 1954). The politics of the post-Stalin era are given special attention in Myron Rush, *The Rise of Khrushchev* (Washington, Public Affairs Press, 1958); in the symposium, "Khrushchev at the Helm," *Problems of Communism,* 1959; in Robert C. Tucker, "The Politics of Soviet De-Stalinization," *World Politics,* July 1957, and in Erich Goldhagen, "Ideology and the Transition to Communism," *Soviet Survey,* April–June 1959. Among the most enlightening journalistic interpretations of contemporary Soviet life are Edward Crankshaw's *Russia without Stalin* (New York, Viking, 1956) and John Gunther's *Inside Russia Today* (New York, Harper, 1958).

The subject of Communism outside Russia must be approached largely through specialized works on various countries and areas or particular aspects of the movement. The only reasonably adequate histories of the international Communist movement as a whole are Franz Borkenau's somewhat dated *World Communism* (New York, Norton, 1939; British edition under the title, *The Communist International,* London, Faber

382 Bibliographical Note

and Faber, 1938); C. L. R. James's pro-Trotsky account, *World Revolution, 1917–1936: The Rise and Fall of the Comintern* (New York, Pioneer Publishers, 1937), and Hugh Seton-Watson's comprehensive but inescapably superficial volume, *From Lenin to Khrushchev: The History of World Communism* (New York, Praeger, 1960; British edition under the title, *The Pattern of Communist Revolution*, London, Methuen, 1953).

Communism in Eastern Europe has been the subject of a voluminous literature, largely country-by-country. The series "East-Central Europe under the Communists" (New York, Mid-European Studies Center and Praeger) includes a volume on each of the Soviet satellites. Hugh Seton-Watson deals with the Communist take-over of the region in *The East-European Revolution* (3rd ed., New York, Praeger, 1956), while developments in the various Communist parties are treated in Adam Ulam, *Titoism and the Cominform* (Cambridge, Harvard University Press, 1952) and in Zbigniew Brzezinski, *The Soviet Bloc: Unity and Conflict* (Cambridge, Harvard University Press, 1960). On Poland, see M. K. Dziewanowski, *The Communist Party of Poland* (Cambridge, Harvard University Press, 1959) and Konrod Syrop, *Spring in October: The Polish Revolution of 1956* (New York, Praeger, 1957). On Yugoslavia, see Hamilton Fish Armstrong, *Tito and Goliath* (New York, Macmillan, 1951); Charles P. McVicker, *Titoism: Pattern for International Communism* (New York, St. Martin's, 1957); Fred W. Neal, "Yugoslav Communist Theory," *American Slavic and East European Review*, Feb. 1960. On Hungary and the crisis of 1956 see Imre Nagy, *On Communism* (New York, Praeger, 1957); Paul Zinner, ed., *National Communism and Popular Revolt in Eastern Europe* (New York, Columbia University Press, 1956); and Tibor Meray, *Thirteen Days that Shook the Kremlin* (New York, Praeger, 1959). An impassioned attack on the overall evolution of society under Communism is made by the deviating Yugoslav Communist leader, Milovan Djilas, in *The New Class* (New York, Praeger, 1957).

On Communism in Western Europe, see particularly Franz Borkenau, *European Communism* (New York, Harper, 1953); Mario Einaudi, ed., *Communism in Western Europe* (Ithaca, Cornell University Press,

1951); Ruth Fischer, *Stalin and German Communism* (Cambridge, Harvard University Press, 1948); David T. Cattell, *Communism and the Spanish Civil War* (Berkeley, University of California Press, 1955). Bernard S. Morris in "Some Perspective on the Nature and Role of the West European Communist Parties," *Review of Politics,* April 1956, demonstrates the essentially nonrevolutionary but firmly pro-Soviet nature of contemporary Communism in the West. Communism in the United States is ably evaluated in Irving Howe and Lewis Coser, *The American Communist Party* (Boston, Beacon Press, 1957); in Morris Ernst and David Loth, *Report on the American Communist* (New York, Holt, 1952); and in Theodore Draper's multi-volume history, of which two volumes, *The Roots of American Communism* and *American Communism and Soviet Russia* (New York, Viking Press, 1957 and 1960), have already appeared. On Latin America, see Robert J. Alexander, *Communism in Latin America* (New Brunswick, Rutgers University Press, 1957), and Ronald M. Schneider, *Communism in Guatemala, 1944–54* (New York, Praeger, 1959). The tactics of the Communist parties in democratic states are analyzed in Philip Selznick, *The Organizational Weapon: A study of Bolshevik Strategy and Tactics* (New York, McGraw-Hill, 1952).

A general view of Asian Communism is available in Malcolm Kennedy, *A History of Communism in East Asia* (New York, Praeger, 1957). Karl A. Wittfogel's *Oriental Despotism* (New Haven, Yale University Press, 1957) offers a provocative Asiatic interpretation of the movement as a whole. China is naturally the subject of most of the specific scholarly attention; among the most useful works on Chinese Communism are Conrad Brant, Benjamin Schwartz, and John K. Fairbank, *A Documentary History of Chinese Communism* (Cambridge, Harvard University Press, 1952); Robert C. North, *Moscow and Chinese Communists* (Stanford, Cal., Stanford University Press, 1953); Benjamin Schwartz, *Chinese Communism and the Rise of Mao* (Cambridge, Harvard University Press, 1951); Peter S. Tang, *Communist China Today* (rev. ed., New York, Praeger, 1960); and "Communist China's First Decade," a symposium, *The New Leader,* Mar. 30–June 29, 1959. Entire volumes of *The Annals of the American Acad-*

emy of Political and Social Science for Sept. 1951 and Jan. 1959 are devoted to Communist China. An illuminating insight into the historical background of the Chinese Revolution is offered by Wolfgang Franke in "Die Stufen der Revolution in China," *Vierteljahrshefte fur Zeitgeschichte,* January 1954. See also Arthur N. Holcombe, *The Chinese Revolution* (Cambridge, Harvard University Press, 1929). The evolving mentality of the Chinese Communist regime is analyzed by Michael Lindsay in *China and the Cold War* (New York, Cambridge University Press, 1955). Mao Tse-tung's own most important writings are available in his *Selected Works* (New York, International Publishers, 1954). On Chinese Communist psychology and indoctrination, see Robert Jay Lifton, *Thought Reform and the Psychology of Totalism; A Study of Brainwashing in China* (New York, Norton, 1961). On economics see Choh-Ming Li, *Economic Development of Communist China* (Berkeley, University of California Press, 1959). On Sino-Soviet relations see H. L. Boorman, Alexander Eckstein, Philip E. Mosely, and Benjamin Schwartz, *Moscow-Peking Axis—Strengths and Strains* (New York, Harper, 1957). China and Soviet Russia are contrasted in my essay, "The Chinese Revolution in Russian Perspective," *World Politics,* Jan. 1961. The principal Chinese Communist documents and policy statements are translated in the series *Current Background* (Hong Kong, US Consulate General).

Representative works on Communism in other Asian countries are: Rodger Swearingen and Paul Langer, *Red Flag in Japan* (Cambridge, Harvard University Press, 1952); Bernard Fall, *The Viet-Minh Regime* (New York, Institute of Pacific Relations, 1956); Justus van der Kroef, "Indonesian Communism under Aidit," *Problems of Communism,* Nov.–Dec. 1958; Gene Overstreet and Marshall Windmiller, *Communism in India* (Berkeley, University of California Press, 1959), and John Kautsky, *Moscow and the Communist Party of India* (New York, Wiley, 1956); Lucian W. Pye, *Guerrilla Communism in Malaya* (Princeton, Princeton University Press, 1956)—a book of great significance in understanding the psychology of Communism throughout Asia; William Z. Laqueur, *Communism and Nationalism in the Middle East* (New York, Praeger,

1956), and A. V. Sherman, "Nationalism and Communism in the Arab World—A Reappraisal," in Walter Z. Laqueur, ed., *The Middle East in Transition* (New York, Praeger, 1958). More general studies with implications regarding the nature of Asian Communism are Daniel Lerner et al., *The Passing of Traditional Society: Modernizing the Middle East* (Glencoe, Ill., The Free Press, 1958); Eduard Heimann, "Marxism and Underdeveloped Countries," *Social Research,* Sept. 1952; Edward Shils, "The Concentration and Dispension of Charisma: Their Bearing on Economic Policy in Underdeveloped Countries," *World Politics,* Oct. 1958. Hostile Asian reactions to Westernization are assessed in E. O. Reischauer, *Wanted: An Asian Policy* (New York, Knopf, 1955); Bernard Lewis, "Communism and Islam," in Ruth N. Anshen, ed., *Mid-East: World Center* (New York, Harper, 1956); and Chitra Fernando, "Asian Xenophobia against the West," *Annals of the American Academy of Political and Social Science,* July 1958. In my article, "Intellectuals and the Russian Revolution," *American Slavic and East European Review,* April 1961, I develop the theory of the "quasi-intelligentsia." A good general introduction to the concept of acculturation is contained in Ralph Linton, *Acculturation in Seven American Indian Tribes* (New York, Appleton, 1940). Some of the cultural problems attending industrialization are set forth in John U. Nef, *Cultural Foundations of Industrial Civilization* (London, Cambridge University Press, 1957). On the concept of alienation in modern industrial society see Daniel Bell, *The End of Ideology* (Glencoe, Ill., The Free Press, 1960).

The relations between Communism and the non-Communist world are dealt with extensively in the general works on Soviet history and the Communist International already cited. The only single-volume survey of Soviet foreign policy as such is George Kennan's *Russia and the West under Lenin and Stalin* (Boston, Little, Brown, 1961). On the Second World War and its aftermath, see William McNeil, *America, Britain and Russia: Their Cooperation and Conflict, 1941–1946* (London, Royal Institute of International Affairs and Oxford University Press, 1953). On recent Soviet foreign policy see John Lukacs, *History of the*

Cold War (New York, Doubleday, 1961), and David Dallin, *Soviet Foreign Policy After Stalin* (Philadelphia, Lippincott, 1961).

A number of books have been devoted to the analysis of Soviet strategy and tactics in relation to the doctrinal intentions of the movement; among these are Stefan Possony, *A Century of Conflict: Communist Techniques of World Revolution* (Chicago, Regnery, 1953); Robert Strausz-Hupé et al., *Protracted Conflict* (New York, Harper, 1959); and Nathan Leites, *The Operational Code of the Politburo* (New York, McGraw-Hill, 1951), which endeavors to set up a catalogue of Soviet tactics. Soviet military thinking is discussed in Byron Dexter, "Clausewitz and Soviet Strategy," *Foreign Affairs,* Oct. 1950, and in R. L. Garthoff, *Soviet Strategy in the Nuclear Age* (New York, Praeger, 1958). For the application of "game theory" to Soviet-Western relations, see Morton A. Kaplan, *System and Process in International Politics* (New York, Wiley, 1957) and "The Calculus of Nuclear Deterrence," *World Politics,* Oct. 1958; Thomas C. Schelling, *The Strategy of Conflict* (Cambridge, Harvard University Press, 1960); and Waldemar Koch, "Geschichtsgesetz und Strategie bei Lenin," in Werner Markert, ed., *Der Mensch im Kommunistische System* (Tübingen, Mohr, 1957). A more traditional power-politics analysis of Communist policy is offered in Robert E. Osgood, *Limited War: The Challenge to American Strategy* (Chicago, University of Chicago Press, 1957) and in Hans J. Morgenthau, "Soviet Policy and World Conquest," *Current History,* Nov. 1959. Julian Towster in "The Dogma of Communist Victory," *ibid.,* undertakes to analyze "world revolution" as a social myth.

The totalitarian aspects of Communism are developed in almost every sort of work on the movement. Useful works dealing generally with totalitarianism include Carl J. Friedrich and Zbigniew Brzezinski, *Totalitarian Dictatorship and Autocracy* (Cambridge, Harvard University Press, 1956); R. H. S. Crossman, "Socialism and the New Despotism," in Hugh Gaitskell, ed., *New Fabian Essays, II* (London, Phoenix, 1953); and R. W. Cassinelli, "Totalitarianism, Ideology, and Propaganda," *The Journal of Politics,* Feb. 1960. On the German parallel, see Franz Neumann, *Behe-*

moth: The Structure and Practice of National Social-
ism (New York, Oxford University Press, 1942). The
nonpolitical trends toward totalitarianism in modern
society are treated explicitly or implicitly in a vast
literature of sociology and economics, but among the
works particularly deserving of mention in this respect
are José Ortega y Gasset, *The Revolt of the Masses*
(New York, Norton, 1932), and Aldous Huxley, *Brave
New World Revisited* (New York, Harper, 1960).

Communism as a faith and the psychology of Communist belief are also treated, at least by implication,
in most of the works on particular branches of the
movement. Studies of the general problem of Communist allegiance include Gabriel Almond, *The Appeals
of Communism* (Princeton, Princeton University Press,
1954); Raymond Aron, *The Opium of the Intellectuals*
(New York, Doubleday, 1957); Francis X. Sutton, "The
Radical Marxist" (Ph.D. dissertation, Harvard University, 1950); and Hadley Cantril, *The Politics of
Despair* (New York, Basic Books, 1958). More specialized books which shed light on the nature of Communist belief include Richard Crossman, ed., *The God
That Failed* (New York, Harper, 1949); Czeslaw Milosz,
The Captive Mind (New York, Knopf, 1953); Tamas
Aczel and Tibor Meray, *The Revolt of the Mind* (New
York, Praeger, 1959); and the works of Arthur Koestler,
particularly *Darkness at Noon* (New York, Macmillan,
1941) and *The Yogi and the Commissar* (New York,
Macmillan, 1945).

Communism is explicitly assessed as a religious
movement in Jules Monnerot, *The Psychology and
Sociology of Communism* (Boston, Beacon Press, 1953);
Eduard Heimann, "Atheist Theocracy," *Social Re-
search,* Fall 1953; Waldemar Gurian, *Bolshevism: An
Introduction to Soviet Communism* (South Bend, Ind.,
Notre Dame University Press, 1952); and Jacques Maritain, *Humanisme integral* (selection reprinted in Joseph W. Evans and Leo R. Ward, eds., *The Social and
Political Philsophy of Jacques Maritain,* New York,
Scribner, 1955). Communism is discussed as the reli-
gion of a new Eastern civilization by P. M. A. Line-
barger in "Communism as a Competing Civilization in
South-East Asia," in P. W. Thayer, ed., *South-East Asia
in the Coming World* (Baltimore, Johns Hopkins Uni-

versity Press, 1953). Works on the general question of
the psychology of belief and the psychology of submission to authority, relevant to Communism whether or
not they refer to it directly, include Theodor Reik,
Dogma and Compulsion (New York, International Universities Press, 1951); Eric Hoffer, *The True Believer*
(New York, Harper, 1951); Erich Fromm, *Escape from
Freedom* (New York, Farrar and Rinehart, 1941); and
T. W. Adorno et al., *The Authoritarian Personality*
(New York, Harper, 1950). On the general question of
religious faith in relation to political power, see Joachim Wach, *Sociology of Religion* (Chicago, University
of Chicago Press, 1944).

I know of only one comprehensive survey of the
various approaches to the understanding of Communism: Daniel Bell's "Ten Theories in Search of Reality
—the Prediction of Soviet Behavior in the Social Sciences," *World Politics,* April 1958.

Index

About the Author

Robert V. Daniels studied at Harvard, received his A.B. degree in 1945, and Ph.D. degree in 1951. He has done research at the Russian Research Center at Harvard, has taught Russian history at Indiana University, Bennington College and the University of Vermont, and has traveled in Russia. He has published articles in the leading scholarly journals dealing with the history of Russia and Communism. His previous books are The Conscience of the Revolution: The Communist Opposition in Soviet Russia *and* A Documentary History of Communism.